Ah! 365 Bruschetta, Crostini, Breads, And Canapes Recipes

(Ah! 365 Bruschetta, Crostini, Breads, And Canapes Recipes - Volume 1)

Lucy Dickert

Copyright: Published in the United States by Lucy Dickert/ © LUCY DICKERT

Published on November, 28 2020

All rights reserved. No part of this publication may be reproduced, stored in retrieval system, copied in any form or by any means, electronic, mechanical, photocopying, recording or otherwise transmitted without written permission from the publisher. Please do not participate in or encourage piracy of this material in any way. You must not circulate this book in any format. LUCY DICKERT does not control or direct users' actions and is not responsible for the information or content shared, harm and/or actions of the book readers.

In accordance with the U.S. Copyright Act of 1976, the scanning, uploading and electronic sharing of any part of this book without the permission of the publisher constitute unlawful piracy and theft of the author's intellectual property. If you would like to use material from the book (other than just simply for reviewing the book), prior permission must be obtained by contacting the author at author@oreganorecipes.com

Thank you for your support of the author's rights.

Content

365 AWESOME BRUSCHETTA, CROSTINI, BREADS, AND CANAPES RECIPES 9

1. 16th Century Crostini With Cheese Recipe ... 9
2. 1970s Bread Bowl Baked Clam Dip Recipe ... 9
3. 3 Tomato Bruschetta With Basil & Garlic Recipe ... 9
4. 3 Cheese Bruschetta Recipe ... 10
5. A Quick Bread App Recipe ... 10
6. APACHE BREAD Recipe ... 11
7. Aciete Y Tomate Español Recipe ... 11
8. Almond Breaded Tilapia Nuggets With Cajun Rub Served With Honey Habanero Bbq Sauce And Greek Style Yogurt Recipe ... 11
9. Almond Bacon Cheese Crostini ... 12
10. Anchovy Canapes Recipe ... 12
11. Anchovy Toasts Recipe ... 13
12. Anchovy Amp Cherry Tomato Bruschetta Recipe ... 13
13. Ants On A Raft Recipe ... 13
14. Appetizer Artichoke Bread Recipe ... 14
15. Appetizer Bread Stuffed With Italian Sausage Recipe ... 14
16. Appetizers Recipe ... 14
17. Apple Goat Cheese Bruschetta Recipe ... 15
18. Apricot Rosemary Crackers Recipe ... 15
19. Apricot Rosemary Crostini With Brie Recipe ... 15
20. Artichoke Bread Recipe ... 16
21. Artichoke Bruschetta Recipe ... 16
22. Artichoke Heart Bread Recipe ... 17
23. Asparagus Bruschetta Recipe ... 17
24. Asparagus, Sundried Tomato And Olive Loaf Recipe ... 18
25. Avotato Canape And Apricream Canape Recipe ... 18
26. BRUSCHETTA DI MAZZANCOLLE DA ZACCARIA Recipe ... 19
27. BRUSCHETTA Recipe ... 19
28. BRUSCHETTA WITH AVOCADO AND GREEN ONION Recipe ... 19
29. Bacon Bread Wraps Recipe ... 20
30. Bacon Canapes Recipe ... 20
31. Bacon Cheese Spread In Bread Bowl Recipe 20
32. Bacon Crisp Recipe ... 20
33. Bagel Cheese Appetizers Recipe ... 21
34. Bagel Chips Recipe ... 21
35. Bagels Recipe ... 21
36. Baked Cheese Dip In Sourdough Bread Bowl Recipe ... 21
37. Baked Lime Chipotle Tortilla Chips Recipe 22
38. Baked Prosciutto And Brie With Apple Butter Recipe ... 22
39. Baked Spinach And Feta Topped Pita Bread Recipe ... 22
40. Balsamic And Oil Bread Dipper Recipe ... 23
41. Beach Bread Recipe ... 23
42. Blackberry Almond Bruschetta Recipe ... 23
43. Blinis With Smoked Salmon & Dill Crème Fraiche Recipe ... 24
44. Blooming Party Bread Recipe ... 25
45. Blue Cheese Canapes Recipe ... 25
46. Blue Cheese Cherry Crostini Recipe ... 25
47. Boar's Head Apple & Smoked Gouda Crostini Recipe ... 26
48. Boursin And Prosciutto Wrapped Breadsticks Recipe ... 26
49. Braunschweiger Canapes Recipe ... 27
50. Bread Bowl Bacon Dip Recipe ... 27
51. Bread Bowl For Dips Recipe ... 27
52. Bread Pot Fondue Recipe ... 27
53. Bread Rolls Filled With Wild Mushrooms Recipe ... 28
54. Bread Topped With Tomato Parsley And Feta Recipe ... 28
55. Breaded Cauliflower Recipe ... 28
56. Breaded Mushrooms Recipe ... 29
57. Breaded Parmesan Chicken Strips Recipe . 29
58. Brick Red Butter Mushroom Crostini With Rosemary Recipe ... 30
59. Brie And Jam Cups Recipe ... 30
60. Brie Bread Bowl Dip Recipe ... 31
61. Brie With Strawberries On Brioche Crostini Recipe ... 31
62. Browned Butter Crab Bruschetta Recipe .. 32
63. Bruchetta Recipe ... 32
64. Bruscetta Recipe ... 32

65. Bruschetta Al Pomodoro Formaggio Bianco Recipe ... 33
66. Bruschetta Al Pomodoro Recipe ... 33
67. Bruschetta Ala Leah Recipe ... 34
68. Bruschetta Crisps Recipe ... 35
69. Bruschetta Italiano Recipe ... 35
70. Bruschetta Pizza Recipe ... 36
71. Bruschetta Polenta ... 36
72. Bruschetta Pomodoro Recipe ... 36
73. Bruschetta Recipe ... 36
74. Bruschetta Topping Recipe ... 37
75. Bruschetta With Roasted Cherry Tomatoes Recipe ... 37
76. Bruschetta With Tomato Salad And Chevre Recipe ... 38
77. Bruschetta With Carmelized Peppers And Onions With Goat Cheese Recipe ... 38
78. Bruschetta With Sauteed Sweet Peppers And Creamy Gorgonzola Recipe ... 39
79. Bruschetta With Sun Dried Tomato Relish Roasted Garlic And Brie Recipe ... 39
80. Bruschetta With Sundried Tomato Jam And Goat Cheese Recipe ... 40
81. Bruschetta With Tomato And Basil Recipe 40
82. Bruschetta With Tomatoes And Basil Recipe ... 41
83. Bruschetta With White Bean Puree And Anchovies Recipe ... 41
84. Bubbly Pizza Bread Recipe ... 41
85. California Beef Crostini Recipe ... 42
86. California Roll Recipe ... 42
87. Canape Recipe ... 43
88. Caramelized Onion And Shrimp Bruschetta Recipe ... 43
89. Caramelized Tomato And Courvoisier Canapes Recipe ... 43
90. Cheddar Biscuits From Scratch Delious! Recipe ... 44
91. Cheddar Mushroom French Bread Rounds Appetizers Recipe ... 45
92. Cheddar Rosemary Crackers Recipe ... 46
93. Cheddar Chive Turnovers Recipe ... 46
94. Cheese Steak Stuffed Bread Recipe ... 47
95. Cheese Stuffed Bread Round Recipe ... 47
96. Cheese And Onion Bread Recipe ... 48
97. Cheesey Spinach Canapes Recipe ... 48
98. Cheesy Artichoke Bread Recipe ... 48
99. Cheesy Bacon Snack Bread Recipe ... 49
100. Cheesy Bread Kabobs Recipe ... 49
101. Cheesy Chicken And Chile Canapes Recipe 49
102. Cheesy Garlic Pull Apart Bread Recipe ... 50
103. Cheesy Twists Recipe ... 50
104. Chewy Pretzel Bites Recipe ... 51
105. Chicken And Veggie Ring Recipe ... 51
106. Chicken Barbecue Pizza Recipe ... 52
107. Chicken Liver Mousse Recipe ... 52
108. Christmas Bread Recipe ... 53
109. Clam Canape Recipe ... 53
110. Classic Bruschetta Recipe ... 54
111. Corn Bread Bites Recipe ... 54
112. Corn Bread Dip Recipe ... 54
113. Crab Garlic Bread Recipe ... 55
114. Crab Crostini Recipe ... 55
115. Crab Crostini With Baby Shrimp Recipe ... 55
116. Crab Crostini With Truffle Oil Recipe ... 56
117. Crabmeat Canapes Recipe ... 56
118. Crabmeat Crostini Recipe ... 56
119. Cranberry Blue Crostini Recipe ... 57
120. Cranberry Bruschetta Recipe ... 57
121. Cranberry Herb Almond Crisps Recipe ... 57
122. Crawfish Bread Recipe ... 58
123. Crawfish Corn Bread Recipe ... 58
124. Crazy Quick Cheesy Bread Recipe ... 59
125. Creamy Dill Cucumber Toasties Recipe ... 59
126. Creme De Brie Mango Cranberry Crostini Recipe ... 59
127. Crockpot Bruschetta Recipe ... 60
128. Crostini Boscaiolo Mushroom Toasts Recipe ... 60
129. Crostini Napolentani Appetizer Toasts Neopolitan Style Recipe ... 61
130. Crostini With Creamy Ricotta And Chorizo Recipe ... 61
131. Crostini With Peaches And Blue Cheese Recipe ... 62
132. Crostini With Sun Dried Tomato Tapenade Recipe ... 62
133. Crunchy Bacon And Rosemary Bites Recipe 63
134. Crusty Croutons Recipe ... 63
135. Crusty Garlic Bread Recipe ... 63
136. Crusty Onion Bruschetta Recipe ... 64

137. Cucumber Canapes 64
138. Curry Toast Recipe 64
139. Custom Creation#17(aka Le Petit Gourmand;) Recipe 65
140. Dawn's Fig Crostini Recipe 66
141. Debs Cajun Bread Recipe 66
142. Delicious Garlic Bread Recipe 67
143. Double Tomato Bruschetta Recipe 67
144. Drunken Cheesy Bread Recipe 68
145. EASY Bruschetta Recipe 68
146. Easiest Anchovey Butter Recipe 68
147. Easter Bunny Bread Easy And Cute Recipe 68
148. Easy Breaded Shrimp Recipe 69
149. Easy Bruschetta Bread Recipe 69
150. Easy Bruschetta Recipe 70
151. Easy Cheesy Bread Stix Recipe 70
152. Easy Smoked Salmon Canapes Recipe 70
153. Egg Salad Bruschetta Recipe 71
154. Eggplant Bruschetta Recipe 71
155. English Pea & Fresh Ricotta Crostini Recipe 72
156. FRENCH BREAD APPETIZER Recipe 72
157. Feta Bruschetta 73
158. Fig And Ricotta Crostini Recipe 73
159. Fig And Goat Cheese Bruschetta Recipe .. 73
160. Fontina N Gorgonzola Crostini Recipe 74
161. French Bread Dip Recipe 74
162. Fresh Bruschetta Recipe 75
163. Fresh Easy Bruschetta Recipe 75
164. Fresh Mozzarella And Tomato Crostini Recipe 75
165. Fresh Peach Salsa & Brie Bruschetta Recipe 76
166. Friendship Bread Recipe 76
167. Fruit Bruschetta Recipe 77
168. GREEK BREAD Recipe 77
169. Gamberi Aragonati Shrimp With Garlic And Toasted Bread Crumbs Recipe 77
170. Garbanzo Bean Bruschetta Recipe 78
171. Garlic Bread Fantastique Recipe 78
172. Garlic Bread Recipe 78
173. Garlic Bread Skewers Recipe 79
174. Garlic Bread With Gorgonzola Sauce Recipe 79
175. Garlic Bread W Cheese Recipe 80
176. Garlic Tomato Bread Recipe 80
177. Garlic And Onion Bruschetta Recipe 80
178. Genuine Bruschetta Recipe 81
179. Goat Cheese And Chorizo Crostini Recipe 81
180. Goat Cheese And Sun Dried Tomato Profiteroles With Herb Oil Recipe 82
181. Goat Cheese Bruschetta With Cherries And Mint Recipe 83
182. Goat Cheese Crostini Recipe 83
183. Goat Cheese Crostini With Wild Mushrooms Recipe 83
184. Goat Cheese Stuffed Mushrooms With Bread Crumbs Recipe 84
185. Goat Cheese, Fig And Proscuitto Crostini Recipe 84
186. Gold Stars Recipe 84
187. Gorgonzola Bread Appetizers Recipe 85
188. Gorgonzola And White Bean And Honey Crostini Recipe 85
189. Grape Relish Recipe 86
190. Greek Flavor Bread Recipe 86
191. Grilled Avocado Recipe 86
192. Grilled Eggplant And Pepper Bruschetta Recipe 87
193. Grilled Grapefruit And Honey Chili Flatbread Recipe 88
194. Grilled Tomato And Fresf Mozzarella Bruschetta Recipe 88
195. Halloumi Cheese Bruschetta Wtomato And Olive Tapenade Recipe 89
196. Ham And Asparagus Toast Rounds With Creamy Smoked Gouda Drizzle Recipe ... 89
197. Ham And Cheese Canapes Recipe 90
198. Hearty Double Pesto Crostini Recipe 90
199. Herb Baguettes Recipe 90
200. Herb Dip And Oil For Bread Recipe 91
201. Herbed Fresh Lobster Bruschetta With Red Pepper Mousseline Recipe 91
202. Herbed Goat Cheese Crostini Recipe 92
203. Hogazas Recipe 92
204. Honey Pear Bruschetta Recipe 92
205. Hong Kong Style Pizza Recipe 93
206. Hot Bruschetta Dip Recipe 93
207. Hot Crab Hero Recipe 94
208. Hot Italian Bread Dip Recipe 94
209. Italian Bread Dip Recipe 94
210. Italian Bread Dipping Oil Recipe 95

211. Italian Salad Sandwich Recipe 95
212. Italian Style Creamy Mushroom Sauce On Sourdough Recipe 95
213. Jarlsberg Onion And Apple Canapes Recipe 96
214. Killer Bread Recipe 96
215. LUSCIOUS APPETIZER BREAD Recipe 96
216. Lavash Cracker Bread Bites Recipe 97
217. Little Puff Ball Breads Recipe 97
218. Lump Crab Crostini Recipe 98
219. Margarita Bread Recipe 98
220. Margherita Pizza Recipe 99
221. Margies Cheese Crusty Canape Recipe 99
222. Marinated Peppers With Crusty Grilled Bread Recipe 100
223. Marinated Peppers Bruschetta Recipe 100
224. Mediterranean Pizza Bites Recipe 100
225. Mediterranean Shrimp Bruschetta Recipe 101
226. Mini Brie And Apple Quiches Recipe 101
227. Mini Pepperoni Bread Recipe 102
228. Mini Spinachoke Bowls Recipe 102
229. Mixed Olive Crostini 103
230. Monkey Bread Recipe 103
231. Mozzarella Impanata Breaded And Fried Mozzarella Recipe 103
232. Mozzarella Pepperoni Bread Recipe 104
233. Mozzarella And Tomato Crostini Recipe 104
234. Muffaletta Bites Recipe 104
235. Muffuletta Appetizer Recipe 105
236. Mushroom Bread Recipe 105
237. Mushroom Canapes Recipe 106
238. Mushroom Garlic Crostini For The Slow Cooker Recipe 106
239. Mushroom Strudel Recipe 106
240. Mushrooms/ Smoked Salmon Bruschetta Recipe 107
241. My Favorite Bruschetta Recipe 107
242. Olive & Roasted Pepper Bruschetta 108
243. Olive Cheese Bread Recipe 108
244. Olive Pesto And Bruschetta Cheese Torta Recipe 109
245. Olive Goat Cheese Bruschetta Recipe 109
246. Onion Bread Recipe 110
247. Onions Au Gratin With Parmesan And Sherry Recipe 110

248. Pan Grilled Bruschetta Pomodoro Recipe 110
249. Pancetta Ricotta Roll Crostini Recipe 111
250. Papas Trashy Fish Bread Recipe 111
251. Parmesan Aioli On Grilled Country Bread Recipe 112
252. Pastel Recipe 112
253. Peach Bread Pudding Recipe 113
254. Pear Walnut And Gorgonzola Bruschetta Recipe 113
255. Pecorino Romano Crostini With Apples And Fig Jam Recipe 113
256. Pepper Crostini Recipe 114
257. Pepperonata Sweet And Sour Peppers On Bruschetta Recipe 114
258. Pepperoni Bread Recipe 115
259. Perfect Bruschetta Recipe 115
260. Pesto Bruschetta 116
261. Pita Bread With Baked Spinach Dip Recipe 116
262. Pizza Bread Sticks Recipe 116
263. Pizza Style Cheese On Toast Recipe 117
264. Pizza Whirls Recipe 117
265. Polenta Bruschetta With Tomato Caper Sauce Recipe 117
266. Pomegranate Pistachio Crostini 118
267. Pomodoro Fresco Sourdough Bruschetta Recipe 118
268. Poor Mans Crab Canapes Recipe 119
269. Pork Tenderloin And Goat Cheese Crostini Recipe 119
270. Port Wine And Sesame Biscuits Recipe . 119
271. Portobello Mushroom And Bread Appetizer Recipe 120
272. Primanti Brothers Sliders Recipe 120
273. Pro Bowl Bread Recipe 121
274. Proscuitto Balsamic Crostini Appetizer Recipe 121
275. Provolone Tomato Bruschetta Recipe 122
276. Pull Apart Cheese Bubble Bread Recipe 122
277. Pumpernickel Bread Dip Recipe 122
278. Pumpernickle Bread Dip Recipe 123
279. Put The Shamalama In Your Ding Dong Bruschetta Recipe 123
280. Quick Fix Focaccia Wedges Recipe 124
281. Rainbow Tomato Bruschetta Recipe 124
282. Raspberry Pistachio Blossoms Recipe 124

283. Red Bell Pepper Crostini Recipe 125
284. Red And Yellow Tomato Crostini With Baby Greens Recipe 125
285. Ricotta And Roasted Tomato Crostini Recipe 126
286. Ricotta Pea Crostini Recipe 126
287. Roasted Pepper Tomato Crostini Recipe 126
288. Roasted Red Pepper And Bocconcini Bruschetta Recipe 127
289. Roasted Red Pepper Bruschetta Recipe .. 127
290. Rob And Ninas Ultimate Bruschetta Recipe 128
291. Rye Bread Bowl Dip Recipe 128
292. Salmon And Cous Cous Rolls With A Spicy Cream Cheese Dip. Recipe 128
293. Salsa Dip In Bread Bowl Recipe 129
294. Sausage Bread Recipe 129
295. Sausage Bruschetta Recipe 130
296. Savory Bruschetta Tart Recipe 130
297. Savoury Parmesan Shortbread Snacks Recipe 131
298. Seafood Bread Bowl Dip Recipe 132
299. Serrano Ham With Crusty Bread And Tomatoes Recipe 132
300. Sheepherders Bread Dip Recipe 133
301. Shiitake Ragout On Chevre Crostini Recipe 133
302. Shrimp Bread Recipe 134
303. Shrimp Canapes Recipe 134
304. Skinny Minis Bruschetta Recipe 134
305. Spam Melt With French Turkish Bread Recipe 135
306. Spanish Crostini Recipe 135
307. Spanish Olive And Cream Cheese Canapes Recipe 135
308. Spanner Crab And Corn Quesadilla Recipe 136
309. Spice And Garlic Bread Recipe 136
310. Spicy Caprese Toasts Recipe 137
311. Spinach Artichoke Crab Dip Served In A Bread Bowl Recipe 137
312. Spinach Bread Recipe 138
313. Spinach French Bread Dip Recipe 138
314. Spinach Shrimp Bread Recipe 138
315. Spinach And Feta Bruschetta Recipe 139
316. Stuffed Bread Italian Appetizer Recipe ... 139
317. Stuffed Bread Jalapeno, Cheese And Bacon Recipe 140
318. Stuffed French Bread Recipe 140
319. Stuffed Mexi Pizza Towers W.avocado Jalapeno Crema Recipe 140
320. Summer Bruschetta Recipe 141
321. Summer Brushcetta Bread Recipe 142
322. Summer Heirloom Tomato Bruschetta Recipe 142
323. Sweet Bacon Crackers Recipe 142
324. Sweet Grape Bruschetta Recipe 143
325. Taste Of Italy Bread Dip Recipe 143
326. Thai Curry Chicken Salad In Phyllo Cups Recipe 144
327. Thick, Buttery Soft Pretzels Recipe 144
328. Tia Rosies Football Bread Recipe 145
329. Toasted Mushroom Bread Recipe 145
330. Toasted Seasoned French Bread For Appetizers Recipe 145
331. Tomato And Ricotta Bruschetta Recipe . 146
332. Tomato Bread Pudding Recipe 146
333. Tomato Bruschetta Recipe 147
334. Tomato Crostini Recipe 147
335. Tomato Garlic Bruschetta Recipe 148
336. Tomato Topped Onion Bread Recipe 148
337. Tomato And Avocado Bruschetta Recipe 149
338. Tomato And Avocado Goat Cheese Crostini Recipe 149
339. Tomato And Olive Bruschetta Recipe 150
340. Tony Merlino's Pizza Dough Recipe 150
341. Tuscan Tuna Bruschetta Recipe 150
342. Upsydaisy Canape Recipe 151
343. Very Berry Bruschetta Recipe 151
344. Vidalia Onion And Ham Bruschetta Recipe 152
345. Vidalia Pitza Recipe 152
346. Walnut Gougeres Recipe 152
347. Walnut Spread Recipe 153
348. Warm Butter Bean And Sage Bruschetta Recipe 153
349. Warm Tomato And Feta Bruschetta Recipe 154
350. Warmed Tomato And Garlic Bruschetta With Balsamic Syrup Recipe 154
351. Wegmans Pumpernickel Bread And Beef Dip Recipe 155
352. Whiskey Grapefruit Glazed Smoked Salmon

Crostini Recipe 155
353. White Bean Bruschetta Recipe 156
354. White Bean Crostini Recipe 156
355. White Bean Sun Dried Tomato Bruschetta Recipe 157
356. Wild Mushroom Bruschetta Recipe 157
357. Wonderul Bruschetta Recipe 157
358. Yummy Tomato Basil Bruschetta Recipe 158
359. Zesty Chicken Sombrero's Recipe 158
360. Zuchinni Bread Recipe 159
361. Cheesy Garlic Bread Recipe 159
362. In Your Face Garlic Bread Recipe 160
363. Mushrooms Over Bread Appetizer Recipe 160
364. Spin Off Of Tastefully Simple Beer Bread Recipe 161
365. Turkey With Dill Spread Canapes Recipe 161

INDEX 162

CONCLUSION 166

365 Awesome Bruschetta, Crostini, Breads, And Canapes Recipes

***

1. 16th Century Crostini With Cheese Recipe

Serving: 18 | Prep: | Cook: 10mins | Ready in:

Ingredients

- 18 slices French bread (1 to 1.5 cm), or some slices of coarse bread you cut small rounds from
- 3 mozzarella cheese made with buffalo milk of 150 gram each
- 60 gram butter
- 1 tablespoon powdered sugar (icing sugar) with 1 teaspoon ground cinnamon
- 1 or 2 tablespoons rose water

Direction

- Toast the slices of French bread or larger slices.
- Then fry them shortly in butter over a slow fire. The bread must be golden, not brown.
- Cut the cheese in 18 slices.
- Preparation:
- Heat the (oven with built-in) grill.
- Cover each piece of bread with a slice of Mozzarella. Place the crostini under the grill until the cheese has melted and is starting to colour.
- Take from the grill, sprinkle sugar with cinnamon over it, and rose water.
- Serve: As soon as possible.

2. 1970s Bread Bowl Baked Clam Dip Recipe

Serving: 8 | Prep: | Cook: 30mins | Ready in:

Ingredients

- 2 cans clam "Pieces"
- 1/4 cup clam juice
- 1/2 cup parmesan cheese
- 1/3 cup Mozzarella (or Ricotta) cheese
- 8 cloves garlic, crushed
- 3 TBS. lemon juice
- 1/2 cup butter
- 1/2 cup Italian bread Crumbs
- 1 Sm onion, Diced
- 1 tsp. Worcestershire
- 1/4 tsp. Tabasco
- parsley, Garnish
- 1 Loaf Sour Dough Round or other round similar bread, hollwed out in center

Direction

- METHOD:
- Melt butter and pour over bread crumbs.
- Mix to cover all crumbs evenly.
- Mix all items together with hand mixer and spoon into the hollowed-out round loaf.
- Bake for approx. 30 minutes at 350°F; will be brown and bubbly.

3. 3 Tomato Bruschetta With Basil & Garlic Recipe

Serving: 4 | Prep: | Cook: 10mins | Ready in:

Ingredients

- 1 cup red cherry tomatoes cut in half

- 1 cup yellow cherry tomatoes cut in half
- 2 sundried tomatoes- packed in oil and diced small
- 1/4 fresh basil leaves- rolled and cut into ribbons
- 4-5 tbsp parmigiana cheese- grated
- 3 cloves garlic- crushed and minced
- 1 tbsp italian seasoning
- 1 tbsp (or to taste) red crushed pepper
- 4 tbsp olive oil
- 2 tbsp red wine vinegar
- coarse black pepper- a few grinds
- 1 tsp salt
- 1/4 tsp sugar
- 1/2 garlic baguette- cut into thin slices and toasted

Direction

- 1. In a large bowl add garlic, sundried tomatoes, crushed red pepper, black pepper, Italian seasoning and red wine vinegar. Mix well. In a slow stream pour olive oil while mixing, so everything is combined.
- 2. Add tomatoes and combine. Add salt and sugar, mix and taste. Last, add basil and cheese and mix until everything is coated.
- 3. Place on a serving platter. Garnish with basil and drizzle bread with a little oil. To eat, top each slice with a generous amount of tomatoes and eat!

4. 3 Cheese Bruschetta Recipe

Serving: 6 | Prep: | Cook: 10mins | Ready in:

Ingredients

- 12 inch pre-made pizza crust
- 2 Tablespoons butter, melted
- 1 Tablespoon garlic salt
- 2 teaspoons dried basil
- 2 tomatoes, thinly sliced
- pepper to taste
- 1 cup shredded mozzarella
- 1 cup shredded cheddar (I generally use just 2 cups mozzarella and omit the cheddar)
- 1/2 cup grated parmesan cheese

Direction

- Brush pizza crust with butter; sprinkle with garlic salt and basil. Arrange tomato slices over pizza and sprinkle with pepper. Top with cheeses.
- Place on a baking sheet.
- Bake in a 400 degree oven of 8-10 minutes or until cheese is melted.

5. A Quick Bread App Recipe

Serving: 1 | Prep: | Cook: 5mins | Ready in:

Ingredients

- 1 slice of a wide bread (I like french or Italian bread)
- 3 or 4 slices of tomato (roma will work)
- Small amount of garlic
- Small amount of oregano (basil or thyme) will work also
- 2 slices of your favorite cheese (I like swiss or mozzarela)
- small amount of olive oil or butter (pam will work)
- 1 small skillet or baking sheet

Direction

- You can bake this if you like and this is only a start you can change this any way you like
- I take the skillet and heat it up
- I spread the bread with olive oil mixed with the garlic and put in the skillet
- I brown both sides and while it is still in the skillet I put on the cheese. I then remove the toast and put on the tomatoes and sprinkle lightly with the herbs and serve quickly.
- You can serve with a marinara sauce or with a bbq meal. Grill the bread if you like.

6. APACHE BREAD Recipe

Serving: 8 | Prep: | Cook: 70mins | Ready in:

Ingredients

- 1 9-inch round loaf of bread (any round, loaf)
- 16 oz grated sharp cheddar cheese
- 8 oz cream cheese, softened
- 8 oz dairy sour cream
- 1/2 cup minced green onion, white and green part
- 1-2 tsp worcestershire sauce
- 2 , 4.5 oz cans chopped green chilies
- 1 cup chopped cooked ham

Direction

- Cut the top off the bread and scoop out the inside, leaving about a half-inch shell on all sides and bottom.
- Reserve top and scooped insides and set aside.
- Combine, cheddar, cream cheese, sour cream, green onion,
- Worcestershire, green chilies and ham; mix well.
- This will be a very stiff mixture.
- Fill the hollow bread with the cheese mixture; replace the top and place, uncovered, on a cookie sheet.
- Bake in a 350*F oven for 1 hour and 10 minutes.
- Guests can use the removed bread for dipping as well as corn chips or tortillas chips.
- Tear off the sides of the bread and eat it as the level of the dip lowers.

7. Aciete Y Tomate Español Recipe

Serving: 0 | Prep: | Cook: 15mins | Ready in:

Ingredients

- Good Quality Extra Virgin Olive Oil - Essential
- Baguette/Crusty bread - Toasted then cut lengthways into around 4 inch/10cm lengths
- Whole clove(s) - Garlic - peeled
- Ripe Plum/Vine/Salad Tomatoes - finely grated - can peel first if wish
- Salt and freshly ground black pepper
- Optional - dried Oregano

Direction

- Finely grate tomatoes - peeled or not in a small bowl
- Lightly pierce the entire surface of the open face of each toasted slice with a fork;
- Rub the face of each slice with garlic clove;
- Lightly pour or sprinkle oil over the face of the toast;
- Spoon and spread the grated tomato over the toast;
- Sprinkle over to taste with salt and pepper;
- If using: Sprinkle over with dried oregano;
- Devour.

8. Almond Breaded Tilapia Nuggets With Cajun Rub Served With Honey Habanero Bbq Sauce And Greek Style Yogurt Recipe

Serving: 4 | Prep: | Cook: 15mins | Ready in:

Ingredients

- Tilapia cut into two-inch by two- inch strips.
- CAJUN RUB:
- 1teaspoon sea salt
- 1teaspoon garlic powder
- 1teaspoon cayenne pepper
- BREADING:
- 2 cups of barley bread crumbs or whole wheat bread crumbs.

- ½ cup sliced almonds course ground
- 4 tablespoons of fresh parsley rough chopped.
- ½-teaspoon cayenne
- ½-teaspoon ground ginger
- ½ cup all purpose flour
- 1-cup buttermilk
- One large egg
- FOR FRYING:
- 4 tablespoons sweet butter
- 4 tablespoons olive oil
- honey habanero BBQ SAUCE:
- ½ cup of honey
- 1/4-cup Habenero Chipotle BB-Q-Sauce Recipe (see my recipe)
- ½-cup Greek style yogurt

Direction

- Beat the egg and add the buttermilk and beat until blended.
- Combine the rub ingredients in a small bowl set aside
- Combine the breading ingredients set aside.
- Sprinkle the Tilapia with the Cajun Rub and rub it evenly on both sides of the fish.
- Add the flour to a bowl and toss the Tilapia to coat shake off excess flour.
- Heat a fry pan with the oil and butter on medium high heat.
- Dip a few pieces at a time into the buttermilk mixture and coat generously with the breadcrumb mixture.
- Fry until golden on each side and place on cookie sheet lined with a paper towel.
- Repeat until all the tilapia is finished.
- Serve on a warmed plate with Honey BBQ Sauce and a dollop of Greek style yogurt.

9. Almond Bacon Cheese Crostini

Serving: 6 | Prep: | Cook: 10mins | Ready in:

Ingredients

- 1 French bread baguette (1 pound), cut into 36 slices
- 2 cups shredded Monterey Jack cheese
- 2/3 cup mayonnaise
- 1/2 cup sliced almonds, toasted
- 6 bacon strips, cooked and crumbled
- 1 green onion, chopped
- Dash salt
- Additional toasted almonds, optional

Direction

- Place bread slices on an ungreased baking sheet. Bake at 400° until lightly browned, 8-9 minutes.
- Meanwhile, in a large bowl, combine the cheese, mayonnaise, almonds, bacon, onion and salt. Spread over bread. Bake until cheese is melted, 7-8 minutes. Sprinkle with additional almonds if desired. Serve warm.
- Nutrition Facts
- 1 each: 120 calories, 8g fat (2g saturated fat), 8mg cholesterol, 160mg sodium, 10g carbohydrate (0 sugars, 1g fiber), 3g protein.

10. Anchovy Canapes Recipe

Serving: 16 | Prep: | Cook: 15mins | Ready in:

Ingredients

- 4 ounces canned flat anchovy fillets
- 2 medium garlic cloves chopped fine
- 1 teaspoon tomato paste
- 1-1/2 tablespoons olive oil
- 2 teaspoons lemon juice or red wine vinegar
- 1 teaspoon freshly ground black pepper
- 8 slices French bread
- 1 teaspoon finely chopped parsley

Direction

- Drain anchovies and place in heavy bowl with garlic and tomato paste.
- Mash mixture to a smooth puree.

- Dribble in oil a few drops at a time stirring until mixture becomes thick and smooth.
- Stir in the lemon juice and pepper.
- Preheat oven to 500.
- Brown bread lightly on one side.
- While bread is still warm spread untoasted side with anchovy mixture.
- Arrange bread on a baking sheet and bake 10 minutes.
- Sprinkle with parsley and serve at once.

11. Anchovy Toasts Recipe

Serving: 16 | Prep: | Cook: 5mins | Ready in:

Ingredients

- 1 (15-ounce) can white beans, drained, rinsed, mashed
- 3 tablespoons extra-virgin olive oil
- 2 tablespoons minced Italian (flat-leaf) parsley
- 2 tablespoons minced onion
- 1 tablespoon + 1 teaspoon lemon juice
- 2 garlic cloves, minced pepper to taste
- 16 small slices French bread, toasted
- 1 can (2 ounces) anchovy fillets in olive oil

Direction

- Mix beans, oil, parsley, onion, lemon juice, garlic and pepper in a small bowl, making make 1 cup spread. Spoon a bit on each slice of toast and top each with 2 anchovies.
- Nutritional Information per Serving:
- Total Fat 4g; Saturated Fat 1g; Cholesterol 5mg; Sodium 330mg; Total Carbohydrate 23g; Dietary Fibre 2g; Sugars 2g; Protein 6g

12. Anchovy Amp Cherry Tomato Bruschetta Recipe

Serving: 10 | Prep: | Cook: 3mins | Ready in:

Ingredients

- 2 mini French bread loafs
- 2-3 cloves garlic, peeled but left whole
- extra virgin olive oil
- sea salt flakes and coarsely ground black pepper
- 8 oz cherry tomatoes, stalks removed and sliced
- 3 oz anchovy fillets in olive oil, drained

Direction

- To Grill the Bread:
- Cut the bread diagonally across into thin slices. Heat a ridged cast iron griddle pan over a medium heat, add some of the bread slices and grill for about 1 minute on each side until golden and very slightly charred in places.
- To season the Bread:
- As soon as each batch of bread is ready, rub one side of each slice with a peeled garlic clove, then drizzle with a little of the olive oil and sprinkle with some sea salt flakes and pepper.
- And Finally:
- Top each slice of bread with 2 slices of tomato and one twisted anchovy fillet. Serve straight away.
- Makes approx 30

13. Ants On A Raft Recipe

Serving: 1 | Prep: | Cook: 5mins | Ready in:

Ingredients

- peanut butter
- Ritz crackers
- raisins

Direction

- 1. Get crackers and smear peanut butter on each

- 2. Place one cracker on top of each peanut butter cracker
- 3. put raisins on the inside of each
- 4. Eat it and enjoy!

14. Appetizer Artichoke Bread Recipe

Serving: 1214 | Prep: | Cook: 25mins | Ready in:

Ingredients

- 1 loaf (1 pound) unsliced French bread
- 1-1/2 cups (12 ounces) sour cream
- 1/2 cup butter, melted
- 2 tablespoons sesame seeds
- 2 cups (8 ounces) shredded monterey jack cheese
- 1 cup (4 ounces) shredded cheddar cheese
- 1/4 cup grated parmesan cheese
- 1 jar (6-1/2 ounces) marinated artichoke hearts, drained and chopped
- 4 garlic cloves, minced
- 2 tablespoons minced fresh parsley
- 2 teaspoons lemon-pepper seasoning
-

Direction

- Cut bread in half lengthwise; hollow out, leaving 1/2-in. shells. Set aside. Place removed bread in a food processor; cover and process until crumbly.
- In a large bowl, combine the bread crumbs, sour cream, butter and sesame seeds; spread onto a baking sheet. Broil 4 in. from the heat for 8-10 minutes or until lightly browned, stirring once.
- In a large bowl, combine the crumb mixture, cheeses, artichokes, garlic, parsley and lemon-pepper. Spoon into bread shells.
- Place on a baking sheet. Bake at 350° for 25 minutes or until golden brown. Slice and serve warm.

15. Appetizer Bread Stuffed With Italian Sausage Recipe

Serving: 16 | Prep: | Cook: 22mins | Ready in:

Ingredients

- 1 package groundor link italian sausage
- 1 loaf frozen white bread dough, thawed
- 1/2 cup softened cream cheese
- 2 large garlic cloves, minced
- 1 jar (7 ounces) roasted red peppers, well drained and sliced
- 1/3 cup kalamata olives, pitted and sliced
- 2 cups shredded swiss cheese
- 1 teaspoon poppy seeds (optional)

Direction

- On lightly floured surface, roll bread dough into 16 x 12-inch rectangle.
- Combine cream cheese and garlic, spread lengthwise over centre third of dough.
- Top with sausage, peppers, olives and Swiss cheese.
- Fold dough over filling, pinching seam to seal.
- Make slits across top of dough every 2 inches.
- Brush lightly with water and sprinkle with poppy seeds.
- Bake at 400°F 20 to 25 minutes or until golden brown.
- Let stand 10 minutes before slicing.

16. Appetizers Recipe

Serving: 4 | Prep: | Cook: 1mins | Ready in:

Ingredients

- salami
- bacon
- chilli cream cheese
- baguette bread

- black olives
- toast cheese slices
- chilli stuffed with cheese
- tuna salad

Direction

- Stuff the bacon with tuna salad. Roll.
- Cut the baguette in medium slices and smear them with chilli cream cheese. Put above them black olives.
- Put a salami slices, then, on it, a cheese slice, a salami, a cheese, till is thick, and finish with a salami slices.
- Then, cut in cubes.
- Arrange them on a plate, and put in the middle a cheese stuffed pepper.

17. Apple Goat Cheese Bruschetta Recipe

Serving: 8 | Prep: | Cook: 2mins | Ready in:

Ingredients

- 1/4 cup crumbled goat cheese
- 1 fuji apple - peeled, cored, and chopped
- 3/4 teaspoon chopped fresh thyme
- 1/2 teaspoon chopped fresh oregano
- 1/4 teaspoon coarse ground black pepper
- 8 thin slices French bread

Direction

- Preheat the oven's broiler and set the oven rack 3 to 4 inches from the heat source.
- Toss together the goat cheese, apple, thyme, oregano, and pepper in a bowl; set aside.
- Arrange the bread slices on a baking sheet; toast the bread under the broiler until golden brown, 1 to 2 minutes.
- Sprinkle the goat cheese mixture evenly over the bread slices.
- Return bread to oven to broil until cheese is softened, about 1 minute more.

18. Apricot Rosemary Crackers Recipe

Serving: 0 | Prep: | Cook: 90mins | Ready in:

Ingredients

- 2 Cups of Oat Flour
- 2 Tsp of baking soda
- 1/2 Tsp of Salt
- 2 Cups of Plain Yogurt
- 1/2 Cup of Raisins
- 1/2 Cup of Dried apricots, chopped
- 1/2 Cup of Pumpkin Seeds
- 1/2 Cup of Sunflower Seeds
- 1/4 Cup of Honey
- 1/4 Cup of brown sugar
- 1 Tsp of Rosemary
- 1/4 Cup of Flax Seeds

Direction

- Mix all ingredients, pour into 2 greased and lined loaf pans. Bake 45 minutes at 350, let cool in pans, then freeze for a few hours. Slice loaf into thin slices. Place on parchment cookie sheet. Bake at 300 for 15 minutes, flip and toast for 10 minutes more.

19. Apricot Rosemary Crostini With Brie Recipe

Serving: 15 | Prep: | Cook: 5mins | Ready in:

Ingredients

- 3/4 cup apricot Spread
- 1 lb . Brie, trim rind off
- 30 rosemary Crostini
- apricot SPREAD
- 3 cups apricot, thawed

- 1 sprig rosemary, leaves minced
- 1 tsp. lemon zest, thawed
- Combine the apricot puree, lemon zest puree and minced rosemary in a saucepot.
- Bring to a boil, reduce to simmer and cook until reduced to 3/4 cup. Remove from the stove. Cool.

Direction

- Preheat oven to 350 degrees.
- Spread one side of the rosemary croutons with the All Apricot Spread.
- Top with a small 1/2 oz. slice of Brie and bake in oven to lightly melt the cheese. Serve.

20. Artichoke Bread Recipe

Serving: 10 | Prep: | Cook: 25mins | Ready in:

Ingredients

- 1 loaf French bread, cut in half lengthwise
- 1½ cups sour cream
- ½ cup butter, melted
- 1 cup shredded cheddar cheese
- 1 cup fresh grated parmesan cheese
- 15 ounce can artichoke hearts, drained and finely chopped
- 3 cloves of garlic, run through garlic press

Direction

- Cut the bread in half the long way, and scoop out just a bit of the middle from each half. Lay halves on cookie sheet (line with foil if you don't want any clean up after baking). Combine remaining ingredients and spread equally between the bread halves, spreading to the very edges of the bread. Bake at 350 degrees until top is golden and bubbly, about 20 to 25 minutes. Remove bread from oven and slice into 2" slices for serving.
- Alternate method:

- Slice a loaf of French bread into 1" slices. Lay the slices on a cookie sheet and bake at 425 degrees until just barely browned - they will brown more when they are baked with the topping (watch the bottoms closely, as they will usually brown first – you only need one side browned, so don't flip them and toast the other side). If you really want an added garlic bang, run the cut side of a garlic clove over the toasted side as soon as you remove the pan from the oven. You can cool and store the toasted slices until you are ready to prepare the appetizers. When ready, spread the un-browned tops of each slice with the cheese and artichoke mixture, and place them on a cookie sheet. Bake at 350 degrees about 12 minutes, and then broil until the tops are browned and bubbly.
- NOTE: you can also use crackers, like Triscuit, spreading them with a thin layer of the spread and popping them under the broiler until browned and bubbly. Experiment any way you like!

21. Artichoke Bruschetta Recipe

Serving: 8 | Prep: | Cook: 2mins | Ready in:

Ingredients

- 1 (6.5 ounce) jar marinated artichoke hearts, drained and chopped
- 1/2 cup grated romano cheese
- 1/3 cup finely chopped red onion
- 5 tablespoons mayonnaise
- 1 french baguette, cut into 1/3 inch thick slices

Direction

- Preheat the broiler.
- In a medium bowl, mix marinated artichoke hearts, Romano cheese, red onion and mayonnaise. Top French baguette slices with equal amounts of the artichoke heart mixture.

- Arrange slices in a single layer on a large baking sheet.
- Broil in the preheated oven 2 minutes, or until toppings are bubbly and lightly browned.

22. Artichoke Heart Bread Recipe

Serving: 12 | Prep: | Cook: 30mins | Ready in:

Ingredients

- 1/4 cup of butter or margarine
- 3-4 cloves of garlic
- 16oz jar of artichoke hearts
- 1 cup of shredded spicy jack cheese
- 1 cup of sour cream
- 1 cup of cream cheese
- 1 cup parmesan cheese
- 1 loaf French bread large
- 3/4 cup shredded cheddar cheese

Direction

- Preheat oven to 375
- Melt butter in pan over med heat
- Add minced garlic cloves
- Cook 10 min or until light brown
- Stir in cheeses (except cheddar) sour cream and artichoke
- Remove from heat
- Cut bread in half lengthwise
- Scoop out centre of bread halves
- Add about half of bread from centre
- Mix well
- Scoop mixture into bread halves
- Sprinkle with cheddar cheese
- Cover with foil and bake 25 min
- Uncover and bake 5-10 more min until cheese is bubbly and done how you like it…I like mine brown.
- Let cool a little then slice

23. Asparagus Bruschetta Recipe

Serving: 12 | Prep: | Cook: 2mins | Ready in:

Ingredients

- 1 pound asparagus, ends trimmed and cut into 2 inch pieces
- 8 ounces gruyere cheese, grated
- 6 ounces good country ham, or 4
- ounces prosciutto, finely chopped or
- ground in food processor
- 1 10 oz french baguette, cut into 1/2-
- inch slices, grilled or toasted
- 3 garlic cloves, peeled and cut in half
- extra-virgin olive oil
- kosher salt
- freshly ground black pepper

Direction

- Preheat broiler.
- Bring a large sauté pan of salted water to a boil over high heat. Add the asparagus and cook until tender crisp, about 2 minutes. Transfer the asparagus to a colander, refresh under cold running water to stop the cooking, and drain well. Set aside.
- In a small bowl, combine the cheese and ham; toss to mix. Set aside.
- Using your fingers to hold the garlic, rub the clove against one side of the toasted bread to flavour the entire surface. Drizzle or brush with a bit of the olive oil.
- Arrange the blanched asparagus on the toasts, then divide the cheese and ham topping evenly over the asparagus. Season with salt and pepper.
- Place bruschetta on a baking sheet and broil just until the cheese melts and begins to brown, about 1-2 minutes. Keep a careful watch so as not to burn.
- Serve immediately.

24. Asparagus, Sundried Tomato And Olive Loaf Recipe

Serving: 0 | Prep: | Cook: 45mins | Ready in:

Ingredients

- 100ml/3 and half fl oz extra virgin olive oil plus extra for greasing.
- 250g/9oz asparagus spears, each cut into 3 pieces.
- 200g/ 8oz self-raising flour
- 1tbsp thyme leaves
- 3 large eggs, lightly beaten
- 100ml/3 and a half fl oz milk
- handful pitted black olives
- 100g/4oz sun dried tomatoes, roughly chopped
- 100g/4oz vegetarian gruyère, grated.

Direction

- Mix the flour and thyme with seasoning in a large bowl. Make a well in the centre, then add the eggs, milk and oil, stirring all the time to draw the flour into the centre. Beat for 1 min to make a smooth batter.
- Reserve 5 asparagus tips and a few olives.
- Add the remaining asparagus, tomatoes, olives and two-thirds of the cheese to the batter. Pour into the tin, then put the reserved asparagus and olives on top.
- Sprinkle with the remaining cheese. Bake for 35-40 mins until the cake feels firm to the touch and is golden and crusty on top. Cool in the tin for 5 mins, then turn out and leave to cool on a wire rack.
- Heat oven to 190c/170c fan/gas 5. Oil and line the base of a loaf tin (approx. 22 x 10 x 5cm) with baking paper. Cook the asparagus in boiling, salted water for 2 mins, drain, then cool quickly under cold running water. Pat dry.

25. Avotato Canape And Apricream Canape Recipe

Serving: 0 | Prep: | Cook: 30mins | Ready in:

Ingredients

- 12 pieces   cheese cracker / salted cracker, as a base of canape
- 1/2 nos   Avocado, For the avocado canape
- 1/2 nos   Potato, For the avocado canape
- 1 pinch   Salt, For the avocado canape
- 1 pinch   Ground pepper, For the avocado canape
- as need   whole pink pepper, For the avocado canape
- as need   Chervil leaves, For the avocado canape
- 3 tablespoon   Cream, For the apricot cream canape
- 2 teaspoon   apricot jam, For the Apricot cream canape
- as need   Salmon roe, For the apricot cream canape
- as need   chervil leaves, For the apricot cream canape

Direction

- CANAPE PREPARATION
- Arrange the base on the plate or pan, where the canapé will not be moved after finished made, as transferring the well-made canapé may collapse it.
- Prepare the dip and sit the dip on the crackers.
- Garnish and light the canapé up.
- MAKING AVOCADO DIP
- AVOCADO DIP CANAPE
- Remove the skin and seed of the avocado, cook and soften the potato in a hot simmering water.
- Mash the potato and avocado in a bowl, then season with salt and paper and mix them well.
- Shape the avocado dip and sit on the crackers, then garnish with whole pink pepper and chervil leaves.
- APRICOT CREAM CANAPE

- Mix well the cream and the apricot jam.
- Pipe the cream mixture on the cracker with a piping bag, or any shape you like.
- Garnish with salmon roe and chervil leaves.

26. BRUSCHETTA DI MAZZANCOLLE DA ZACCARIA Recipe

Serving: 8 | Prep: | Cook: 10mins | Ready in:

Ingredients

- 4 tablespoons virgin olive oil
- 2 garlic cloves peeled and sliced thin
- 12 large shrimp peeled and deveined
- 1 lemon juiced and zested
- 2 ounces limoncello liqueur
- 4 ounces dry white wine
- 1 bunch chives snipped
- 4 slices country style bread cut 3/4inch thick

Direction

- In 14 inch sauté pan heat oil over medium heat until just smoking.
- Add garlic and toast until light brown then add shrimp and cook 3 minutes.
- Turn shrimp over and add lemon juice, limoncello and wine then cook 1 minute.
- Meanwhile grill bread and place 1 slice on each plate then divide shrimp over bread.
- Add chives to pan and divide sauce over shrimp.
- Sprinkle with lemon zest and serve immediately.

27. BRUSCHETTA Recipe

Serving: 4 | Prep: | Cook: 8mins | Ready in:

Ingredients

- 2 tomatoes, cubed
- 1 teaspoon dried basil
- 4 tablespoons grated parmesan cheese
- 2 tablespoons olive oil
- 1 clove garlic, crushed
- seasoned salt to taste
- ground black pepper to taste

Direction

- In a medium bowl, mix tomatoes, basil, Parmesan cheese, olive oil, garlic, seasoned salt and ground black pepper.
- Cover and chill in the refrigerator 8 hours, or overnight, before serving.

28. BRUSCHETTA WITH AVOCADO AND GREEN ONION Recipe

Serving: 8 | Prep: | Cook: 10mins | Ready in:

Ingredients

- 1 ripe avocado
- 1 teaspoon fresh lemon juice
- 1 teaspoon salt
- 2 slices country bread thick slices
- 1 garlic clove peeled cut in half
- 2 green onions tops trimmed and thinly sliced
- extra virgin olive oil

Direction

- Peel avocado then place in a bowl and mash coarsely with a fork adding lemon juice and salt.
- Grill bread and rub with the cut side of the garlic clove and drizzle with olive oil.
- Mound avocado mixture on top of bread slices and sprinkle with green onions.
- Drizzle a few drops of olive oil over the top.

29. Bacon Bread Wraps Recipe

Serving: 12 | *Prep:* | *Cook: 20mins* | *Ready in:*

Ingredients

- 15 slices of bread
- 5 strips bacon, cut into thirds
- 1 can cream of mushroom soup
- toothpicks

Direction

- Cut the crusts off each piece of bread.
- Cut each piece of bread into thirds.
- Lay a piece of bacon down, top with one piece of bread.
- Spread soup over; wrap up bacon & bread and secure with a toothpick.
- Repeat for all the bacon and bread.
- Bake on cookie sheet at 375 degrees 15 to 20 minutes.

30. Bacon Canapes Recipe

Serving: 15 | *Prep:* | *Cook: 4mins* | *Ready in:*

Ingredients

- 1 cup mayonnaise
- 1 cup of cheddar or swiss cheese, grated
- 1 pound of crisply cooked bacon, crumbled
- 1 roll of thin party pumpernickel or rye bread

Direction

- Oven temperature 400 degrees
- Mix mayonnaise, cheese, and bacon together and spread on bread.
- Put in oven on cookie sheet and bake for 4 minutes until bubbly and hot.
- Spread may be made ahead. Bacon must be very crisp.

31. Bacon Cheese Spread In Bread Bowl Recipe

Serving: 6 | *Prep:* | *Cook: 60mins* | *Ready in:*

Ingredients

- 1 loaf round bread, any flavor
- 12 bacon slices, crisply cooked and crumbled
- 8 ounces shredded cheese
- 1 cup parmesan cheese
- 1 cup mayo (I use the free type)
- 1 small onion, finely chopped (I have to leave this out because of my husbands tummy)

Direction

- Cut top off the bread loaf and remove the centre.....make sure you leave enough for the shell. Cut up bread from centre into small pieces.
- Mix remaining ingredients in small bowl. Spoon into bread bowl. Cover with top of bread. Place on baking sheet.
- Bake 350 degrees for one hour

32. Bacon Crisp Recipe

Serving: 24 | *Prep:* | *Cook: 10mins* | *Ready in:*

Ingredients

- 1/2 c fresh grated Parmesan cheese
- 1 sleeve buttery rectangular crackers(recommended:Waverly Wafers)
- 1 lb sliced bacon cut in 1/2

Direction

- Preheat oven to 250'
- Place 1 tsp. of cheese on each cracker and wrap tightly with a piece of bacon. Place wrapped crackers on broiler rack on baking sheet and put baking sheet in the oven.

- Bake for 2 hours or till bacon is done. Do not turn. Drain on paper towels. Serve hot or at room temperature.
- Note: You can bake at 350' for 40 mins. If you are in a hurry.

33. Bagel Cheese Appetizers Recipe

Serving: 0 | Prep: | Cook: 20mins | Ready in:

Ingredients

- 1 bag mini bagels
- 1-2 tubs veggie cream cheese
- Sliced red onion
- Peeled & sliced cucumber
- Sliced roma tomatoes
- provolone cheese-quartered

Direction

- Split Bagels
- Spread cream cheese on each bagel half
- Top with a cucumber slice, a few onion pieces, & a tomato slice.
- Top with a piece of cheese
- Broil till cheese is melted

34. Bagel Chips Recipe

Serving: 0 | Prep: | Cook: 20mins | Ready in:

Ingredients

- Thinly sliced bagels - anykind
- 1/4 cup olive oil
- dried basil
- sea salt

Direction

- Placed the bagels on a baking sheet and brush with olive oil and then sprinkle on the basil and sea salt and bake in the oven for 15 minutes or golden brown

35. Bagels Recipe

Serving: 8 | Prep: | Cook: 40mins | Ready in:

Ingredients

- 16 Rhodes™ dinner rolls, thawed but still cold
- 1 tablespoon baking soda
- grated cheese, seeds or spices

Direction

- Combine 2 rolls together into a nice round ball.
- Put both pointer fingers through centre of the ball and stretch to form a large hole.
- Repeat with remaining rolls.
- Place bagels on a large sprayed baking sheet.
- Cover with sprayed plastic wrap and let rise 30-45 minutes.
- In a large saucepan, bring 6 inches of water with baking soda to a boil.
- Slip bagels, one or two at a time into gently boiling water.
- Boil for 30 seconds on each side.
- Remove with slotted spoon; drain on cooling rack for a few seconds.
- Return to sprayed baking sheet and sprinkle with cheese or seeds if desired.
- Bake at 375°F 15-20 minutes or until golden brown.

36. Baked Cheese Dip In Sourdough Bread Bowl Recipe

Serving: 8 | Prep: | Cook: 75mins | Ready in:

Ingredients

- 1 round sourdough bread, hollowed out (10 in.)
- 1 can artichokes, not marinated, chopped
- 1 cup cheddar cheese, shredded
- 1 clove garlic, minced
- 1 cup mayonnaise
- 1 cup monterey jack cheese, shredded
- 1 small onion, finely chopped
- 1 cup parmesan cheese, grated
- .

Direction

- Preheat oven to 350
- Hollow out sourdough bread (save insides)
- Mix rest of ingredients together
- Put mixture into bread
- Put lid back on bread
- Bake 1 1/4 hours
- Cube bread and place around bowl

37. Baked Lime Chipotle Tortilla Chips Recipe

Serving: 10 | Prep: | Cook: 20mins | Ready in:

Ingredients

- corn tortillas
- fresh lime juice
- Chipotle Chille powder
- salt optional

Direction

- There is really no set amounts of the above ingredients just use what you like
- Preheat oven to 375 degrees
- Place a stack of about 10 tortillas on chopping board and cut into triangles then place them on a sprayed/oiled cookie sheet and then brush with the lime juice and sprinkle with chipotle chilli powder and then bake in the oven for 7 minutes and then turn over and bake another 7 minutes or until crisp

38. Baked Prosciutto And Brie With Apple Butter Recipe

Serving: 0 | Prep: | Cook: 30mins | Ready in:

Ingredients

- 1 loaf crusty French bread
- 4 Tbs butter, softened
- 1 cup apple butter
- 16 thin slices prosciutto, about 1/4 pound
- 2 pears or apples, thinly sliced
- 1 lb Brie, thinly sliced
- kosher salt and freshly ground black pepper
- extra-virgin olive oil, for drizzling (or drizzle honey_- my note)

Direction

- 1. Heat the oven to 450 degrees F.
- 2. Cut 16 (1/2-inch thick) slices out of the loaf.
- 3. Butter each side of the slices and put them onto a baking sheet.
- 4. Spread 1 tablespoon of apple butter onto each slice.
- 5. Top this with 1 slice of prosciutto and 3 or 4 slices of pear or apple.
- 6. Cover this with the Brie slices, season with salt and pepper, and drizzle with olive oil.
- 7. Bake until the cheese is melted, about 8 to 10 minutes.
- 8. Wonderful served with champagne

39. Baked Spinach And Feta Topped Pita Bread Recipe

Serving: 4 | Prep: | Cook: 12mins | Ready in:

Ingredients

- 6 (6 inch) whole wheat pita breads

- 1 (6 ounce) tub sun-dried tomato pesto
- 2 roma (plum) tomatoes, chopped
- 1 bunch spinach, rinsed and chopped
- 4 fresh mushrooms, sliced
- 1/2 cup crumbled feta cheese
- 2 tablespoons grated parmesan cheese
- 3 tablespoons olive oil
- 1 pinch ground black pepper to taste

Direction

- Preheat the oven to 350 degrees F (175 degrees C).
- Spread tomato pesto onto one side of each pita bread, and place them pesto side up on a baking sheet.
- Top with tomatoes, spinach, mushrooms, feta cheese, and Parmesan cheese.
- Drizzle with olive oil and season with pepper.
- Bake for 12 minutes in the preheated oven or until pita breads are crisp.
- Cut into quarters and serve

40. Balsamic And Oil Bread Dipper Recipe

Serving: 4 | Prep: | Cook: | Ready in:

Ingredients

- Balsamic Vineagar, mid-sweetness if you can
- extra virgin olive oil (use enough to balance out the balsamic)
- dried basil
- Dried oregano
- S&P (fresh cracked if you can)
- dried red chili peppers (optional but worth it!)
- Tools:
- Mortar and Pestle
- Flattish plate for easy bread dipping

Direction

- Finley grind all herb ingredients using a mortar and pestle (or your thumb and index finger). Set aside.
- Pour balsamic in plate first, use as much as you like.
- Add EVOO over the balsamic. I usually don't measure this because it depends on the type of balsamic I use. Take a fork and mix it up a bit.
- Add crushed herbs. Take fork and mix again. Let stand for 10 mins.
- Just before serving, add S&P if you haven't already and mix with fork again.
- Serve with a warm baguette and some oven roasted garlic!

41. Beach Bread Recipe

Serving: 0 | Prep: | Cook: 20mins | Ready in:

Ingredients

- French bread, sliced
- Chunky blue cheese dressing
- garlic & onion powder
- parmesan cheese, grated
- mozzarella cheese, sliced
- Fresh Chopped tomato and herbs (basil, parsley, etc.)

Direction

- Lightly toast bread with a drizzle of olive oil in 350 oven. Spread with dressing, sprinkle lightly with garlic and onion, add Parmesan Cheese, Mozzarella slices, and return to oven to melt. Top with tomato and herbs.

42. Blackberry Almond Bruschetta Recipe

Serving: 24 | Prep: | Cook: 20mins | Ready in:

Ingredients

- 1 can pillsbury refrigerated Crusty French loaf
- butter-flavor cooking spray
- 2T. granulated sugar
- 8oz. pkg. reduced fat cream cheese
- 1&1/2t. almond extract
- 1 pkg. frozen blackberries; thawed & well drained
- 1/3c. sliced almonds; toasted
- 3T. powdered sugar

Direction

- Preheat oven to 350F.
- Bake bread as directed on can. Cool 5 min.
- Cut ends off of loaf.
- Cut remaining loaf into 24 1/2" slices.
- Arrange slices on ungreased cookie sheet.
- Spray each slice lightly with cooking spray & sprinkle with granulated sugar.
- Bake 8-10 min. until lightly toasted.
- Meanwhile, beat cream cheese, extract & powdered sugar until combined.
- Spread cheese mixture onto toasted bread slices.
- Top each slice with 3 or 4 berries & sprinkle with almonds.
- Dust each bruschetta with powdered sugar.
- NUTRITIONAL DATA:
- 1 appetizer =
- 90 calories (30 from fat)
- Total fat: 3.5g
- Saturated Fat: 1.5g
- Trans Fat: 0g
- Cholesterol: 5mg
- Sodium: 115mg
- Total Carbs: 11g
- Fibre: 0g
- Sugar: 5g
- Protein: 2g

43. Blinis With Smoked Salmon & Dill Crème Fraiche Recipe

Serving: 10 | Prep: | Cook: 30mins | Ready in:

Ingredients

- 2 cups all purpose flour
- 1 teaspoon baking powder
- 3 cage-free eggs, separated
- 1 1/2 cups buttermilk
- 4 tablespoons unsalted butter, melted
- 1/4 cups chopped green onions
- 2 heaping tablespoons chopped fresh dill
- 1 teaspoon kosher salt
- 3 tablespoons each of canola oil & melted butter - for brushing on the griddle (or nonstick pan)
- For Topping:
- 1 cup Crème fraiche
- 1 1/2 teaspoons white pepper
- 2 tablespoons chopped fresh dill
- 4 to 5 ounces smoked salmon
- 8 to 10 dill sprigs for garnish

Direction

- In a small bowl, whisk together the crème fraiche and dill and season with salt and pepper to taste. Refrigerate until needed.
- In a small bowl, sift together the flour and baking powder. Reserve.
- In a separate bowl, whisk together the egg yolks, buttermilk, and melted butter. Add to the dry ingredients, along with the green onions and dill. Stir gently until incorporated.
- Using a wire whisk or an electric mixer, whisk the egg whites until shiny and firm but not dry. Stir a little into the batter, and then fold in the remaining whites.
- In a small bowl, combine 3 tablespoons melted butter with 3 tablespoons oil. Heat a 10-inch non-stick skillet or griddle and brush with some of the butter mixture. For each pancake, using 2 tablespoons of batter, make 2-1/2-inch pancakes onto the griddle and, over a medium flame, cook until brown on one side. Turn and

brown the other side, brushing the skillet or griddle with the butter mixture as necessary. As the pancakes are cooked, transfer to a tray lined with a clean towel and keep warm in a low oven while preparing the remaining pancakes.
- Presentation: Place pancakes on heated plates. Spread some of the cream mixture over the pancake and arrange a slice of smoked fish on the cream. Garnish with a sprig of dill. Serve immediately.

44. Blooming Party Bread Recipe

Serving: 8 | Prep: | Cook: 5mins | Ready in:

Ingredients

- 16 ounces monterey jack cheese
- 1 loaf sourdough bread, unsliced
- 1 stick butter, melted
- 1/2 teaspoon garlic powder
- 3 green onions, thinly sliced
- cooking spray

Direction

- Make one slice down the top of the bread two thirds of the way through.
- Then, make a bunch of cuts 1-inch apart and also two thirds through all the way down the bread to create the "blooming bread" effect.
- Place the bread on a cookie sheet sprayed with cooking spray.
- Mix the melted butter and garlic powder and pour evenly over bread in between cuts.
- Take 1/2 green onion and sprinkle between slices. Tuck the cheese between cracks over onions.
- Sprinkle the remaining green onion on top. Place in the oven on broil until cheese is melted and turning brown and bubbly. Serve immediately.

45. Blue Cheese Canapes Recipe

Serving: 24 | Prep: | Cook: 20mins | Ready in:

Ingredients

- 1 pound crumbled blue cheese
- 1 cup toasted walnuts
- 1/4 cup heavy cream
- 1 teaspoon salt
- 1 teaspoon ground white pepper
- 2 tablespoons olive oil
- 1 cup thinly-sliced white onions
- 1 cup julienned granny smith apples
- 3 teaspoons rice wine vinegar
- 24 French bread rounds toasted
- fresh parsley for garnish

Direction

- In food processor fitted with metal blade combine cheese, walnuts and cream.
- Puree until smooth and season with salt and pepper.
- In small sauté pan over medium heat add oil.
- When oil is hot add onions and apples and sauté until caramelized.
- Remove from heat and stir in vinegar.
- Spread heaping spoonful of cheese mixture over each toasted round.
- Garnish with small pile of apple onion mixture and parsley.

46. Blue Cheese Cherry Crostini Recipe

Serving: 8 | Prep: | Cook: 5mins | Ready in:

Ingredients

- 1-1/2 cups cashews
- 1 cup dried cherries
- 1/2 pound blue cheese

- 1/2 teaspoon freshly ground black pepper
- 1 Tablespoon fresh parsley, diced
- 1 12- to 16-ounce loaf baguette-style French bread
- 2 Tablespoons fresh chopped parsley

Direction

1. Preheat the oven to broil.
2. Add the cashews and cherries to a food processor.
- Process on high for a short 3 to 5 seconds.
3. Add the cashew and cherry mixture to a bowl.
- Crumble the blue cheese into the bowl, and add the pepper using a wooden spoon, mix everything until it is well combined.
4. Slice, carefully, the baguette into 1/4-to-1/2-inch slices.
- Place the slices on a baking sheet, and place the baking sheet in the oven.
- Watching it closely, broil for a minute per side to lightly brown.
5. Remove the toasts from the oven, and top each with a large dollop of the blue cheese mixture.
- Broil 1 to 2 minutes more to heat cheese mixture.
6. Place the crostini on a platter, and sprinkle the platter with parsley.

47. Boar's Head Apple & Smoked Gouda Crostini Recipe

Serving: 12 | Prep: | Cook: 20mins |Ready in:

Ingredients

- 2 Tbsp olive oil
- 1 Loaf French bread
- 2 granny smith apples
- ¼ LB Natural gouda cheese

Direction

- Turn oven onto broil.
- Slice the French bread into thin rounds and place into large bowl.
- Pour olive oil into the bowl over rounds and toss until all rounds are well covered in oil.
- Core the apple and slice the apple into thin rounds. Slice the Smoked Gouda into thin slices as well.
- Place a piece of apple on top of your French bread rounds, followed by a piece of Smoked Gouda.
- Spread the rounds out on your baking sheet and place in the oven. Broil the rounds for two to three minutes. Pay careful attention as you don't want to burn the bread or melt the cheese too much.
- Remove the baking sheet from the oven and allow rounds to cool for five minutes before serving.

48. Boursin And Prosciutto Wrapped Breadsticks Recipe

Serving: 0 | Prep: | Cook: 10mins |Ready in:

Ingredients

- 8 prosciutto slices (cut paper thin)
- 1/2 pkg. (75g) any flavour boursin cheese
- 16 bread sticks (about 5" long)

Direction

- Lay Prosciutto slices out on a countertop. Cut each slice in half lengthwise. Spread each piece of prosciutto with about 1 tsp. of cheese. Roll up 1 piece of prosciutto diagonally around the bread stick, leaving the ends uncovered. Repeat with remaining breadsticks. Arrange on a platter and serve within 1 hour of preparing.

49. Braunschweiger Canapes Recipe

Serving: 8 | Prep: | Cook: | Ready in:

Ingredients

- 8 ounces Braunschweiger
- 1/4 cup ketchup
- 1 tablespoon pickle juice
- 4 each sweet pickle, sliced 1/8-inch thick
- 45 each Ritz crackers

Direction

- Mix Braunschweiger, Ketchup & Pickle Juice in a bowl. Blend together.
- Spread mixture on Ritz Cracker and top with pickle slice.

50. Bread Bowl Bacon Dip Recipe

Serving: 6 | Prep: | Cook: | Ready in:

Ingredients

- 1 large round loaf of bread
- 1 cup mayonnaise
- 1 cup sour cream
- 1 cup cooked lean bacon ; crumbled
- 10 ounces package frozen chopped
- spinach ; thawed with
- water squeezed out
- 2 tomatoes ; chopped

Direction

- Pull out the centre of the loaf of bread; you may save these pieces to use later. Combine remaining ingredients and mix well. Place dip in the refrigerator until ready to use, then spoon into hollowed out bread loaf and serve with bread pieces and crackers.

51. Bread Bowl For Dips Recipe

Serving: 12 | Prep: | Cook: 15mins | Ready in:

Ingredients

- 1 Loaf Round sourdough bread (or any round bread you prefer)

Direction

- Cut a slice across the top of the bread loaf and set aside
- Remove center, leaving 1 inch thick shell
- Cut removed bread into bite sized pieces
- Cover the shell opening with the sliced off top
- Place on baking sheet along with bread pieces
- Bake at 350 for 15 mins, until lightly toasted
- Cool slightly
- Fill with your favorite party dip. I'll be posting a few of my favorites.

52. Bread Pot Fondue Recipe

Serving: 8 | Prep: | Cook: 70mins | Ready in:

Ingredients

- 1 each   Loaf round white or pumpernickel bread
- 2 cups   Shredded sharp or mild cheddar cheese
- 2 pkg   3 oz packages cream cheese, softened
- 1 1/2 cups sour cream
- 1 cup   cooked ham, diced small or ground
- 1/2 cup   green onion, chopped
- 4 oz   Can green chilies, drained chopped
- 1 tsp   worcestershire sauce

Direction

- Slice off top of bread; hollow out centre, leave half shell. Combine ingredients and spoon filling into hollowed loaf and replace top. Wrap loaf tightly with two or three layers of heavy duty aluminum foil. Set on cookie sheet and bake 1 hour and 10 minutes at 35OF. Remove from oven; place on platter. Stir gently. Serve with raw vegetables and crackers.

53. Bread Rolls Filled With Wild Mushrooms Recipe

Serving: 4 | Prep: | Cook: 20mins | Ready in:

Ingredients

- 4 round good quality white bread rolls
- 2 large garlic cloves peeled and halved
- 2 ounces olive oil
- 7 ounces wild mushrooms
- 1 ounce unsalted butter
- 2 ounces water mixed with 1-1/2 teaspoons lemon juice
- 1 teaspoon salt
- 2 teaspoons freshly ground black pepper
- 1 teaspoon fresh chervil chopped
- 1 teaspoon fresh tarragon leaves blanched and chopped
- 1 teaspoon chopped fresh parsley
- 2 ounces whipping cream whipped

Direction

- Preheat oven to 350.
- Take each bread roll and slice off the top about one-third of the way down.
- Reserve tops.
- Scoop out the soft insides and rub inside hollow and top inside of the lid with garlic then brush olive oil over same surfaces.
- Place in preheated oven to dry out and crisp for 10 minutes.
- Sauté wild mushrooms in the butter for 1 minute.
- Add water and lemon juice and cook 1 minute longer with the lid on.
- Season with salt and pepper the reserve.
- Add chopped herbs to the whipped cream then taste and season with salt and pepper.
- Just before serving whisk the whipped cream into the mushrooms and their juices.
- Divide the mushrooms between the hollows in each bread roll and spoon the sauce on and around then top with lids and serve.

54. Bread Topped With Tomato Parsley And Feta Recipe

Serving: 8 | Prep: | Cook: 10mins | Ready in:

Ingredients

- 1 loaf French bread sliced
- 2 fresh tomatoes petite diced
- 1 banana pepper chopped
- 1/2 cup crumbled feta cheese
- 1/3 cup black olives pitted and chopped
- 1 egg
- 1/3 bunch parsley finely chopped
- 1/2 teaspoon black pepper
- 1/2 teaspoon crushed pepper
- 1 teaspoon paprika
- 1/2 tablespoon olive oil
- 1/2 teaspoon salt

Direction

- Mix all ingredients except bread in a bowl.
- Place tomato mixture on bread slices with a spoon.
- Place the bread slices on a broiler tray
- There will be some juice left in the bowl so put some on top of each slice
- Broil 6 inches below heat for 10 minutes.

55. Breaded Cauliflower Recipe

Serving: 4 | Prep: | Cook: 5mins | Ready in:

Ingredients

- 1 head of cauliflower, cleaned and broken into florets to have about 5 cups.
- 4 egg yolks
- 1 teaspoon garlic powder
- 1 teaspoon onion powder
- 1 teaspoon Minced fresh parsley
- 1/2 teaspoon sugar
- 1/2 teaspoon salt
- 1/4 teaspoon pepper
- 1 cup seasoned bread crumbs
- Grated parmesan cheese
- 3/4 -1 cup butter
- Naturally Fresh honey mustard dressing for dipping (if you can't find the Naturally Fresh brand, use your favorite dipping sauce)

Direction

- Place cauliflower and a small amount of water in a skillet.
- Bring to a boil.
- Reduce heat, cover and simmer until crisp-tender, takes about 8 minutes.
- Drain and set aside.
- In a bowl, whisk egg yolks and seasonings.
- Put bread crumbs and about 3 tablespoons parmesan cheese in a large, resealable plastic bag.
- Add a few cauliflower florets at a time to the egg mixture and coat.
- Using a slotted spoon, put coated florets into bread crumb mixture and toss to coat.
- In a skillet, melt the butter over medium-high heat. Using a slotted spoon, put coated florets into batches and cook until golden brown.
- Remove and drain on paper towel-covered plate.
- Place on serving dish with dipping sauce and enjoy.

56. Breaded Mushrooms Recipe

Serving: 24 | Prep: | Cook: 5mins | Ready in:

Ingredients

- 2 cups mushrooms (cleaned)
- 1/2 cup milk
- 1 egg
- 1/2 cup flour
- 1/2 cup Italian bread crumbs
- salt and pepper to taste

Direction

- Beat egg with milk in a bowl and add clean, dry mushrooms. I use a bowl with a lid and shake the mushrooms until they are coated.
- Mix dry ingredients together and add the mushrooms coated with the egg mixture. Again shake the mushrooms until they are covered thoroughly with bread crumb mix.
- Put in hot oil and cook until golden brown... under 5 minutes.

57. Breaded Parmesan Chicken Strips Recipe

Serving: 2 | Prep: | Cook: 30mins | Ready in:

Ingredients

- 1 pkg of chicken breast Tenderloins (cut into strips)
- 1 cup of Italian bread crumbs
- 3/4 parmesan cheese
- 3/4 garlic powder
- 2 eggs
- 1 Teaspoon of oil

Direction

- Take a Ziploc bag and put in the Parmesan cheese, garlic, and Italian bread crumbs.
- Mix it well by shaking the bag.
- Next, break two eggs and beat them.

- Take a cookie sheet pan and coat it with the oil.
- Preheat your oven to 400 degrees.
- Dip three chicken tenderloins strips in the egg and put them in the bag with the bread crumb mixture.
- Shake well.
- Make sure the bread crumbs are fully covering the chicken.
- Then place them side by side in the pan.
- Continue the dipping cycle with three chicken strips at a time.
- Put it in the oven for 30 minutes until golden brown.

58. Brick Red Butter Mushroom Crostini With Rosemary Recipe

Serving: 8 | Prep: | Cook: 10mins | Ready in:

Ingredients

- 1 stick Unsalted organic grade AA sweet cream butter
- 1 stick salted organic grade AA sweet cream butter
- 1/4 cup non-fat dried milk
- 2 lbs button mushrooms
- 4 sprigs fresh rosemary
- 1 french baguette

Direction

- Slice the baguette on a bias into 1/3" thick slices
- Place slices on cookie sheet
- Spray slices with olive oil
- Place cookie sheet into oven at 350F for 12-15 minutes
- Remove crostini when golden brown
- Get a small very fine mesh sieve (one with a handle), a mesh strainer, and a copper pan
- On low heat, begin to melt two stick of organic AA quality butter, one unsalted, one salted
- Add 1/4 cup dried non-fat milk, stir
- Continue over low heat, allowing the water to evaporate
- As the butter begins to froth, start stirring, keeping the heat very low
- If the froth is clouding your view from keeping an eye on the colour of the milk solids, occasionally remove from heat and return
- Scrape down the side of the pan for any lingering or crusted milk solids
- As the milk solid turns golden brown, you're now in the zone
- Keep stirring constantly, removing from heat every few seconds to widen the window to catch the change to brick
- As brick redness begins to surface, remove from heat
- Quickly use the mesh strainer to recover as much of the milk solids from the now clarified butter as possible
- Repeat this process with the fine sieve and drain of any of the hot butter from the solids
- Reserve the solids separately from the clarified (though now nutty) butter
- The whole straining process took 15-20 seconds, you have to move quickly or you will burn the milk solids
- Slice the mushrooms into 1/4" thick slices
- Pull the rosemary leaves from the sprigs and chop finely
- In a large flat sided sauté pan, add the mushroom slices and clarified butter
- Sauté the mushrooms in the clarified butter
- Add the finely chopped fresh rosemary near the end of cooking
- Remove from heat and incorporated the brick red milk solids

59. Brie And Jam Cups Recipe

Serving: 10 | Prep: | Cook: 20mins | Ready in:

Ingredients

- 2 15 count packages of frozen phyllo cups
- 8 oz wedge of brie
- 1/2 cup of jam or preserves, I like raspberry jam or mango chutney
- 1/4 cup sliced almonds

Direction

- Preheat oven to 350
- Place phyllo cups on baking sheet
- Drop about 1/2-1 tsp. of brie into each
- Top with 1/2 tsp. jam
- Top with a few sliced almonds
- Bake for 10-15 minutes until cheese is melted and shells are crisp

60. Brie Bread Bowl Dip Recipe

Serving: 8 | Prep: | Cook: 30mins | Ready in:

Ingredients

- 1 1/2 tsp chili powder
- 1/2 tsp ground mustard
- 1/2 tsp garlic powder
- 1/2 tsp sugar
- 1 round soft bread such as sourdough, Italian, French, 1 lb.
- 1 Tbs. butter
- 1, 8-oz wheel of brie cheese

Direction

- Mix seasonings and set aside.
- Cut out a hollow from centre of bread and remove bread centre to make room for the Brie.
- Spread butter on the bread and sprinkle 2 tsp. of the seasoning.
- With knife make 2 inch cuts at one inch intervals around the bread.
- Remove rind from Brie and place into bread.
- Sprinkle Brie with the remaining seasonings.
- Replace top of bread. Place on baking sheet and bake 350F about 30 minutes.
- To serve, remove top of bread and break into bite size pieces.
- Dip bread into the hot brie.

61. Brie With Strawberries On Brioche Crostini Recipe

Serving: 12 | Prep: | Cook: 5mins | Ready in:

Ingredients

- 12 slices brioche bread sliced 1/4-inch thick (I make my own, recipe is on my grouprecipes page)
- 6 ounces whipped cream cheese, at room temperature
- 1 teaspoon chopped chives
- 3 large strawberry
- 1 small (about 2 inches diameter) Brie wheel
- fresh edible flowers for garnish

Direction

- Preheat the oven to 325 degrees F.
- Using a 1 1/2-inch diameter biscuit cutter, cut the sliced bread into 24 circles and put on a baking sheet. Toast the brioche circles in the oven for 3 to 5 minutes, until golden brown.
- With a rubber spatula, fold together the cream cheese and chopped chives and place in a small pastry bag with star tip. Pipe out about 1/2-ounce of cream cheese and chive mixture onto each toasted brioche circle. Cut off top of strawberry, slice in half lengthwise, and then cut each half into 3 wedges. Cut the 1/2 wheel of Brie into 6 triangle wedges. Place 1 wedge of strawberry and 1 wedge of Brie standing up on the cream cheese. Garnish with additional chives/edible flowers

62. Browned Butter Crab Bruschetta Recipe

Serving: 6 | Prep: | Cook: 30mins | Ready in:

Ingredients

- 8oz cooked lump crab
- 1 1/2 sticks butter
- 1 large or 2 small shallots, diced
- 2 cloves garlic, minced
- 1/4 cup white wine
- 2T heavy cream
- 1t Old Bay Seasoning
- 1 roasted red pepper, chopped
- 3T fresh parsley, chopped
- 1 large French or Italian baguette, sliced on the bias in 12, 1 inch slices
- 1/4 cup fresh Parmesan, grated
- salt and fresh ground pepper

Direction

- Melt butter in medium sauté pan over medium heat.
- Add shallots and cook, stirring often, until shallots are dark brown and butter is nutty brown. You are not looking for a burned outcome: shallots and butter will be dark, but their taste should not be burnt
- Add garlic, wine, Old Bay salt and pepper. Lower heat and simmer to reduce by about half.
- Add cream and stir to combine and heat through.
- Remove from heat.
- Let cool slightly while mixing crab and slicing bread.
- In medium glass bowl, combine crab, roasted red pepper and parsley.
- Dip one cut side of each piece of bread into melted butter mixture then place, dry side down, on baking sheet or stone.
- Bake at 400 for about 10-12 minutes until bread is toasted around the edges.
- Meanwhile, add rest of the butter/shallot mixture to the crab mixture and mix well.
- Remove from oven and top each slice with an equal amount of the crab topping.
- Sprinkle each piece with grated Parmesan.
- Bake another 5 minutes or so just to warm and slightly melt cheese.

63. Bruchetta Recipe

Serving: 8 | Prep: | Cook: 15mins | Ready in:

Ingredients

- 1 pint cherry tomatoes, quartered
- 1 small yellow onion, finely chopped
- 3 cloves garlic, finely chopped
- basil, chopped
- 3 tbs. olive oil
- fresh cracked black pepper
- sea salt
- 5.2 oz block boursin cheese
- Italian bread, sliced and toasted

Direction

- In a medium bowl, mix tomatoes, onion, garlic, basil, and olive oil. Season with salt and pepper and toss to incorporate.
- Spread the boursin chees on toasted bread and top with bruschetta mixture right before serving.
- Enjoy!

64. Bruscetta Recipe

Serving: 4 | Prep: | Cook: 10mins | Ready in:

Ingredients

- 1 loaf - Italian bread
- 1 tsp - Garlic
- 20ml - Olive Oil
- 1 ½ - Tomatoes (Cut into 1cm pieces)
- 1 Tbs - Basil (Finely chopped)

Direction

- Slice bread into diagonal pieces 2cm thick.
- Mix half the oil and the garlic, and brush over both sides of the bread.
- Char grill lightly on both sides.
- Mix remaining oil, basil and tomatoes and toss until well combined.
- Spoon onto bread.

---

65. Bruschetta Al Pomodoro Formaggio Bianco Recipe

Serving: 1 | Prep: | Cook: 17mins | Ready in:

Ingredients

- For toasted bread
- Slices of baguette bread : 2 pieces
- olive oil : 05 Ml
- For feta cheese & tomato salsa
- tomatoes, finely diced : 50 gm
- feta cheese : 25 gm
- black olive Slice : 10 gm
- garlic, peeled : 05 gm
- Dry red peppers : 01 gm
- extra-virgin olive oil : 20 ml
- salt : to taste
- basil leaves : 02 gm
- black pepper : 01 gm
- For skewers
- black olive : 50 gm
- Cherry tomato : 50 gm
- wooden skewers : 1 piece
- For pesto sauce
- basil : 100 gm
- olive oil : 50 ml
- Chopped garlic : 05 gm
- pine nuts : 02 gm
- parmesan cheese grated : 05 gm
- salt : 01 gm
- Pepper : 01 gm
- For honey Balsamic Reduction
- balsamic vinegar : 100 ml
- honey : 30 gm

Direction

- For Toasted Bread
- Grill the bread on both sides until golden brown. Lightly rub the garlic on the surface of the bread.
- For Feta cheese & tomato Salsa
- In a bowl mix tomato, cheese, slice olive basil, extra-virgin olive oil, salt, and pepper.
- For Skewers
- Using wooden skewers, soak them in plenty of water for about 10 minutes. Alternate the Cherry Tomato with Olive black on wooden and grill in pan medium-high heat.
- For Pesto sauce
- Place basil leaves in small batches in food processor and whip until well chopped. Add pine nuts and garlic, blend again. Add parmesan cheese blend while slowly adding olive oil, stopping to scrape down sides of container. Process basil pesto it forms a thick smooth paste. Repeat until all ingredients are used, mix all batches together well.
- For Honey Balsamic Reduction
- On medium heat, bring the balsamic vinegar and honey to a boil. Reduce heat and simmer until the mixture is reduced to half. Should take about 10 minutes of simmering. Mixture will thicken as it cools so be sure to time this correctly with your meal.
- Assemble
- Arrange bread on plate Distribute uniformly Feta cheese & tomato Salsa on the bread. Arrange skewer aside and drizzle pesto and balsamic. Garnish with fresh lettuce.

---

66. Bruschetta Al Pomodoro Recipe

Serving: 8 | Prep: | Cook: 20mins | Ready in:

Ingredients

- 8 slices hearty, rustic Italian bread - sliced 1/2 inch thick
- 2 cloves garlic, peeled and cut in half
- 6 roma tomatoes, thinly diced
- 8 basic leaves, cut into thin strips
- 4 T. extra virgin olive oil
- kosher salt
- Crushed red pepper (if desired)

Direction

- Place bread on baking sheet, in single layer. Drizzle with small amount of olive oil. Bake in 400 degree oven until lightly browned on one side. Turn bread over and repeat olive oil, and cook for a few minutes until lightly browned.
- Note: If you want to grill your bread over an open flame or on a stovetop grill pan, that is great. Either method works perfectly well. The objective is to have grilled bread that has been drizzled with olive oil to help in the browning.
- When bread has been baked or grilled, rub both sides (generously) of bread with cut side of a garlic clove. Set aside.
- In small bowl, place tomatoes and basil. Drizzle well with olive oil and sprinkle with kosher salt. Add small sprinkle of peperoncino (crushed red pepper) if desired. Mix well.
- Top each piece of bread with substantial layer of tomato and basil mixture. Drizzle with additional olive oil and serve immediately.

67. Bruschetta Ala Leah Recipe

Serving: 12 | Prep: | Cook: 10mins | Ready in:

Ingredients

- 1 cup olive oil
- 1/3 cup balsamic vinegar
- 12 or more leaves of fresh basil
- 3 medium on the vine tomatoes or 4-5 plum tomatoes
- 1 good teaspoon kosher salt
- 1/2 teaspoon fresh cracked pepper
- 2 shakes of dried crushed red pepper flakes
- juice of one lemon
- 3-5 garlic cloves
- 1-2 teaspoons white sugar
- 1 good loaf of Italian bread, sliced thin
- 1/2 pound or more of fresh mozzarella cheese (please use the fresh stuff, ok?)
- 1 large cookie sheet
- 1 med bowl to mix 'dressing in'
- 1 potato masher

Direction

- This 'dressing' is one of those that is great to throw over pasta, marinate steaks and chicken in for the grill, etc. as it keeps for 2 weeks in a sealed container in the fridge. Let it come to room temperature before using.
- Also this 'dressing' gets stronger in its garlic flavour as the ingredients meld - so start with three garlic cloves or less if you want it less garlicky.
- Though I like to have my bruschetta bite me in my mozzarella if you know what I mean... ok here we go...enough of my yapping....
- Minced garlic and add to bowl, add salt, fresh cracked pepper, dried crushed red pepper and lemon juice.
- Pile rinsed fresh basil leaves upon each other and roll them up like a cigar. Slice (chiffonade) the basil then cut lengthwise once and throw into bowl.
- Take half of your tomatoes and slice up as small as possible. I do not mind the seeds or juices - in fact you want as much as the fresh tomato juices as you can.
- With potato masher, mash up your ingredients to 'pulverize' and mash your tomatoes and garlic with the basil. The added salt helps this process.
- Add vinegar and white sugar and stir.
- Add remaining tomatoes sliced as small as you can muster, add all seeds and juices to the mix.

- Slowly pour and add the olive oil, stirring all the while to create an emulsion as best as you can.
- Set aside - taste test if you like - yummy, yes?!
- I like to let my 'dressing' set out covered on the counter an hour at least before using so that the garlic really comes out. - If using as a marinade for later, simply seal and place into fridge until you are ready to use.
- ***Back to bruschetta - slice your Italian bread into 1/2 inch slices on the diagonal.
- Put slices onto cookie sheet and place in oven to brown on one side - say at 350 for 5 minutes - then flip bread and toast the other side till light brown.
- Slice fresh mozzarella and place slices onto toast - place back into oven and let melt for another 5 minutes just before it starts to bubble.
- Put toast with melted mozzarella onto serving plates or platter.
- Spoon 'dressing' on top over melted cheese and Perfecta Bruschetta ala Leah is served, ready to be gobbled up!

68. Bruschetta Crisps Recipe

Serving: 12 | Prep: | Cook: 4mins | Ready in:

Ingredients

- 1/2 cup virgin olive oil
- 2 Tablespoons finely chopped fresh basil
- 2 baguette-style French bread, cut into 1/4-inch slices
- 1/2 cup grated parmesan cheese

Direction

- Preheat the oven to 425 degrees.
- Warm the oil and basil in a saucepan. Brush each piece of bread with the oil and sprinkle with Parmesan cheese.
- Arrange bread on the baking sheet and bake for 4 minutes or until golden brown.

69. Bruschetta Italiano Recipe

Serving: 8 | Prep: | Cook: 5mins | Ready in:

Ingredients

- 1 loaf of fresh Italian bread.
- 8 plum tomatoes chopped
- 1 cup of fresh chopped basil
- 1 red onion chopped
- 3 or 4 or 5 cloves of garlic crushed
- 1 teaspoon of dried oregano
- extra-virgin olive oil
- fresh ground black pepper or red pepper flakes
- salt to taste
- Variations include: Top with capers, use sun dried tomatoes instead of fresh, top with fresh buffalo mozzarella, top with a slice of "prociutto de parma", use your imagination.

Direction

- Slice bread on the diagonal around a half inch thick.
- Spread crushed garlic on top of bread.
- Drizzle or brush with a little extra-virgin olive oil
- Arrange bread on a cooking sheet and broil until toasted, around 5 minutes.
- In a mixing bowl combine tomatoes, onions, basil and oregano and toss gently.
- Season with fresh ground black pepper or red pepper flakes.
- Salt to taste.
- Arrange toasted bread on a platter and generously top with tomato mixture.
- Serve immediately so the bread doesn't have time to get soggy.
- You want the crunch to be part of the experience.

70. Bruschetta Pizza Recipe

Serving: 4 | Prep: | Cook: 1mins | Ready in:

Ingredients

- 1/2 lb. bulk pork sausage
- 1 prebaked Italian bread shell crust
- 1 (6 oz) pkg sliced turkey pepperoni
- 2 C. shredded mozzarella cheese
- 1 1/2 C. chopped plum tomatoes
- 1/2 C. fresh basil leaves thinly sliced
- 1 T. olive oil
- 2 garlic cloves minced
- 1/2 t. minced fresh thyme or 1/8 t. dried thyme
- 1/2 t. balsamic vinegar
- 1/4 t. salt
- 1/8 t. pepper
- additional fresh basil leaves, optional

Direction

- In a small skillet cook sausage over medium heat until no longer pink; drain. Place crust on an ungreased baking sheet. Top with pepperoni, sausage and cheese. Bake at 450 for 10-12 minutes or until cheese is melted.
- In a small bowl combine the tomatoes, sliced basil, oil, garlic, thyme, vinegar, salt and pepper. Spoon over the pizza. Garnish with additional basil if desired.

71. Bruschetta Polenta

Serving: 0 | Prep: | Cook: | Ready in:

Ingredients

- 1 tube (1 pound) polenta, cut into 1/2-inch slices
- 1 tablespoon olive oil
- 1 cup bruschetta topping
- 3 tablespoons shredded Parmesan cheese

Direction

- In a large skillet, cook polenta slices in oil over medium heat for 2 minutes on each side or until golden.
- Place the bruschetta topping in a microwave-safe bowl; cover and cook on high for 1 minute. Spoon 1 tablespoon onto each slice of polenta; sprinkle with cheese.
- Note: Look for bruschetta topping in the pasta aisle or your grocer's deli case.
- Nutrition Facts
- 2 each: 116 calories, 5g fat (1g saturated fat), 2mg cholesterol, 603mg sodium, 16g carbohydrate (2g sugars, 1g fiber), 2g protein.

72. Bruschetta Pomodoro Recipe

Serving: 6 | Prep: | Cook: | Ready in:

Ingredients

- 2 cups minced roma tomatoes
- 1 1/2 teaspoons capers
- 2 tablespoons chopped kalamata olives
- 1 tablespoon chopped fresh basil
- 1 tablespoon extra-virgin olive oil
- 1/4 teaspoon salt
- 1/4 teaspoon balsamic vinegar
- 1/8 teaspoon pepper

Direction

- Combine all the ingredients; cover and let stand 30 minutes. Drain the tomato mixture.

73. Bruschetta Recipe

Serving: 8 | Prep: | Cook: 5mins | Ready in:

Ingredients

- 1 8 oz loaf baguette-style French bread

- Nonstick spray coating
- 1 1/2 cups firmly packed torn fresh spinach
- 1/4 cup grated parmesan cheese
- 3 tablespoons almonds
- 3 tablespoons snipped fresh basil or 1 tablespoon dried basil, crushed
- 1 large clove garlic, quartered
- 1/8 teaspoon salt
- 2 tablespoons olive oil
- 2 tablespoons water
- 1 cup chopped red and/or yellow tomato
- 2 tablespoons thinly sliced green onion
- 2 teaspoons olive oil
- 1/8 teaspoon pepper
- fresh basil (optional)

Direction

- For the toasts, cut bread into 1/2-inch-thick slices. Spray both sides of each slice lightly with non-stick coating. Place on an ungreased baking sheet. Bake in a 425 degrees oven about 5 minutes or until crisp and lightly browned, turning once. (If desired, transfer the cooled toasts to a storage container. Cover and store the toasts at room temperature for up to 24 hours.)
- For pesto, in a blender container or food processor bowl combine the spinach, Parmesan cheese, almonds, basil, garlic, and salt. Cover and blend or process with several on-off turns until a paste forms, stopping the machine several times and scraping the sides. With machine running, gradually add the 2 tablespoons olive oil and the water, blending or processing until the mixture is the consistency of soft butter. (If desired, cover and chill the pesto for up to 2 days.)
- For the tomato topper, in a small bowl stir together chopped tomato, green onion, the 2 teaspoons olive oil, and the pepper.
- To assemble, spread each toast with a thin layer of pesto; top each with some of the tomato topper. If desired, garnish with fresh basil.
- Makes 18-20 slices.

74. Bruschetta Topping Recipe

Serving: 16 | Prep: | Cook: 1hours | Ready in:

Ingredients

- 2 cups diced tomatoes, peeled if fresh
- 2 cloves garlic, minced
- 3 green onions, minced
- ⅔ cup minced fresh basil (I used lime basil)
- ¼ cup minced fresh oregano
- 1 tbsp white wine
- ½ tbsp white wine vinegar
- 1 tsp lime juice
- 1 tsp kosher salt
- ¼ tsp coarse black pepper
- 2 tbsp tomato paste

Direction

- Combine all the ingredients in a pot and bring to a simmer.
- Cook 5-10 minutes, stirring occasionally.
- If preserving for shelf-storage: can in a water bath for 20 minutes.
- Otherwise, refrigerate up to 2 weeks or freeze up to 6 months.

75. Bruschetta With Roasted Cherry Tomatoes Recipe

Serving: 6 | Prep: | Cook: 25mins | Ready in:

Ingredients

- 1 pound cherry tomatoes
- 1 garlic clove crushed
- 1/4 teaspoon red pepper flakes
- 1/4 cup extra virgin olive oil
- 1 tablespoon balsamic vinegar
- 1/4 teaspoon salt
- 1/4 teaspoon freshly ground black pepper
- 4 slices day old bread 1/2" thick

- 1 garlic clove halved
- extra virgin olive oil

Direction

- Preheat oven to 400 then combine tomatoes, garlic, red pepper flakes, oil and vinegar in roaster.
- Sprinkle with salt and pepper then toss well to coat then roast 20 minutes.
- Toast bread on a preheated ridged cast iron grill pan 2 minutes per side.
- Rub one side of each slice with cut garlic and drizzle olive oil over each slice.
- Spread tomatoes over bread then serve at room temperature.

76. Bruschetta With Tomato Salad And Chevre Recipe

Serving: 4 | Prep: | Cook: 3mins | Ready in:

Ingredients

- tomatoes, grape or cherry halved, or your favourite large variety cut into manageable bites
- red onion, finely minced
- garlic, finely minced or microplaned (optional)
- basil, in fine strips (chiffonade)
- parsley, finely minced
- salt and pepper
- red wine vinegar (optional)
- olive oil
- Slices of Calabrese bread, or any other crusty bread you like
- garlic (left whole)
- Chèvre

Direction

- Combine tomatoes, onion, garlic and herbs in a bowl. Season to taste with salt and pepper and a scant splash of red wine vinegar. Pour over a good-quality olive oil, mixing gently to combine. Allow to sit at room temperature while you prepare the bruschetta.
- Under a hot broiler, toast bread on one side until golden brown. Turn and toast the second side until just starting to turn colour. Remove from oven and, working quickly, rub the cut side of the whole garlic clove all over the lightly toasted side. Top with crumbled chevre, and return to the broiler until the cheese is starting to melt.
- Serve topped with tomato salad and a final drizzle of olive oil.

77. Bruschetta With Carmelized Peppers And Onions With Goat Cheese Recipe

Serving: 30 | Prep: | Cook: 15mins | Ready in:

Ingredients

- 1 long baguette, cut into 30 (½ in) slices
- ¼ cup olive oil
- 2 Tbsp butter
- ¼ cup brown sugar
- 1-16oz bag Birds Eye Frozen pepper Stir-Fry
- 1½ Tbsp balsamic vinegar
- salt & black pepper
- 4 oz fresh goat cheese, crumbled
- fresh basil leaves, cut into a strips (optional)

Direction

- Heat oven to 350°F. Put baguette slices on baking sheet and brush tops with oil. Bake in oven until golden brown. In large skillet melt the butter and brown sugar, add the pepper stir-fry and cook over MEDIUM heat for 10 to 12 minutes, or until all the moisture has evaporated and the vegetables are caramelized. Season with salt and pepper to taste. Top each baguette slice with a portion of the pepper mixture and some of the crumbled goat cheese. Sprinkle on basil. Serve while warm.

- Return to oven 1-2 minutes and warm through

78. Bruschetta With Sauteed Sweet Peppers And Creamy Gorgonzola Recipe

Serving: 8 | Prep: | Cook: 8mins | Ready in:

Ingredients

- EVOO
- 1 red bell pepper, seeded and sliced into thin strips
- 1 yellow bell pepper, seeded and sliced into thin strips
- 1/2 tsp sugar
- 1 TBS capers, drained
- 2 TBS julienned fresh basil leaves
- kosher salt
- black pepper
- baguette
- 3 oz creamy gorgonzola or other bleu cheese at room temperature

Direction

- Preheat oven to 375
- Heat 2 Tbsp. EVOO in sauté pan over med-high heat
- Add peppers and cook until soft, about 12 minutes
- Sprinkle with sugar and cook 2 more minutes
- Stir in capers and basil, season to taste with salt and pepper
- Set aside
- Slice baguette crosswise into 18 thin slices
- Brush rounds with EVOO on one side
- Arrange in rows, oil side up on sheet pan lined with parchment or foil
- Toast in oven until lightly browned, about 7 minutes
- Top each toast round with teaspoonful of pepper mixture
- Place 2 small pieces of gorgonzola on top of each

79. Bruschetta With Sun Dried Tomato Relish Roasted Garlic And Brie Recipe

Serving: 8 | Prep: | Cook: 60mins | Ready in:

Ingredients

- Tomato Relish:
- • 2 T balsamic vinegar
- • 3 T olive oil
- • 4 finely chopped kalamata olives
- • 4 cups diced tomatoes
- • ¼ cup finely chopped sun-dried tomatoes, reconstituted or 3 T sun-dried tomato paste
- Roasted Garlic:
- • 3 bulbs garlic
- • olive oil for drizzling
- 4 oz Soft Brie or Chevre
- 1 loaf crusty bread, sliced on the diagonal

Direction

- Relish:
- Combine vinegar, oil, olives, and sun-dried tomatoes. (Can be made 6 hours ahead. Cover; chill.) Add fresh tomatoes; toss to coat. Season with salt and pepper.
- Makes 8 servings.
- Alternative – replace the olives with ½ cup finely diced mango and 2 T chopped cilantro.
- Garlic:
- Cut the top off each garlic bulb (just to where the tops of each cloves are showing). Drizzle with olive oil, salt and pepper. Place on a foil square (about 10" x 10") and enclose the garlic, sealing the foil. Place in a 375 F oven for 1 hour. Serve warm.
- Brie (or Chevre):
- Take 4 oz. of soft brie and whip it until it is soft and creamy. Cover and refrigerate until

ready to use. If desired, add 4 oz. whipped cream cheese.
- If using the mango relish alternative, substitute camembert or other sweeter cheese for the brie.
- Bread:
- 1 loaf French bread or rustic Italian Bread, sliced on the diagonal, brushed with olive oil and slightly toasted.
- To Serve:
- On a platter, arrange the bread around one side, place the garlic in the middle. On the other side, mound the relish and place a container of brie. If desired, garnish the plate with sprigs of parsley.

80. Bruschetta With Sundried Tomato Jam And Goat Cheese Recipe

Serving: 8 | Prep: | Cook: 45mins | Ready in:

Ingredients

- 2 3 oz sundried tomatoes (not oil or water packed just dehydrated)
- 1 medium onion, halved and thinly sliced
- 2 cloved garlic thinly sliced
- 1 teas dried thyme or 1 Tbs fresh thyme
- 1 teas salt
- 1 teas black pepper
- 4 Tbs sugar
- 1/2 c red wine vinegar
- 1 can chicken broth (14 oz)
- 8 oz water
- 3 Tbs olive oil
- Bruschetta
- 1 loaf crusty bread (your favorite) cut in 1/2" slices
- 1/4 c olive oil
- salt
- 1 clove of garlic
- Crumbled feta or chevre goat cheese (I prefer herbed or crack pepper varieties)

Direction

- Julienne the sundried tomatoes. In a pot add the 3 Tbsp. olive and bring to medium heat. Add the sliced onion, sundried tomatoes, and garlic and sauté for 3-4 minutes. Add the rest of the ingredients and stir well. Cover and simmer over low for 30 minutes. Uncover and reduce most of the liquid (another 10 minutes). Cool to room temperature.
- Preheat oven to 400 F. Brush one side of the bread slices with olive oil and place on a cookie sheet with the oiled side up. Sprinkle with salt. Bake for 10 minutes and remove (it will crust up). Rub the garlic clove on the bruschetta. Let cool.
- Top a slice of bruschetta with a tablespoon or more of the sundried tomato. Top with a teaspoon of crumbled goat cheese. Enjoy.
- Great on burgers and hotdog or any meat.

81. Bruschetta With Tomato And Basil Recipe

Serving: 10 | Prep: | Cook: 2mins | Ready in:

Ingredients

- 1 loaf(s) (8 ounces) Italian bread
- 1 clove(s) (large) garlic, cut in half
- 1 1/4 pound(s) (8 medium) ripe plum tomatoes, seeded and cut into 1/4-inch pieces
- 2 tablespoon(s) fresh basil leaves, thinly sliced
- 2 tablespoon(s) extra-virgin olive oil
- 1/4 teaspoon(s) salt
- 1/8 teaspoon(s) ground black pepper

Direction

- Preheat oven to 350 degrees F.
- Meanwhile, slice bread diagonally into scant 1/2-inch-thick slices; reserve ends for making bread crumbs another day. Place bread slices on 2 cookie sheets.

- Toast bread on 2 oven racks 15 minutes or until crusty and dry, turning slices over once and rotating cookie sheets between upper and lower racks halfway through baking. Transfer bread to wire racks to cool slightly. When bread is cool enough to handle, rub 1 side of each toast slice with cut side of garlic. Discard garlic.
- Meanwhile, in small bowl, gently toss tomatoes, basil, oil, salt, and pepper until combined.
- To serve, spoon 1 heaping tablespoon tomato mixture on garlic-rubbed side of each toast slice.

82. Bruschetta With Tomatoes And Basil Recipe

Serving: 8 | Prep: | Cook: 5mins | Ready in:

Ingredients

- 4 med ripe tomatoes (about 1 2/3 pounds) cored&cut 1/2" dice
- 1/3 c shredded fresh basil leaves
- salt and pepper
- 1 12x5-inch loaf country bread,sliced crosswise into 1" thick pieces (ends removed)
- 1 or 2 large garlic cloves,peeled
- 3 tbl. extra virgin olive oil

Direction

- Heat broiler
- Mix tomatoes, basil, salt and pepper (to taste) in medium bowl, set aside
- Broil bread until golden brown on both sides
- Place toasted slices on large platter
- Rub garlic over tops
- Brush with oil
- Use slotted spoon to divide tomato mixture on toasted slices
- Serve immediately

83. Bruschetta With White Bean Puree And Anchovies Recipe

Serving: 8 | Prep: | Cook: |Ready in:

Ingredients

- 1 can cannellini beans
- 3 cloves garlic
- 1 tbsp butter
- 1 tin anchovies in olive oil
- 1 baguette or loaf of crusty bread
- 1 lemon
- olive oil
- chives
- salt

Direction

- Peel and chop the garlic. In a small frying pan, heat the butter and add the garlic. When the garlic is lightly browned, add the beans, reserving some of the liquid. Cook over medium heat until the flavours have mingled and some of the bean liquid has reduced. Salt to taste.
- Remove bean mixture from heat, allow to cool somewhat, and puree in a food processor.
- Slice the bread thinly. Rub the bread a slice of garlic and drizzle each slice with olive oil. Toast the slices of bread under the broiler until light brown.
- Spread some of the bean puree on each piece of toast. Add a slice of anchovy on top of the puree. Zest the lemon or cut some tiny, paper-thin slices, and add some zest or lemon slices on top of the anchovies. Garnish with chopped chives.
- Serve warm or cold.

84. Bubbly Pizza Bread Recipe

Serving: 6 | Prep: | Cook: 20mins | Ready in:

Ingredients

- 6 frozen Texas rolls or 10 dinner rolls, thawed and risen
- 1/3 cup grated parmesan cheese
- 1/2 cup grated mozzarella cheese
- Salad Supreme seasoning, if desired

Direction

- Sprinkle bread board with Parmesan cheese.
- Press rolls into a ball, place on top of cheese and begin rolling out into a 12 to 14-inch circle.
- Turn dough over a few times as you continue to roll the cheese into the dough.
- Place on a sprayed 12-inch pizza pan.
- Sprinkle with mozzarella cheese and Salad Supreme.
- Cover with sprayed plastic wrap.
- Let rise 30 minutes.
- Remove wrap and bake at 350°F 15-20 minutes.
- Serve warm or store up to 2 days.
- Use the crust for your favourite pizza if you wish

85. California Beef Crostini Recipe

Serving: 30 | Prep: | Cook: 20mins | Ready in:

Ingredients

- 10 small (about 2-inch) Yukon gold or red potatoes*****
- 1 TBSP. olive oil
- 1/2 teasp. garlic salt
- 1/4 cup mayonnaise
- 1 teasp. wasabi powder or prepared horseradish, or to taste
- 1/4 teasp. minced garlic
- dash of pepper
- 1/4 LB. shaved lean roast beef from the deli,
- 30 slices pimiento-stuffed green olives
- ****** it looks nice on the platter to have both kinds of potatoes

Direction

- Cut off the ends of each potato. Discard ends.
- Cut potatoes into 3/8 inch thick slices (about 3 per potato)
- Place slices on ungreased cookie sheet.
- Brush slices with oil. Then sprinkle each with the garlic salt
- In a preheated 400'F, bake for 15 to 20 minutes or until tender and golden brown
- Cool 20 minutes or until completely cool
- Meanwhile in small bowl: combine the mayonnaise, wasabi powder, garlic and pepper. Mix well
- To serve place potato slices on serving platter. Top each with about 1/2 tsp. mayonnaise mixture. Then the roast beef. Then the slice of green olive

86. California Roll Recipe

Serving: 32132 | Prep: | Cook: | Ready in:

Ingredients

- See Direction!

Direction

- California roll
- With great taste and covetable display, California roll is here for you. It is a sushi roll usually made inside out, containing cucumbers, crab meat and avocado. A hub of Fusion food in Japanese and western food. Here you can get food of your own choice and taste. We have for you the Sushi Roll, Rice wine and many other party foods with great test. Our outstanding services make us unique throughout the Hawthorn, California.

87. Canape Recipe

Serving: 6 | Prep: | Cook: 10mins | Ready in:

Ingredients

- 1(7oz.)Can water Packed tuna
- 12 anchovy fillets,chopped
- 3/4 Cup sweet green pepper,chopped
- 1/2 Cup pimento,chopped
- 1 Fresh egg,hard boiled,chopped
- 1 Cup Russian Dressing
- 1-1/2 Tablespoon cognac
- 6 Tablespoon butter
- 6 Thin bread Slices,remove the crusts
- 1 Tablespoon worcestershire sauce

Direction

- Combine tuna, anchovies, green pepper, pimento, egg and 2 tablespoons Russian dressing.
- Mix completely and set to the side.
- In another bowl, mix the remaining Russian dressing with the cognac and set this to the side.
- Place butter in a pan, melt, sauté the bread slices until well browned and butter has been absorbed.
- In this same pan, spread tuna mixture over each bread slice.
- Cover with the Russian dressing mixture.
- Sprinkle with 1/2 teaspoon Worcestershire sauce over each.
- Heat over low heat for about 5 to 10 minutes (or) until very hot.

88. Caramelized Onion And Shrimp Bruschetta Recipe

Serving: 24 | Prep: | Cook: 45mins | Ready in:

Ingredients

- 1/2 cup golden raisins
- 2 tablespoons canola oil
- 4 cups chopped yellow onions
- 2 tablespoons capers, rinsed and chopped
- 2 tablespoons minced fresh dill
- 1/2 teaspoon freshly ground pepper
- 1/4 teaspoon salt
- 24 thin slices baguette, toasted
- 24 peeled and deveined cooked shrimp, (26-30 per pound)

Direction

- 1. Place raisins in a small bowl and cover with boiling water; set aside for 30 minutes.
- 2. Meanwhile, heat oil in a large skillet over medium heat. Add onions and cook, stirring often, until the onions are softened and beginning to colour, 5 to 10 minutes. Cover, reduce heat to medium-low, and continue cooking, stirring occasionally, until the onions are golden brown, 15 to 25 minutes more.
- 3. Drain and chop the raisins; add to the onions along with capers, dill, pepper and salt. Cook uncovered, stirring, for 5 minutes. Transfer to a bowl and let cool for at least 30 minutes.
- 4. Top each slice of toasted bread with 1 tablespoon onion spread and 1 shrimp.
- Make Ahead Tip:
- Prepare through Step 3, cover and refrigerate for up to 3 days. Bring the spread to room temperature before assembling.

89. Caramelized Tomato And Courvoisier Canapes Recipe

Serving: 20 | Prep: | Cook: |Ready in:

Ingredients

- Crisps
- 1 cup flour
- 1/2 tsp raw sugar
- 1/2 tbsp coarse sea salt or kosher salt
- 1/2 tsp coarsely ground black pepper

- 1 tbsp olive oil
- 2 tbsp Courvoisier VS cognac
- 3 tbsp water or more, as needed
- cornstarch for rolling
- Caramelized Tomato Topping
- 2 tbsp dark raisins
- 3 tbsp Courvoisier VS cognac
- 5 large plum tomatoes, quartered and seeded
- 1/2 tsp coarse sea salt or kosher salt
- 1/4 tsp freshly ground black pepper
- 1 tbsp olive oil
- 1 tsp raw sugar
- 1/2 tbsp thyme
- 1 tsp rosemary
- zest of 1/2 lemon
- 2 tbsp ground almonds
- 2 tbsp fine, dry breadcrumbs
- 1 green onion, minced, plus some for garnish

Direction

- Crisps
- Preheat oven to 425°F.
- In a large bowl, combine flour, raw sugar, salt and pepper.
- Add the olive oil, Courvoisier VS and just enough water to form a stiff but sticky dough.
- Turn mixture out onto a cornstarch-dusted counter, knead briefly and form into a ball.
- Divide dough in half and let rest 15 minutes (uncovered).
- Working with one portion at a time, Place on a sheet of parchment dusted generously with cornstarch and roll until paper-thin.
- Transfer the parchment to a baking sheet. Repeat with remaining dough and another sheet of parchment.
- Bake, 1 sheet at a time, for 15 minutes, rotating sheet after 7 minutes.
- Cool on the sheet.
- Once cool, break into "rustic", uneven pieces.
- Crisps can be stored in an airtight container up to 2 days.
- Caramelized Tomato Topping
- In a small container, combine raisins and Courvoisier VS. Cover and let steep overnight.
- Preheat oven to 350°F and lightly oil a baking sheet.
- Place the tomatoes, cut side up, on the sheet and sprinkle with salt and pepper. Drizzle with the olive oil.
- Roast for 35 minutes.
- Remove from the oven and sprinkle with raw sugar, thyme and rosemary.
- Return to the oven and roast a further 10 minutes.
- Let cool 10 minutes, then scrape the entire pan contents into a blender or small food processor and add the raisins (with liquid), lemon zest, ground almonds, breadcrumbs and green onion.
- Puree until smooth and thick.
- Let cool, then scrape into a bowl and chill before serving.
- Assembly
- Place 1-2 tsp. of the Caramelized Tomato Topping on top of each crisp. Garnish with green onion.
- Serve within 3 hours of assembly.

90. Cheddar Biscuits From Scratch Delious! Recipe

Serving: 0 | Prep: | Cook: 45mins | Ready in:

Ingredients

- baking mix
- 1 1/2 Cups flour
- 2 Teaspoons baking powder
- 1/3 Cup powdered milk
- Mix
- 1/3 Cup lard
- Mix
- 1 teaspoons sugar
- 1/4 teaspoon cream of tartar
- 1/8 teaspoon salt
- Mix
- 4 Tablepoons unsalted butter
- Mix

- 1/8 teaspoon red pepper
- 1/4 teaspoon garlic powder
- 1/8 teaspoon old bay spice
- 3/4 Cup Sharp Cheddar 6 oz
- Mix
- Wet Ingredients
- 1/4 Cup sour cream
- Stir in lightly
- 2/3 Cup COLD milk
- Hand mix
- Topping
- 6 Tablespoons butter melted
- 1 clove garlic crushed or 1 teaspoon garlic powder
- 1 teaspoon dried parsley
- 1/2 Teaspoon oregano
- 1/2 Teaspoon salt

Direction

- Starting from the top of the baking mix list add each ingredient mixing as described in List. The Lard/Butter should be mixed in Dry not melted. Use a pastry cutter or a potato smasher to work it into the flour. You want chunks of butter/lard throughout the flour.
- Once you get to the Wet ingredients start working with your hands. Add all the sour cream and work in lightly. Start slowly adding the COLD milk without working the dough too much. You don't want dough that is too wet. If it starts to look too wet don't add any more milk! Cook immediately!
- Forum 1 1/2' inch balls and place on greased or non-stick baking dish. I press them down to flatten the bottom then prick top with a fork. Using 1/2 the Topping mixture coat with a brush the top of each biscuit before cooking. Cook @ 425 for 15-20 min till tops are golden . When they golden up a little coat again with remaining topping and continue cooking for another 2-5 minutes.
- Tip: Using a Thicker pan or Darker colored pan will cause the bottoms to burn.
- Don't use a Flat pan to bake because Butter will drip off.
- Keeping the butter and milk Extra cold makes them so much better.
- Using too much milk will cause the dough to be a wet mess.
- Fresh Baking Powder will make them rise correctly. To test the Baking powder drop a small amount in water it should have a slight bubbling reaction.
- Air Bake Pans or Glass baking dishes work best for keeping the bottoms not burnt.
- A pizza stone or a brick in the bottom of the oven can help moderate the temperature of the oven, keeping it more consistent

91. Cheddar Mushroom French Bread Rounds Appetizers Recipe

Serving: 10 | Prep: | Cook: 10mins | Ready in:

Ingredients

- 2 Tbs butter
- 4 oz mushrooms coarsely chopped. Chopped they measure 10 oz by volume. Why are we told to dry wipe mushrooms clean? If washed in water "methinks they absorb too much". Well, I hate dry wiping ... chasing tiny black dirt specks around the cap, so I wiped this batch clean with my fingers under a slow running tap. Fast and easy. I shook the drips off and weighed them again. They gained less than one quarter of an ounce. Well, my wife and I already ate this batch, so it's too late for the Iron Chef to arrest me.
- 4 tsp flour
- 2 Cups shredded cheddar cheese
- 1 tsp worcestershire sauce
- 1 tsp prepared yellow mustard
- 10 slices of French bread, cut across into 3/4 inch thick rounds. (I made them one inch once and they were too thick.) I much prefer using sub sandwich buns. Cut three buns into 20 slices. They make smaller pieces that are more

convenient. French bread slices end up being cut in half. Too much putsy work.
- parsley flakes shaker
- paprika shaker
- pepper shaker

Direction

- Melt the butter in a saucepan.
- Add mushrooms and cook gently 2 minutes, stirring now and then.
- Add flour to the pan and stir in.
- Add the cheese, Worcestershire and mustard, shake in pepper to taste. Stir over the same gentle heat until all is melted together. Remove from heat.
- Throw bread slices onto a cookie sheet and toast one side LIGHTLY under the broiler.
- Spread the cheese mixture onto the untoasted side. Pick up one tablespoon of the mix and spread it with the back of the spoon. It goes on easily, but reminds me of filling a grease cup with stiff bearing grease.
- Broil again until the top bubbles.
- Sprinkle with parsley flakes and paprika. Serve hot.

92. Cheddar Rosemary Crackers Recipe

Serving: 0 | Prep: | Cook: 2hours1mins | Ready in:

Ingredients

- • 250g chilled butter, chopped
- • 1 tsp Dijon mustard
- • 300g (2 cups) plain flour
- • 105g (1 1/4 cups) coarsely grated vintage cheddar
- • 2 tbs chopped fresh chives
- • Cheddar, to serve

Direction

1. Preheat oven to 180°C. Line 2 baking trays with non-stick baking paper. Use an electric beater to beat the butter and mustard in a bowl until pale and creamy.
2. Stir in the flour, cheddar and chives. Turn onto a lightly floured surface. Use your hands to bring the dough together.
3. Divide into 2 equal portions. Roll out 1 portion onto a lightly floured surface until about 5mm thick. Use a round 5.5cm-diameter pastry cutter to cut discs from the dough. Place on the lined trays. Place in the fridge for 10 minutes to chill.
4. Bake in oven, swapping trays halfway through cooking, for 18-20 minutes or until golden. Set aside on the trays for 5 minutes to cool before transferring to a wire rack. Repeat with the remaining dough portion. Serve with cheddar and Thai Sweet Chili Sauce or a spicy, sweet jelly.

93. Cheddar Chive Turnovers Recipe

Serving: 10 | Prep: | Cook: 25mins | Ready in:

Ingredients

- 3 TB melted butter
- pinch of salt
- pinch of cayenne pepper
- shredded cheddar cheese
- chopped chives
- 1 can refrigerated biscuits

Direction

- Mix butter with salt and cayenne. Lay out rounds of dough on a parchment-lined baking sheet. Brush with butter; top with cheese and chives
- Fold into half-moons and crimp to seal then bake as label directs. Brush with more butter.

94. Cheese Steak Stuffed Bread Recipe

Serving: 0 | Prep: | Cook: 40mins | Ready in:

Ingredients

- 2 1lb balls of prepared bread/pizza dough(can used frozen or "tubed" version, if desired, as long as it's raw)
- 1lb left over sliced roast beef(can use rare deli cuts, too, if desired, but not sliced too thin)
- 1 large onion, sliced thin
- 2-3 bell peppers, sliced into thin half rings or chopped
- 12oz fresh mushrooms, sliced
- lil olive oil
- 1/4 cup favorite mustard(rec whole grain, spicy, or something else with a lil character :)
- several dashes hot sauce
- several dashes worcestershire sauce
- 1lb provolone cheese, sliced or grated
- kosher or sea salt and fresh ground pepper

Direction

- Roll bread doughs to form 2 rectangles, about 16X12(this is approx. :)
- Place them on large sheet pans (sprayed with no cook spray) or baking stones and set aside
- In medium skillet, sauté onions, peppers and mushrooms in a bit of olive oil just until beginning to soften, about 5-10 min.
- Add beef, mustard, hot sauce, Worcestershire sauce, salt and pepper and stir to combine.
- Layer the cheese over 1/2 of each of the bread rectangles. (Reserve some for top)
- Using a slotted spoon (the mushrooms are going to let out a lot of liquid... you don't want all this in the bread :), transfer 1/2 the beef/veggie mixture to each of the breads, over the cheese.
- Fold other side of the bread over the mixtures and seal the edges.
- Cut small slits in the tops of the breads.
- Top with remaining cheese.
- Bake at 400 until bread and cheese are golden brown and heated through.
- Let rest about 5-7 minutes, then slice into "sticks" to serve.

95. Cheese Stuffed Bread Round Recipe

Serving: 7 | Prep: | Cook: 60mins | Ready in:

Ingredients

- 1 round loaf of Italian bread, about 6 inches in diameter
- 1 cup coarsely shredded mozzarella cheese
- 3/4 cup ricotta cheese
- 1 small green bell pepper, cored, seeded, and chopped fine
- 1 small red bell pepper, cored, seeded, and chopped fine
- 1/4 cup freshly grated Parmesan or romano cheese
- 1 tsp ground cumin
- 1/2 tsp garlic powder
- 1/4 tsp salt
- 1/4 tsp pepper

Direction

- Place oven rack in middle position in oven, and place a second rack in next lowest position, preheat oven to 400F. Slice 1 inch off the top of the loaf, and set it aside. Scoop out the centre of the bread, leaving a 1/2 inch shell, set aside. Cut the scooped out bread into 1 and 1/2 inch cubes.
- Combine Mozzarella and Ricotta cheeses, green and red peppers, Parmesan, cumin, garlic powder, salt and pepper in a medium bowl. Spoon the mixture into the bread shell and replace the top. Wrap bread snugly in foil, then place on an ungreased baking sheet and bake for 1 hour on middle oven rack.

- Spread the bread cubes on an ungreased baking sheet, place on lower rack, and bake, uncovered, until crisp and golden - about 10 minutes.
- Carefully remove the foil, lift off the top, and stir the cheese mixture until creamy. Replace top, tilting it slightly to the side, and place loaf on serving platter. Surround with bread cubes for dipping. Serve immediately.

96. Cheese And Onion Bread Recipe

Serving: 46 | Prep: | Cook: 30mins | Ready in:

Ingredients

- 1 loaf of French or sour dough bread
- 1 1/2 C grated cheese
- 1/2 minced onion
- 2 large tomatoes sliced
- 1 c mayonnaise

Direction

- Turn oven on to 375
- Cut the bread in half (long width), then set aside.
- In a bowl mix the grated cheese, minced onion and mayonnaise until well mixed.
- Now place bread on a baking sheet, and spread the cheese mixture on bread fully covering the top. Then place the tomato slices on it placed strategically so when sliced everyone gets a piece of tomato.
- ** Tomatoes are optional......
- Bake in oven for 30 mins and let cool, prior to slicing in pieces (to make sure cheese stays on bread.

97. Cheesey Spinach Canapes Recipe

Serving: 12 | Prep: | Cook: 15mins | Ready in:

Ingredients

- 6 eggs, beaten
- 3/4 c. soft butter
- 1/2 c. parmesan cheese
- 1/2 c. romano cheese, shredded
- 2 c. pepperidge Farm herb stuffing mix
- 3 T onion, chopped fine
- 3 T chopped garlic
- 3 T red pepper, chopped fine
- 3 T chopped mushrooms
- seasoned salt
- garlic pepper
- 1 T Worcestershire
- 2 (10 oz.) pkgs. frozen chopped spinach

Direction

- Thaw and drain spinach.
- Mix all of above ingredients together and let sit in refrigerator 2 hours.
- Roll into small bite-size balls.
- Bake at 350 degrees for 15 minutes on large greased cookie sheets.
- Serve warm as hors d'oeuvre.

98. Cheesy Artichoke Bread Recipe

Serving: 812 | Prep: | Cook: 20mins | Ready in:

Ingredients

- 1 can atrichoke hearts drained and chopped
- 1 cup Hellmans real mayo (this is the best brand I have tried of Mayo)
- 3-5 cloves of garlic (adjust to taste) finely chopped
- 1 1/2 cups grated parmesan cheese (best to use fresh grated!!)
- 1 loaf french or italian loaf halved lengthwise

Direction

- Combine all ingredients except bread and mix well (I used my food processor)
- Spread on the bread and close
- Bake at 350 F 20 min or until golden

99. Cheesy Bacon Snack Bread Recipe

Serving: 20 | Prep: | Cook: 15mins | Ready in:

Ingredients

- 1 lb loaf frozen white bread dough, thawed according to package directions.
- 2 Tbsp Land O' Lakes butter, melted
- 1/2 tsp onion salt
- 1/2 tsp liquid smoke, if desired
- 8 oz pkg (2 cups) Land O' Lakes Chedarella cheese, shredded
- 5 slices (1/3 cup) crispy bacon, crumbled
- 2 Tbsp chopped fresh parsley

Direction

- Press room temperature dough into greased 15x10x1-inch jelly roll pan.
- Combine melted butter, onion salt and liquid smoke in a small bowl. Brush evenly over dough. Cover and let rise in a warm place until double in size (45 to 60 minutes).
- Prick dough carefully all over with fork.
- Sprinkle with cheese and bacon.
- Bake for 15 to 20 minutes or until edges of dough are golden brown and cheese begins to brown.
- Sprinkle with parsley.
- Cool 10 minutes and cut into serving pieces. Serve warm.

100. Cheesy Bread Kabobs Recipe

Serving: 8 | Prep: | Cook: 7mins | Ready in:

Ingredients

- 1 5oz jar sharp American cheese spread
- 1T butter, softened
- 1T sliced green onion
- 1/2tsp drie tarragon, crushed
- Dash garlic powder
- 8 slices French bread

Direction

- Preheat both sides of grill on HIGH for 10 minutes.
- Combine cheese spread, butter, onion, tarragon, and garlic.
- Make two 4-layer sandwiches with the bread, spreading cheese mixture between slices and on top and bottom of each stack.
- Cut each stack into quarters.
- Using 8 skewers in all, thread each sandwich quarter on a skewer.
- Turn both sides of grill to MEDIUM.
- Place kabobs on cooking grids; close hood and cook 6 to 7 minutes, turning often.
- Makes 8 servings.

101. Cheesy Chicken And Chile Canapes Recipe

Serving: 12 | Prep: | Cook: 5mins | Ready in:

Ingredients

- 2 c. cooked chopped chicken
- 1 c. mayonnaise, more if needed to moisten
- 1/4 c. minced fresh onions
- 1 (4 oz.) can green chilies (may use jalapeños)
- 1 c. cheddar cheese, grated
- garlic salt, to taste
- miniature party rye rounds

Direction

- Preheat oven to Broil.
- Combine all ingredients and place on the bread.
- Broil 5 minutes or until brown and bubbly.

102. Cheesy Garlic Pull Apart Bread Recipe

Serving: 0 | Prep: | Cook: 30mins | Ready in:

Ingredients

- 1 oblong loaf of sourdough or italian bread unsliced
- 1 stick of butter- make it very soft and spreadable
- 1 glove minced garlic (or to taste)
- 1 tbsp fresh parsley
- 1-2 tbsp chopped green onion
- 1 - 1/2 (8 oz) blocks of monterey jack cheese grated(you can always use more!)
- all ingredients for the garlic butter and cheese are flexible and can be made to your taste!

Direction

- 1. Slice the bread in cross- cuts diagonally in one direction. Do not cut through the bottom. Then cut diagonally the other direction- leaving a crisscross pattern on the bread. Don't cut all the way through- you want the bread to stay intact as a loaf. (There are many references on the net that show how to cut it).
- 2. Mix your butter/garlic/green onion/parsley so it is nice and spreadable
- Spread it into each crevice in the bread and rub some on top- its ok to be sloppy!!
- 3. Take your shredded cheese and also fill all the crevices
- 4. Double wrap in foil and bake 15- 20 mins at 350 degrees.
- 5. Unwrap and bake another 5 minutes or so to get it nice and golden and bubbly on top.
- 6. Unwrap and serve- Enjoy the cheesy buttery goodness!!!

103. Cheesy Twists Recipe

Serving: 36 | Prep: | Cook: 30mins | Ready in:

Ingredients

- 1 ½ cups flour
- 1 ½ cups spelt flour
- 1 tsp bakers ammonia
- 2 tsp baking powder
- 1 tsp sugar
- ¼ cup cheese powder (like Kraft or Frontier Natural Products)
- 2 tbsp parmesan cheese
- pinch salt
- ½ tsp cream of tartar
- ¼ cup canola oil
- 1 cup whole milk
- 1 tbsp melted butter

Direction

- Preheat oven to 425F.
- In a medium bowl, mix together flours, baker's ammonia, baking powder, sugar, cheese powder, Parmesan, salt, and cream of tartar.
- Mix in oil and milk to form a soft dough.
- Turn dough onto a lightly floured surface. Knead until smooth.
- Roll dough into a 16" x 8" rectangle.
- Brush dough with melted butter and cut into ½" wide strips.
- Twist each strip and place twists 1" apart on an ungreased baking sheet.
- Bake 8-10 minutes, until golden brown and crisp.

104. Chewy Pretzel Bites Recipe

Serving: 0 | Prep: | Cook: 1hours | Ready in:

Ingredients

- 2 1/2 cups (10 1/2 ounces) all-purpose flour
- 1/2 teaspoon salt
- 1 teaspoon sugar
- 2 1/4 teaspoons instant yeast *
- 1 cup (8 ounces) very warm water
- Topping:
- 1/2 cup (4 ounces) warm water
- 2 tablespoons baking soda
- coarse salt (optional)
- 3 tablespoons butter, melted

Direction

- In a large bowl or the bowl of an electric mixer, place the flour, salt, sugar and yeast. Mix to just combine. Add the water and mix well, adding more flour, as needed, a bit at a time to form a soft, smooth dough that clears the sides and bottom of the bowl. Knead the dough, by hand or machine, for about 5 minutes, until it is soft, smooth and quite slack. The goal is to get a really soft dough that isn't overly sticky. Lightly flour the dough and place it in a plastic bag; close the bag, leaving room for the dough to expand, and let it rest for 30 minutes or up to 60 minutes.
- Preheat your oven to 500°F. Don't be afraid of the high heat! This is what will help those pretzels to brown up perfectly and stay soft on the inside. Prepare two baking sheets by lining them with parchment paper or lightly greasing them.
- Transfer the dough to a lightly greased work surface, and divide it into about four strips of equal length. Allow the pieces to rest, uncovered, for 5 minutes. While the dough is resting, combine the 1/2 cup warm water and the baking soda in a liquid measuring cup (deep enough to dip the pretzel bites into). Make sure the baking soda is thoroughly dissolved. Sometimes I have a hard time getting the baking soda completely dissolved, so I just lightly stir up the mixture right before adding each pretzel.
- Cut each strip of dough into about 6-8 pieces, about 1 to 1-½ inches in width. You don't have to be completely exact, just eyeball it. Dip each pretzel bite in the baking soda solution (this will give the pretzels a nice, golden-brown colour), and place them on the baking sheets. Sprinkle them lightly with coarse, kosher, or pretzel salt. Allow them to rest, uncovered, for 10 minutes.
- Bake the pretzels for 7-8 minutes or until they're golden brown. Bake one sheet at a time - it won't hurt the other pretzels to chill out for a little longer.
- Remove the pretzels from the oven, and brush them thoroughly with the melted butter. Keep brushing the butter on until you've used it all up; it may seem like a lot, but that's what gives these pretzels their ethereal taste. Eat the pretzels warm, or reheat them in an oven or microwave on low heat.
- *Note: if using active dry yeast, increase the yeast to 1 tablespoon. Proof the yeast in the warm water and sugar (let it bubble and foam - maybe about 5 minutes) before adding it to the flour and salt.
- ** Just made these, and just about polished off the whole batch - my husband and kids disappeared them before I could get a picture, even! I think I would reduce the amount of baking soda in the water bath a little. I could taste the soda on the final product - I have not noticed this with other homemade pretzels.

105. Chicken And Veggie Ring Recipe

Serving: 8 | Prep: | Cook: 50mins | Ready in:

Ingredients

- 8 Rhodes™ dinner rolls, thawed to room temperature
- 2 cups cooked, cubed chicken, seasoned with salt & pepper
- 1 cup frozen vegetable mixture of peas, corn, carrots & beans
- 1/2 cup grated cheddar cheese
- 1/4 cup mayonnaise
- 1 tablespoon Dijon mustard
- 1 1/2 teaspoons dried minced onion
- 1 teaspoon italian seasoning
- fresh parsley, if desired

Direction

- Spray counter lightly with non-stick cooking spray.
- Combine rolls into a ball and roll into a 12-inch circle.
- Cover with plastic wrap and let rest.
- In a medium bowl combine chicken, frozen vegetables, cheese, mayonnaise, mustard, onion and Italian seasoning.
- Mix well.
- Remove wrap from dough and cut into 8 equal pie shaped pieces.
- Place on a sprayed 12-inch pizza pan, forming a ring with pointed ends facing outer edge of pan and wide ends overlapping slightly.
- Lightly press overlapping ends together.
- Spoon filling over wide ends of ring.
- Fold points over filling and tuck under wide ends.
- Filling will still be visible.
- Bake at 375°F 15-20 minutes or until golden brown.
- Garnish with fresh parsley, if desired.

106. Chicken Barbecue Pizza Recipe

Serving: 4 | Prep: | Cook: 15mins | Ready in:

Ingredients

- 2 english muffin
- 8 oz Chicken: Breast, Skinless, roasted
- 1/4 cup Hickory Smoke Barbeque Sauce
- 1 cup Shredded Wisconsin Extra Sharp Cheddar
- 12 Kosher dill pickle chips

Direction

- Split the English muffins in half and toast them
- Chop the chicken and put it in sauce pan to heat mixing in the BBQ sauce. Heat thoroughly.
- Top each muffin half with dill pickle chips, bbq chicken and then with the shredded cheese.
- Serving suggestions: coleslaw and orange wedges.

107. Chicken Liver Mousse Recipe

Serving: 6 | Prep: | Cook: | Ready in:

Ingredients

- 1/2 pound (2 sticks) plus 4 tablespoons of unsalted butter
- 1 pound of chicken livers
- 1 large egg
- 2 teaspoons of salt
- Pinch of Quatres épices
- Pinch of white pepper
- 1 baguette, sliced and toasted
- 2 tablespoons of cognac

Direction

- 1. Preheat the oven to 300°
- 2. Coat the inside of six of 4-ounce ramekins with 4 tablespoons of unsalted butter with a pastry bush

- 3. Put the livers in a blender, add the eggs, salt, quatre épices, white pepper and the Cognac for about 20 seconds.
- 4. Add the butter and continue blending for 15 seconds
- 5. Put the mixture in the ramekins until three-fourths full. Place them in a baking dish and fill the dish with warm water to half the height of the ramekins.
- 6. Carefully transfer to the oven and bake for 30 minutes
- 7. Let them cool and refrigerate until needed.
- Serve chilled with baguette toast!
- 8. SUBSCRIBE!

108. Christmas Bread Recipe

Serving: 16 | Prep: | Cook: 30mins | Ready in:

Ingredients

- 1 c nonfat milk
- 1/2 c sugar
- 2 pk yeast
- 1/2 c Warm water (105 115'F.)
- 1/2 c Nonfat egg substitute
- 1 ts vanilla
- 1 1/2 ts salt
- 6 c flour
- 1 Grated lemon zest
- 1 c mixed candied fruit
- 1 c golden raisins
- 1 tb butter, melted
- powdered sugar
- Red candied pineapple

Direction

- Heat milk and sugar in saucepan to scalding, then cool to lukewarm. Combine yeast and warm water in mixing bowl, stirring until yeast is dissolved. Add cooled milk mixture to yeast mixture in mixing bowl. Stir in egg substitute, vanilla and salt. Beat in 3 cups of flour and lemon zest. Beat in remaining flour to make soft dough.
- Knead in mixed candied fruit and raisins. Knead about 10 minutes, until smooth and elastic.
- Put dough in greased bowl and let rise in warm place until doubled in bulk, about 1 hour. Punch down. Divide dough in half. Roll first half of dough on lightly floured surface into oval about 1/4" thick. Fold in half lengthwise. Place on greased baking sheet. Brush with half of melted butter. Repeat with second half of dough.
- Cover loaves and let rise until doubled, about 45 minutes. Bake at 375'F. 25 30 minutes, until golden brown. Let cool to warm. Sprinkle with powdered sugar and decorate with candied pineapple or cherries. Makes 2 loaves, or 16 servings.

109. Clam Canape Recipe

Serving: 20 | Prep: | Cook: 4mins | Ready in:

Ingredients

- 1 tall can minced clams
- 2/3 small package cream cheese
- Dash salt and pepper
- Dash tabasco OR horseradish sauce
- bread rounds

Direction

- Preheat broiler.
- Drain and mash clams.
- Add the cheese and seasonings.
- Toast bread rounds on one side.
- Put clam mixture on other side.
- Place under broiler for about 2 minutes.

110. Classic Bruschetta Recipe

Serving: 0 | Prep: | Cook: 20mins | Ready in:

Ingredients

- 1 baguette
- 2 containers fresh grape tomatoes
- about 30 large fresh basil leaves
- at least 1/2 cup shaved or shredded parmesan
- 1/2 cup olive oil
- salt & pepper to taste

Direction

- Preheat oven to 400 degrees Fahrenheit. Line 2 baking sheets with aluminum foil, set aside.
- Cut baguette into thin, flat slices; about 1/4 of an inch thick. Arrange baguette slices on baking sheets, making sure not to overlap. Brush slices generously with olive oil. Top each slice with a small amount of parmesan, saving some for garnish. Bake baguette slices for 6 minutes, or until golden & crispy.
- Meanwhile, dice tomatoes & set aside in a small bowl. Chop basil into thin slices & add to bowl. Mix together, adding salt & freshly ground pepper to taste.
- Once baguette slices are done, spoon a small amount of tomato mixture onto each, then top with freshly shaved parmesan. Arrange on a platter & serve at room temperature.

111. Corn Bread Bites Recipe

Serving: 12 | Prep: | Cook: 17mins | Ready in:

Ingredients

- 2/3 cup all-purpose flour
- ½ cup yellow cornmeal
- 1 tbsp sugar
- 1 ½ tsp baking powder
- ¼ tsp salt
- 1/2 cup sharp cheddar, grated
- ½ cup sour-cream
- ¼ cup green onions, thinly sliced
- 1 can (8 ¾ oz.) cream style corn
- dash of hot sauce
- 1 lrg. egg, lightly beaten
- cooking spray

Direction

- Preheat oven to 375
- Combine flour and next 4 ingredients (through salt) in a large bowl
- Combine cheese and remaining ingredients in a smaller bowl
- Stir with whisk, add to flour mixture; stir until just moistened
- Coat muffin cups with cooking spray
- Divide batter evenly among muffin cups
- Bake for 10 minutes or until golden brown
- Cool on wire racks

112. Corn Bread Dip Recipe

Serving: 8 | Prep: | Cook: 35mins | Ready in:

Ingredients

- 2 boxes Jiffy cornbread mix (Cooked by directions on box)
- 1 onion, chopped
- 1 bell pepper, chopped
- ! can Rotel tomatoes
- 1 can mexicorn
- 2 cans chicken broth
- 12 oz grated cheddar cheese

Direction

- Mix and cook cornbread according to package directions.
- Sauté onion and bell pepper until tender.
- Crumble cornbread and add Rotel, mexicorn, chicken broth, and cheese to onion and pepper mixture.
- Place in a greased baking dish.

- Bake at 350 degrees until firm.

113. Crab Garlic Bread Recipe

Serving: 6 | Prep: | Cook: 45mins | Ready in:

Ingredients

- 1 loaf French bread
- 1 cube butter, soft
- 1 c. mayonnaise
- 2 c. grated cheddar cheese
- Sm. bunch green onions, chopped
- 1/4 c. parsley, chopped
- As much garlic as you like, never less than 2 lg. cloves!
- 1 can crab meat (6 oz.), washed, drained and patted dry, or more if desired

Direction

- Cut the bread lengthwise and spread the butter evenly on both halves.
- Mix the mayonnaise, cheese, onions, parsley, garlic, and crab together, then spread them evenly over the butter.
- Cover with foil, folded high above the surface of the bread so as not to touch the mixture.
- Bake at 375 half an hour.
- Take off the foil and put the bread back in the oven for another 15 minutes OR until nicely brown.

114. Crab Crostini Recipe

Serving: 8 | Prep: | Cook: 6mins | Ready in:

Ingredients

- 8 oz lump crabmeat
- 1/2 cup diced red bell pepper
- 2 Tbsp plus 2 tsp reduced calorie mayonnaise
- 2 Tbsp chopped fresh parsley
- 1 Tbsp chopped fresh chives
- 1 Tbsp fresh lime juice
- 1 Tbsp Djion mustard
- 2 tsp grated parmesan cheese
- 4 to 5 drops hot pepper sauce (1 like more!)
- 4 oz Italian bread, cut into 16 slices

Direction

- Preheat the broiler.
- Line a broiler pan with foil.
- Pick over crabmeat to remove any cartilage.
- In a medium bowl, combine the crabmeat, bell pepper, mayonnaise, parsley, chives, lime juice, mustard, Parmesan cheese and hot sauce and blend well.
- Spread 1 Tbsp. of the crab mixture on each slice of bread.
- Place crostini on the broiler pan and broil 4 inches from the heat for 5 to 6 minutes, or until lightly browned.
- Serving size: 2 crostini
- 88 calories, 7 g protein, 2 g fat, p g carbohydrates, 30 mg cholesterol, 255 mg sodium.

115. Crab Crostini With Baby Shrimp Recipe

Serving: 6 | Prep: | Cook: 3mins | Ready in:

Ingredients

- 6 slices baguette-style bread, sliced thinly
- 1/2 pound gruyere cheese, grated
- 1/2 cup sour cream
- 1 teaspoon Dijon mustard
- 1 tablespoon minced scallions
- 1 tablespoon fresh lemon juice
- 1 teaspoon Old Bay Seasoning
- 8-10 dashes Tabasco sauce
- 1/2 teaspoon salt
- 1/2 teaspoon freshly ground black pepper
- 1/2 pound lump crabmeat

- 1/4 pound baby shrimp

Direction

- Grill the thinly sliced bread or place it under the broiler until toasted. Turn and toast the other side. Set aside.
- Combine the half of the cheese, the sour cream, mustard, scallions, lemon juice, Old Bay seasoning, Tabasco sauce, salt, and pepper in a medium mixing bowl and mix thoroughly.
- Check the crabmeat for any small pieces of shell and discard them.
- Gently add the crab to the mixture. Don't over mix; you want the lumps of crab to remain intact.
- Cover the mixture with plastic wrap and refrigerate for several hours so that the flavours meld.
- Remove the crab from the refrigerator and spoon it onto the toasts. Top each with a portion of the remaining cheese and a few baby shrimp.
- Sprinkle a small amount of the cheese over the shrimp and place under the broiler for 2 to 3 minutes, until melted and bubbly.

116. Crab Crostini With Truffle Oil Recipe

Serving: 30 | Prep: | Cook: 10mins | Ready in:

Ingredients

- 16 oz - crab meat (flaked)
- Mirco-Greens or arugula
- Stracchino cheese
- truffle oil
- Crostini
- chives

Direction

- With a fork cream together the flaked crab meat and stracchino cheese until well blended.
- Add a few drops of truffle oil to taste.
- Put about 1 tbsp. on top of each crostini, sprinkle with chives and micro-greens.
- Serve warm or cold.

117. Crabmeat Canapes Recipe

Serving: 32 | Prep: | Cook: | Ready in:

Ingredients

- 18 oz cream cheese
- 1 tbl creamed horseradish
- 1/2 tsp lemon juice
- 1/4 tsp onion powder
- 1/4 tsp garlic powder
- pepper and salt
- 1 1/2 cup (6 1/2 oz) flaked crab meat
- 1 cup chopped cucumbers

Direction

- Mix cream cheese, horseradish, lemon juice, and seasonings
- Add crab meat and cucumbers
- Refrigerate until ready to serve

118. Crabmeat Crostini Recipe

Serving: 4 | Prep: | Cook: | Ready in:

Ingredients

- 8- 1/2 inch-thick slices La Brea baguette
- 2 cups snow crab meat from the legs
- 2 tablespoons mayonnaise
- 2 teaspoons sour cream
- 1/2 teaspoon Dijon mustard
- ½ teaspoon horseradish

- 4 teaspoons finely chopped chives
- Freshly ground pepper

Direction

- Grill the bread until the bread is golden brown. In a mixing bowl combine the crab meat, mayonnaise, sour cream, mustard, and 2 teaspoons of the chives. Season to taste with pepper. Spread each crisp with one-eighth of the crabmeat mixture. Sprinkle with the remaining chives, and serve.

119. Cranberry Blue Crostini Recipe

Serving: 24 | Prep: | Cook: 15mins | Ready in:

Ingredients

- 24 1/4-inch thick slices of French bread, each slice about the size of a business card
- 2 T. walnut oil
- 1/2 c. finely chopped walnuts
- 8 oz. blue cheese, crumbled
- 4 T. minced shallots
- 1/3 c. dried cranberries

Direction

- Place walnuts in dry non-stick sauté pan over medium heat, stirring occasionally, until toasted brown (about 6 minutes).
- Preheat oven to 400 degrees. Arrange bread slices on baking sheet. Brush slices with walnut oil. Bake about 5 minutes or until crisp.
- Mix toasted walnuts, blue cheese, shallots and cranberries. Spread mixture on toast slices. Bake just until cheese melts, about 4 minutes. Serve warm from the oven. Good with a nice Zinfandel--Sapphire Hill is an excellent match.

120. Cranberry Bruschetta Recipe

Serving: 16 | Prep: | Cook: 30mins | Ready in:

Ingredients

- 14 oz can Ocean Spray Whole cranberry sauce
- 1/4 cup sugar
- 1/4 cup red wine vinegar
- 1/2 red onion, thinly sliced into rings
- 2 garlic cloves, minced
- 2 Tbsp minced fresh basil
- 1 tsp oregano
- 8 oz loaf of French bread
- olive oil

Direction

- Combine all ingredients, except bread and oil, in a medium saucepan.
- Cook on medium heat, stirring occasionally, until onion is soft and sauce has thickened, about 30 minutes.
- Cool to room temperature.
- Cut bread diagonally into 3/4-inch slices; brush both sides with oil.
- Broil each side of bread for 1 to 2 minutes or until golden brown.
- Top each slice with cranberry mixture.

121. Cranberry Herb Almond Crisps Recipe

Serving: 22 | Prep: | Cook: 3hours | Ready in:

Ingredients

- 1 cup whole wheat flour
- 1 tsp baking soda
- 1/4 tsp salt
- 1 cup unsweetened almond milk
- 2 tbsp brown sugar

- 2 tbsp agave nectar (I used Amoretti Organolicious blood orange Flavored agave nectar)
- ½ cup dried cranberries
- ¼ cup raisins
- ¼ cup slivered almonds
- 2 tbsp ground flax seed
- 1 tsp dried rosemary
- 1 tsp dried thyme

Direction

- Preheat oven to 350° F and line an 8x4" loaf pan with parchment.
- In a large bowl, stir together the flour, baking soda and salt.
- Add the almond milk, brown sugar, and agave and stir. Add the cranberries, raisins, almonds, flaxseed and herbs and stir just until blended.
- Bake for about 35 minutes, until golden and springy to the touch. Remove from the pans and cool completely on a wire rack.
- Slice the loaves as thin as you can and place the slices in a single layer on an ungreased cookie sheet.
- Reduce the oven heat to 300° F and bake them for 25 minutes, then flip them over and bake for another 20 minutes, until crisp and deep golden.
- Turn off the oven and allow crisps to cool inside

122. Crawfish Bread Recipe

Serving: 24 | Prep: | Cook: 15mins | Ready in:

Ingredients

- 2 tbs. butter
- 1 chopped onion
- 1 chopped bell pepper
- garlic, to taste
- 1/2 cup green onions
- 1 pound of crawfish (leftover boiled is great)
- 1 1/2 cups mayonnaise
- 3 oz. of each cheese: Provolone, Mozarella, Cheddar, & America
- 1 stick of melted butter(mixed with a little honey)
- 2 loaves of French bread, cut in half

Direction

- Sauté first 6 ingredients in 2 tbsp. of butter until wilted
- Add mayonnaise and cheese until melted
- Spread over each half of the French bread
- Put breads back together
- Baste with honey butter mixture
- Bake at 250 degrees for 15 mins.
- Cut into slices and enjoy!

123. Crawfish Corn Bread Recipe

Serving: 810 | Prep: | Cook: 30mins | Ready in:

Ingredients

- 1 cup cornmeal
- 1 can cream-style corn
- 1 onion, finely chopped
- 1/2 pound shredded cheddar cheese
- 1/3 cup oil
- 2 eggs
- 2 jalapeno peppers with seeds removed, finely chopped
- 1 teaspoon salt
- 1/2 teaspoon baking soda
- 1 pound crawfish or shrimp

Direction

- Combine all ingredients together, put in greased pan, and bake at 375 degrees for 30 minutes or until done. Use toothpick in the centre to test; when it comes out clean, cornbread is done. Cool before cutting into squares.

- Serve with a salad and it becomes a full meal. May be reheated.

124. Crazy Quick Cheesy Bread Recipe

Serving: 8 | Prep: | Cook: 25mins | Ready in:

Ingredients

- 2 cups shredded cheese
- 1 small can chopped green chiles, undrained
- 1/2 tsp onion powder
- 1/2 tsp black pepper
- 1 jar (5 oz) olive-pimento cheese spread
- 1/4 cup mayo
- 1 loaf of frech bread cut in half
- sliced green olives, if desired

Direction

- Heat broiler.
- Mix all ingredients except olives
- Broil bread on a cookie sheet until lightly toasted
- Spread cheese mixture on the toasted sides and place back under broiler until hot and melted.
- Sprinkle with olives and cut into slices to serve.
- ** Great on the grill as well!

125. Creamy Dill Cucumber Toasties Recipe

Serving: 12 | Prep: | Cook: 2hours | Ready in:

Ingredients

- 1 (8 ounce) package cream cheese, softened
- 1 (.7 ounce) package dry Italian-style salad dressing mix
- 1/2 cup mayonnaise
- 1 French baguette, cut into 1/2 inch thick circles
- 1 cucumber, sliced
- 2 teaspoons dried dill weed

Direction

- In a medium bowl, mix together cream cheese, dressing mix and mayonnaise.
- Spread a thin layer of the cream cheese mixture on a slice of bread, and top with a slice of cucumber. Sprinkle with dill. Repeat with remaining ingredients.

126. Creme De Brie Mango Cranberry Crostini Recipe

Serving: 10 | Prep: | Cook: 10mins | Ready in:

Ingredients

- 20 thin (¼ inch) slices french baguette
- 2 tbsp. olive oil
- 1 pkg. (5 oz.) Alouette Crème de Brie, Original
- ¼ cup purchased mango chutney
- 2 tbsp. sweetened dried cranberries
- 1 tbsp. snipped fresh mint leaves, if desired

Direction

- Heat oven to 375° F.
- Arrange baguette slices on large ungreased cookie sheet. Brush with olive oil. Bake 5 to 7 minutes or until lightly toasted and crisp.
- Place on 2 serving plates and cool 1 minute. Spread each with about ½ tablespoon Alouette Crème de Brie.
- In small bowl, combine chutney, and cranberries. Spoon small dollops over cheese. Garnish sparingly with mint.

127. Crockpot Bruschetta Recipe

Serving: 4 | Prep: | Cook: 60mins | Ready in:

Ingredients

- 3 Medium tomatoes, cored, seeded, diced
- 1 celery Stalk, trimmed and chopped
- 1 shallot, chopped
- 2 pepperoncini peppers, chopped
- 1 tsp tomato paste
- 1/2 tsp salt
- 1/4 tsp Pepper
- 1 T olive oil
- 4-6 Slices Italian bread, or any round bread will do
- 1 clove Garlic

Direction

- In Crockpot, add tomatoes (drain off juice as much as possible)
- Add celery, shallots, pepperoncini, tomato paste, salt pepper and oil
- Cover and Cook on LOW 1 hour
- Put sliced bread rounds in oven at 300 until lightly toasted
- When bread is toasted, immediately rub each slice with garlic
- Spread tomato topping on bread and Serve.
- (I serve the bread and the tomato mixture separately for parties so the mixture stays warm to eat.)
- Note: Pepperoncini peppers can be found fresh in produce section or in the grocery store aisle with pickles, etc. Usually have them whole or sliced in a jar. Also known as 'banana peppers'.

128. Crostini Boscaiolo Mushroom Toasts Recipe

Serving: 8 | Prep: | Cook: 30mins | Ready in:

Ingredients

- 1/2 lb cremini or portabella mushrooms(can substitute others, play around!), washed and dried and sliced thin
- 3 T extra virgin olive oil
- 1 medium spanish onion, finely diced
- 3 sprigs thyme
- 1/2 cup white wine or white vermouth
- 1 cup low sodium or homemade chicken stock
- 1/4 cup cream
- S&P to taste
- 1 baguette
- 1 clove garlic
- parmigiano reggiano for grating

Direction

- Heat 1 T extra virgin olive oil in large sauté pan over medium heat until it slides easily across the bottom
- Add mushrooms just so that they cover the pan in one layer, sprinkle salt and pepper over them and let them brown without moving them too often, really let them colour.
- As the mushrooms are cooked remove and reserve them and add a new batch, sprinkling with salt & pepper again and adding oil. It usually takes me 3 batches in a large skillet
- When all of the mushrooms are browned add the onion (may need to add more oil) and sauté until softened
- Strip the leaves from the thyme and add them to the onions, sauté until you smell the aroma of the thyme
- Now deglaze with the white wine, cook the wine down for a minute and add the stock
- Cook the liquid down until it starts to slightly thicken and then add the reserved mushrooms
- Cook until the liquid coats the mushrooms nicely, then add the cream and cook another minute to meld the flavours, adjust seasoning at this point
- The above may done ahead and reheated to top the toasts at the last minute

- Now make the crostini: slice the baguette about 1/4 inch thick and rub one side with the peeled garlic clove
- Broil the baguette slices until just starting to brown
- Top the garlic side of the baguette with a few tablespoons of the mushroom mixture
- Grate a light snowfall of Parmigiano (could use asiago or Romano but please no waxy green can 'parmesan'!) over the toasts and stick back under the broiler just to melt the cheese- yummy

129. Crostini Napolentani Appetizer Toasts Neopolitan Style Recipe

Serving: 8 | Prep: | Cook: 10mins | Ready in:

Ingredients

- 1/2 cup extra virgin olive oil
- 16 slices Italian bread, sliced 1/2 inch thick
- 16 slice mozzarella cheese, sliced 1/4 inch thick
- 32 anchovy fillets, rinsed and patted dry, chopped
- 1 lb fresh plum tomatoes, cut into 16 thin slices
- salt and pepper, to taste

Direction

- Preheat oven to 400F.
- Brush oil on one side of bread slices and place oiled side up on flat baking sheet. Cover each slice of bread with a slice of mozzarella, sprinkle with chopped anchovy, and top with a slice of tomato. Brush with oil and sprinkle with salt and pepper. Bake 10 minutes.
- Variation: In place of anchovies and plum tomatoes, use 1/4 cup black or green pureed olives, and 2 large roasted red peppers cut in 1/4 inch strips. Spread bread with olive puree, lay on Mozzarella cheese, and cover with two crossed strips of red pepper. Bake as above.

130. Crostini With Creamy Ricotta And Chorizo Recipe

Serving: 6 | Prep: | Cook: 30mins | Ready in:

Ingredients

- 1 cup fresh ricotta cheese
- 3 tablespoons extra-virgin olive oil, plus more for brushing
- salt and freshly ground pepper
- Six 1/2-inch-thick slices of Italian peasant bread
- 2 small garlic cloves, 1 minced
- 1/4 small red onion, thinly sliced
- 6 tablespoons balsamic vinegar
- 1 small dry chorizo (about 3 ounces), thinly sliced
- 1 tablespoon chopped tarragon
- 1 tablespoon chopped parsley
- 1 small head of frisée, tender white and light green leaves only

Direction

- Put the ricotta in a fine sieve set over a bowl. Cover with plastic wrap and refrigerate overnight (about 10-12 hours).
- Discard the liquid in the bowl. Wipe out the bowl, add the thickened ricotta and stir in 1 tablespoon of the olive oil and season with salt and pepper.
- Preheat a grill pan.
- Lightly brush both sides of the bread slices with oil and grill, turning once, until toasted, about 3 minutes. Transfer the toasts to a platter and rub them with the whole garlic clove.
- In a small bowl, toss the red onion with 2 tablespoons of the balsamic vinegar and let stand for 10 minutes; drain the onion, discarding the vinegar.

- Meanwhile, in a small saucepan, boil the remaining 1/4 cup of balsamic vinegar until reduced to 1 tablespoon, about 5 minutes.
- In a medium skillet, combine the remaining 2 tablespoons of oil with the minced garlic, chorizo, tarragon and parsley. Cook over low heat, stirring occasionally, just until warmed through, about 5 minutes.
- Spread the ricotta on the toasts and top with the warm chorizo. Garnish with the frisée and pickled onions.
- Drizzle with the reduced balsamic vinegar and serve.

131. Crostini With Peaches And Blue Cheese Recipe

Serving: 12 | Prep: | Cook: 15mins | Ready in:

Ingredients

- 12 thin slices baguette or similar bread (stale bread is fine)
- olive oil, for brushing
- 3 to 4 ripe peaches
- 2 tablespoons balsamic vinegar
- 3/4 to 1 cup crumbled blue cheese
- Freshly ground black pepper (optional)

Direction

- Brush the bread with just a bit of olive oil, then toast, bake, grill, or broil the bread until it's almost dry.
- To peel the peaches, boil them for 30 seconds, then immediately transfer them to a bowl of ice water. The skin will come off easily. Slice the peaches into very small and thin pieces and combine them with the balsamic vinegar.
- Preheat the broiler to low.
- Arrange the bread on a rimmed baking sheet. Top the bread slices with the peaches and their juices. Put the crumbled cheese on top of the peaches, and add just a touch of pepper, if desired.

- Broil the crostini until the cheese is hot, soft and just touched with brown. Serve at any temperature, preferably within a couple hours of being made.

132. Crostini With Sun Dried Tomato Tapenade Recipe

Serving: 8 | Prep: | Cook: 10mins | Ready in:

Ingredients

- Crostini with Sun-Dried-Tomato tapenade
- Ingredients:
- 1 cup pitted kalamata olives or other brine-cured black olives
- 3/4 cup drained oil-packed sun-dried tomatoes
- 2/3 cup extra virgin olive oil
- 1/4 cup drained capers
- 3/4 teaspoon dried oregano
- 1 French-bread baguette, cut into 1/2-inch-thick slices
- Additional extra virgin olive oil

Direction

- Directions:
- Using on/off turns, finely chop olives and tomatoes in processor.
- Add 2/3 cup olive oil, capers, and oregano; blend to coarse puree.
- Transfer to bowl. (Tapenade can be made 3 days ahead. Cover; refrigerate. Bring to room temperature before using.)
- Preheat oven to 350°F.
- Place bread slices on baking sheet.
- Brush lightly with additional olive oil.
- Bake until golden, about 10 minutes.
- Spread tomato tapenade on toasts and serve. Makes about 36.
- That's it!

133. Crunchy Bacon And Rosemary Bites Recipe

Serving: 24 | Prep: | Cook: 1hours | Ready in:

Ingredients

- • 12 strips of naturally smoked bacon
- • 24 Great Value rosemary and olive oil wheat crackers
- • fresh rosemary

Direction

- 1. Preheat oven to 300F (190C). Line a sturdy baking tray with aluminum foil; top with a wire rack sprayed with non-stick canola oil cooking spray.
- 2. Cut the strips of bacon in half widthwise.
- 3. Top each cracker with a cluster of rosemary leaves. Wrap loosely with half a strip of bacon. Transfer to wire rack on prepared baking tray, seam side down, leaving about 1" (2.5 cm) in between. Repeat with remaining ingredients.
- 4. Bake in centre of oven for 55-65 minutes or until nicely browned and crispy. Serve warm or at room temperature.
- Tips:
- • For a beautiful presentation, garnish the serving platter with sprigs of fresh rosemary as an added touch.
- • Don't wrap the bacon too tightly around the crackers; the bacon strips shrinks as they bake, if they're too tight, the crackers will bend.

134. Crusty Croutons Recipe

Serving: 0 | Prep: | Cook: 35mins | Ready in:

Ingredients

- 6 Rhodes Warm-N-Serv™ Crusty rolls, baked following package instructions
- 2 tablespoons butter, melted
- 1 tablespoon olive oil
- 1 teaspoon italian seasoning
- 1/4 cup grated parmesan cheese
- garlic salt

Direction

- Cut rolls into 1/2 to 1-inch cubes.
- Place in a large bowl.
- Combine butter and oil and drizzle over roll cubes.
- Toss until all cubes are evenly coated.
- Sprinkle with seasoning and Parmesan cheese and toss again until well coated.
- Spread on a baking sheet and sprinkle lightly with garlic salt.
- Bake at 350°F 10-15 minutes or until nicely browned.

135. Crusty Garlic Bread Recipe

Serving: 10 | Prep: | Cook: 15mins | Ready in:

Ingredients

- 2 cloves garlic, minced
- 2 tsp. olive oil
- 2 Tbs. chopped fresh parsley
- 2 Tbs. chopped fresh thyme or 2 tsp. Dried thyme
- 2 tsp. Chopped fresh marjoram or 1 tsp. dried marjoram
- ½ tsp. paprika
- 2 Tbs. grated parmesan cheese (optional)
- 2 small loaves (4oz each) of French or Italian bread

Direction

- 1) Preheat oven to 350°. In a small bowl, combine the garlic and oil; mix well.
- 2) In another small bowl, combine parsley, thyme, marjoram, and paprika. Add Parmesan; mix well. Cut each loaf crosswise into diagonal slices, without cutting all the

way through. Brush cut sides of slices with garlic oil. Sprinkle herb mixture between slices. Wrap each loaf in foil; place on a baking sheet.

- 3) Bake until heated through, about 10 to 15 minutes. Unwrap the loaves and place them on a breadboard or in a basket. Serve immediately.

136. Crusty Onion Bruschetta Recipe

Serving: 8 | Prep: | Cook: 20mins | Ready in:

Ingredients

- 1 French bread baguette
- 4 ounces cream cheese
- 1/2 cup ricotta cheese
- 2 teaspoons dried oregano
- 2 teaspoons dried basil
- 1 cup pizza sauce
- 1 medium onion cut into paper thin wedges
- 1/4 cup parmesan cheese grated

Direction

- Split bread in half lengthwise.
- Pull out some bread from centre of each half leaving a 1/2-inch shell.
- Beat cheeses and herbs with fork and spread mixture along length of both bread halves.
- Place a ribbon of pizza sauce and a single layer of onions over cheese mixture.
- Sprinkle with parmesan and bake on baking sheet at 400 for 30 minutes.
- Cut crosswise into narrow strips.

137. Cucumber Canapes

Serving: 1233 | Prep: | Cook: 221mins | Ready in:

Ingredients

- 1 cup mayonnaise
- 3 ounces cream cheese, softened
- 1 tablespoon grated onion
- 1 tablespoon minced chives
- 1/2 teaspoon cider vinegar
- 1/2 teaspoon Worcestershire sauce
- 1 garlic clove, minced
- 1/4 teaspoon paprika
- 1/8 teaspoon curry powder
- 1/8 teaspoon each dried oregano, thyme, basil, parsley flakes and dill weed
- 1 loaf (1 pound) white or rye bread
- 2 medium cucumbers, scored and thinly sliced
- Diced pimientos and additional dill weed

Direction

- In a blender or food processor, combine the mayonnaise, cream cheese, onion, chives, vinegar, Worcestershire sauce, garlic and seasonings. Cover and process until blended. Cover and refrigerate for 24 hours.
- Using a 2-1/2-in. biscuit cutter, cut out circles from bread slices. Spread mayonnaise mixture over bread; top with cucumber slices. Garnish with pimientos and dill.
- Nutrition Facts
- 1 canape: 120 calories, 9g fat (2g saturated fat), 7mg cholesterol, 134mg sodium, 8g carbohydrate (1g sugars, 1g fiber), 2g protein.

138. Curry Toast Recipe

Serving: 0 | Prep: | Cook: 9mins | Ready in:

Ingredients

- 1 package of engish muffins(6 muffins)
- 5 Tb butter
- 1 C of shredded american or cheddar cheese
- 1 C of shredded Swiss cheese
- 1/4-1/3 C mayonaisse

- 1 bunch of green onions chopped up (into the green parts)
- 1 tsp. hot or sweet (regular) Curry powder
- 1-2 garden tomatoes (optional)

Direction

- Preheat oven to low broil. Open the muffins and place cut side- up on lined baking sheet.
- Put in the oven and toast the muffins as dark as you would like them (2-4 minutes).
- Remove from the oven and butter all 12 muffins.
- Mix the cheeses gently with the mayonnaise. Mix in the green onions and Curry powder.
- If you choose to use fresh tomatoes slice thinly and blot the extra juice on paper towels, and divide the sliced tomatoes among the muffins.
- Cover the muffins with the cheese mix and toast under the broiler until golden brown 4-8 minutes.
- For hors d'oeuvres, slice in quarters and serve hot or leave as- is serve with soup or salad for a nice filling lunch.

139. Custom Creation#17(aka Le Petit Gourmand;) Recipe

Serving: 12 | Prep: | Cook: 1hours | Ready in:

Ingredients

- 1 lb cooked lobster meat(can sub cooked crawfish meat)
- 24 asparagus tops
- 6 large fresh mushrooms, whole
- 3 slices bacon, fried crisp and broken into very small pieces
- 1/2 cup olive tapenade(recipe follows, or your favorite)
- 3-4T melted(clarified is even better) butter
- 12 2inch diameter, about 1/2inch thick fried tortillas(recipe follows, or use your own)
- salt and pepper
- 1T olive oil
- For Tapenade
- 1/2 cup kalamata olives(measured whole)
- 1 roasted red pepper
- 1T capers
- 1 clove garlic
- 1t olive oil
- squirt of lemon or lime juice
- 1T fresh cilantro
- For Tortillas
- 2 cups instant mesa
- 2 cups room temperature water
- 1T salt(yes, really)
- 2T flour
- oil heating for frying

Direction

- For Tortillas
- Combine all ingredients in glass bowl, mixing with wooden spoon until just mixed.
- With wet hands, work dough between your hands to "knead" it, for about 10 minutes, creating a smooth ball. Dough will not get elastic as bread dough, do
- Pinch off dough and form to create 2 inch rounds, about 1/2 inch thick. Smooth edges and surfaces as much as possible.
- Deep fry in hot oil until golden brown, about 5 minutes.
- Drain on paper towels or paper bag
- For Tapenade
- Add all ingredients to food processor and process into small chunks, evenly.
- For Mushrooms
- Slice mushrooms on mandoline
- Drop into hot oil and fry until golden brown, about 1 minute.
- Drain on paper towel or paper bag.
- For Asparagus
- Toss spear tops with olive oil and sprinkle with salt and pepper.
- Broil for about 5 minutes until tender and tops are crisp.
- For Lobster
- Toss lobster meat in clarified butter and let rest while preparing to stack the finished dish.
- To Stack

- Place 2 asparagus tops crosswise on each tortilla
- Top with slightly drained lobster meat.
- Add about 1 teaspoon tapenade to lobster
- Top with a few slices of fried mushroom
- Sprinkle with a few pieces of bacon

140. Dawn's Fig Crostini Recipe

Serving: 8 | Prep: | Cook: 15mins | Ready in:

Ingredients

- fig topping:
- 1 c. dried black mission figs (6 oz)
- 1 t. lemon juice
- 2 c. water
- 2 T. maple syrup
- dash of salt
- onions:
- olive oil
- 2 c. vertically sliced yellow onions
- 2 T. chocolate balsamic vinegar
- 1 t. chopped fresh thyme
- 1/4 t. salt
- remaining ingredients:
- 1/2 c. (4 oz) gorgonzola cheese, softened (or brie)
- 24 (1 inch thick) slices diagonally cut French bread baguette, brushed with olive oil + toasted (12 oz)
- 1 t. fresh thyme leaves

Direction

- Preparation:
- To prepare fig topping, remove stems from figs. place fig and juice in food processor; process until figs are coarsely chopped. Place fig mixture, 2 c. water, syrup, and dash of salt in a medium saucepan; bring to a boil. Reduce heat and simmer 25 minutes or until thick. Cool completely.
- To prepare onions, heat a large non-stick skillet coated with cooking spray or oil over medium heat. Add onion, vinegar, 1/2 t. thyme, and 1/4 t. salt; cover and cook 5 minutes. Uncover and cook 20 minutes or until onion is deep golden brown, stirring occasionally.
- Spread 1 t. cheese over each baguette slice. Top each slice with about 1 t. jam + 1 t. onions. Sprinkle evenly with thyme leaves.
- *The changes I made were: I didn't use the food processor to chop the figs, just chopped them coarsely by hand. I used about 1 c. onion instead of 2 c. because I used mini baguettes for an appetizer size. I used brie cheese (because it's what I had on hand, and I accidently grabbed gorgonzola cheese instead of goat cheese-shoot!). I adjusted the amounts of everything on the bread because they were smaller. I also topped the cheese with a little bit of store bought fig jam, but next time I'd probably skip it!

141. Debs Cajun Bread Recipe

Serving: 8 | Prep: | Cook: 12mins | Ready in:

Ingredients

- 1 roll breakfast sausage, mild(such as Jimmy Dean or Bryan)
- 1 stick butter
- 1 can black olives, chopped
- 1 bunch green onions, chopped
- 8 oz. cream cheese, softened
- dash of creole or cajun seasoning
- 8 oz. shredded cheddar cheese
- 1 package brown and serve rolls cut lengthwise or 1 loaf French bread cut in half.(if using both halves, double the filling recipe)

Direction

- Brown sausage

- Add butter, green onions, and black olives and cook one minute longer.
- Pour mixture into a large bowl.
- Add cream cheese and seasoning
- Refrigerate until ready to put together and serve
- Before serving, preheat oven to 350 degrees.
- Place rolls side by side on a baking pan.
- If using French bread, place on cookie or baking pan. (I have a cooking stone and place it on that to cook)
- Spread mixture over each roll or on French bread half.
- Sprinkle with cheese and bake until golden brown (about 10 to 12 minutes)
- Serve warm.

the highest rack. Broil on high heat for 2-3 minutes until the edges of the bread begin to toast and the cheese (if you are using cheese) bubbles. Watch very carefully while broiling. The bread can easily go from un-toasted to burnt.
- Remove from oven, let cool a minute. Remove from pan and make 1-inch thick slices. Serve immediately.
- For Soft version:
- Preheat oven to 350°F. Make the butter, garlic, parsley mixture as above. Make 1-inch thick slices into the bread, but do not go all the way through, just to the bottom crust. Put a teaspoon or two of the butter mixture between each slice. Add the cheese, then wrap the bread in aluminum foil and heat for 15 minutes in the oven.

142. Delicious Garlic Bread Recipe

Serving: 6 | Prep: | Cook: 12mins | Ready in:

Ingredients

- 1 16-ounce loaf of Italian bread or French bread
- 1/2 cup (1 stick) unsalted butter, softened
- 2 large cloves of garlic, smashed and minced
- 1 heaping tablespoon of freshly chopped parsley
- 1/4 cup freshly grated parmesan cheese(or asiago) secret!

Direction

- Preheat oven to 350°F.
- Cut the bread in half, horizontally. Mix the butter, garlic, and parsley together in a small bowl. Spread butter mixture over the two bread halves. Place on a sturdy baking pan (one that can handle high temperatures, not a cookie sheet) and heat in the oven for 10 minutes.
- Remove pan from oven. Sprinkle Parmesan (or Asiago cheese) over bread. Return to oven on

143. Double Tomato Bruschetta Recipe

Serving: 12 | Prep: | Cook: 7mins | Ready in:

Ingredients

- 6 roma (plum) tomatoes, chopped
- 1/2 cup sun-dried tomatoes, packed in oil
- 3 cloves minced garlic
- 1/4 cup olive oil
- 2 tablespoons balsamic vinegar
- 1/4 cup fresh basil, stems removed
- 1/4 teaspoon salt
- 1/4 teaspoon ground black pepper
- 1 french baguette
- 2 cups shredded mozzarella cheese

Direction

- Preheat the oven on broiler setting
- In a large bowl, combine the roma tomatoes, sun-dried tomatoes, garlic, olive oil, vinegar, basil, salt, and pepper. Allow the mixture to sit for 10 minutes

- Cut the baguette into 3/4-inch slices. On a baking sheet, arrange the baguette slices in a single layer. Broil for 1 to 2 minutes, until slightly brown.
- Divide the tomato mixture evenly over the baguette slices. Top the slices with mozzarella cheese.
- Broil for 5 minutes, or until the cheese is melted.

144. Drunken Cheesy Bread Recipe

Serving: 4 | Prep: | Cook: 20mins | Ready in:

Ingredients

- butter for the pan
- 1/2 baguette, cut into 2 inch slices
- 1 to 2 green onions, chopped
- 4 slices bacon, cooked and crumbled
- 3/4 cup dry white wine
- 1/4 tsp. cayenne
- 1 1/2 cups grated cheese (gruyere, Swiss, Monterey Jack, fontina or white Cheddar or mixture)

Direction

- Preheat oven to 400°F.
- Place the bread in a buttered ovenproof skillet, a 9" square baking dish, or casserole. Scatter the onion and bacon over the bread. Pour the wine over the onion and bacon and sprinkle with the cayenne and Gruyere.
- Bake until the cheese has melted and begun to brown at the edges, about 20 minutes.
- Spoon onto individual plates

145. EASY Bruschetta Recipe

Serving: 20 | Prep: | Cook: | Ready in:

Ingredients

- 10 plum tomatoes
- 2 Ugly or Large beef Stake tomatoes
- 1 Medium red onion
- 1 Cup Fresh Chopped basil
- 1 Medium sized block of EXTRA Sharp provolone cheese
- 1 Large Bottle Ken's Lite Caesar Dressing
- 1 Loaf French bread

Direction

- Dice all ingredients by hand
- Mix in a large mixing bowl
- Cover with Dressing
- Chill 15 minutes and serve with sliced French bread

146. Easiest Anchovey Butter Recipe

Serving: 0 | Prep: | Cook: | Ready in:

Ingredients

- three anchovies
- 1 stick unsalted butter
- toasted artisan bread

Direction

- Put anchovies and butter into a blender or Cuisinart and blend until smooth
- Spread on toasted bread
- EAT and ENJOY!

147. Easter Bunny Bread Easy And Cute Recipe

Serving: 24 | Prep: | Cook: 25mins | Ready in:

Ingredients

- Ingredients:
- 2 loaves (1 pound each) frozen bread dough, thawed
- 2 raisins
- 2 sliced almonds
- 1 egg, lightly beaten
- lettuce leaves
- Dip of your choice

Direction

- Directions:
- Cut a fourth off of one loaf of dough; shape into a pear to form head. For body, flatten remaining portion into a 7-in. x 6-in. oval; place on a greased baking sheet. Place head above body. Make narrow cuts, about 3/4 in. deep, on each side of head for whiskers.
- Cut second loaf into four equal portions. For ears, shape two portions into 16-in. ropes; fold ropes in half. Arrange ears with open ends touching head. Cut a third portion of dough in half; shape each into a 3-1/2-in. oval for back paws. Cut two 1-in. slits on top edge for toes. Position on each side of body.
- Divide the fourth portion of dough into three pieces. Shape two pieces into 2-1/2-in. balls for front paws; shape the remaining piece into two 1-in. balls for cheeks and one 1/2-in. ball for nose. Place paws on each side of body; cut two 1-in. slits for toes. Place cheeks and nose on face. Add raisins for eyes and almonds for teeth.
- Brush dough with egg. Cover and let rise in a warm place until doubled, about 30-45 minutes. Bake at 350° for 25-30 minutes or until golden brown. Remove to a wire rack to cool.
- Place bread on a lettuce-lined 16-in. x 13-in. serving tray. Cut a 5-in. x 4-in. oval in centre of body. Hollow out bread, leaving a 1/2-in. shell (discard removed bread or save for another use). Line with lettuce and fill with dip. Yield: 1 loaf.

148. Easy Breaded Shrimp Recipe

Serving: 2 | Prep: | Cook: 10mins | Ready in:

Ingredients

- olive oil for frying
- 10 large shrimp, peeled and deveined
- 1 egg, beaten
- 2 cups plain bread crumbs
- garlic (i didnt measure)
- Old Bay Seasoning (i didnt measure)
- paprika (i didnt measure)

Direction

- Heat oil in large skillet.
- Mix bread crumbs and seasonings
- Dip shrimp in egg, then coat in bread crumbs
- Fry the shrimp in the oil.
- Place fried shrimp on paper towel to soak up some of the grease.
- (Obviously you can make more than 10 shrimp...it is just my fiancé and so I just made a few and some fish as well for dinner)

149. Easy Bruschetta Bread Recipe

Serving: 10 | Prep: | Cook: 20mins | Ready in:

Ingredients

- 1 loaf of French bread
- 1 can diced tomatoes
- 1/2 onion
- oregano
- black olives, chopped
- feta cheese
- butter flavored cooking spray

Direction

- Preheat oven to 350.

- Cut French bread into medium sized slices and arrange on a cookie sheet. Spray tops of slices with butter flavored cooking spray. Flip each slice over so that the sprayed side is facing down. Spray the unsprayed sides as well.
- Bake bread slices for 10 minutes.
- Meanwhile, add 1/2 can diced tomatoes and onion to a food processor. Process until onions are fairly chopped up. Add enough oregano to your liking.
- Pull slices out of oven, then flip them over so the cooked sides are now facing up.
- Spread tomato mixture on all of the slices. Sprinkle black olives and feta cheese over the slices.
- Back for 10 more minutes, or until bottom sides are nicely toasted.
- Serve hot!

150. Easy Bruschetta Recipe

Serving: 6 | Prep: | Cook: 5mins | Ready in:

Ingredients

- 1 loaf baguette
- 1 cups zesty Italian dressing
- 2 roma tomatoes, chopped
- freshly grated parmesan cheese

Direction

- Slice baguette diagonally into 1 inch slices. Arrange slices on cookie sheet.
- Brush each slice with Italian dressing.
- Sprinkle with tomatoes and Parmesan.
- Broil until cheese is melted and bread is golden brown.
- Serve immediately.

151. Easy Cheesy Bread Stix Recipe

Serving: 20 | Prep: | Cook: 45mins | Ready in:

Ingredients

- 1 1/2 cup grated extra sharp cheddar cheese
- 3/4 cup all purpose flour
- 1/4 cup of butter, cut in pieces and softened
- 1/2 teaspoon kosher salt
- 1/2 teaspoon garlic powder
- 1/2 teaspoon cayenne pepper
- 1 tablespoon milk

Direction

- Place all ingredients except milk in food processor. Pulse until mixture looks like fine crumbs
- Add milk and process until ball of dough forms
- Roll out on floured board to an 8 x 12 rectangle, 1/8 inch thick
- Cut in strips 1/4 - 1/2 inch wide.
- Place 1 inch apart on parchment lined baking sheet.
- Bake at 350 F for 12 minutes or until ends are golden brown.
- Allow to stand on baking sheet for a couple of minutes before transferring to a wire rack to cool.

152. Easy Smoked Salmon Canapes Recipe

Serving: 0 | Prep: | Cook: 10mins | Ready in:

Ingredients

- 1 cup sour cream
- 1/4 teasp. finely grated lemon peel
- 1 loaf of party size light rye bread
- 4 TBSP. unsalted butter, melted

- 1/2 pound smoked salmon, sliced and cut into 1/2 - 1-inch strips
- 2 scallions, thinly sliced

Direction

- Combine the sour cream and the lemon zest.
- Chill for at least 2 hours or over night
- Brush the bread slices with butter and cut each slice in half diagonally
- Arrange the bread triangles on a baking sheet
- Bake at 350' F for about 10 minutes, or until lightly toasted
- Let cool completely
- Spread generously but not goopy, the chilled lemon cream on top of each triangle.
- Place a strip of salmon on top of each... be decorative...
- Garnish with the scallions...

153. Egg Salad Bruschetta Recipe

Serving: 24 | Prep: | Cook: 15mins | Ready in:

Ingredients

- - 1 baguette, sliced in 1/2" pieces (or purchase prepared bruschetta toast)
- egg SALAD:
- - 4 eggs
- - 4 tablespoons mayonnaise
- - 2 teaspoons sweet pickle relish
- - 2 tablespoons green onion, finely chopped
- salt and freshly ground pepper to taste
- OPTIONAL GARNISH:
- parsley or favorite edible green
- sliced olives

Direction

- Bruschetta: Preheat oven to 400° F.
- Brush both sides of each slice of baguette with olive oil. Place on an ungreased baking sheet and bake 5 minutes, turn. Bake an additional 5 minutes or until both sides are golden brown. Cool.
- Egg Salad: Fill a small sauce pan with enough water to just cover eggs and bring to a full boil.
- Reduce heat to low and cover. Cook eggs for about 10 minutes.
- Remove from heat, drain and immediately cool eggs with cold running water.
- Peel eggs and finely chop.
- Add mayonnaise, pickle relish, chopped onion, salt, and pepper.
- Place a heaping tablespoon of egg mixture on each toast.

154. Eggplant Bruschetta Recipe

Serving: 0 | Prep: | Cook: 1hours | Ready in:

Ingredients

- 1 large eggplant, peeled and cubed
- 1 shallot
- 2 green onions or two tablespoons chives
- 4 cloves of minced garlic, or more depending what you like
- 2 tbsp. kosher salt
- 1 tsp. chili flakes or other hotness you like
- Ground black pepper
- ¼ cup Romano cheese (or cheese of your choice)
- 1 ½ cups tomato sauce
- ¼ cup fresh parsley (chopped)
- 1 bunch basil
- Good olive oil
- For my version I added the following with the above ingredients
- Finely chopped serrano pepper and thai chili
- Dried red chili
- Ancho chili powder
- Smoked paprika
- Italian seasoning
- cayenne pepper

- Oregano
- Dried basil

Direction

- On medium low heat, sauté ¼ cup of good olive oil, shallots, green onions, garlic, (peppers if using) and eggplant until the eggplant starts to soften. Add all your seasoning. Then take a potato masher and just break it down a bit. Taste and add more salt if necessary.
- Add your tomato sauce. Let it cook for about 10 minutes and taste it. If it needs more salt or more olive oil, don't be scared to add it. Then add the cheese, parsley and basil and simmer for about 40 minutes. Make sure most of the moisture is gone. Should be thick.
- You can add mozzarella cheese on top when serving on crostini or a baguette when you're done.
- You can also use with pasta!

155. English Pea & Fresh Ricotta Crostini Recipe

Serving: 6 | Prep: | Cook: 30mins | Ready in:

Ingredients

- 1 pound of fresh English peas (about 1 cup shelled)
- 1 clove of garlic, crushed
- 1/2 cup finely grated parmigiano-reggiano
- 3-4 tablespoons extra virgin olive oil
- sea salt and fresh ground black pepper to taste
- 1 local baguette, sliced into cross sections on the bias
- 1 8 oz. container fresh whole milk ricotta
- additional olive oil for garnish

Direction

- Bring a medium pot of water to a boil. Add the shelled peas to the water once boiling, and cook for 5 minutes. Add to ice bath to cool, drain peas and transfer to food processor.
- Add garlic, parmesan, salt and pepper to food processor and blend until the mixture forms a paste. Slowly drizzle in each tablespoon of olive oil, pulsing the food processor along the way, until the pea puree reaches your desired consistency. Add more olive oil for saucier, less for more of a spread.
- Toast baguettes under broiler until golden brown (or in a 350 degree oven for 5-7 minutes). Spread the pea puree on the toasts, then dollop of ricotta on each. Finish with a pinch of coarse salt, freshly ground pepper, and a drizzle of olive oil. Serve immediately.

156. FRENCH BREAD APPETIZER Recipe

Serving: 2 | Prep: | Cook: 65mins | Ready in:

Ingredients

- 1 c. shredded Jack cheese
- 3 oz. cube cream cheese
- 1/3 c. butter
- 2 egg whites
- 30 1" cubes French bread

Direction

- Cook and melt Jack cheese, cream cheese and butter (microwave works great for this). Beat egg whites until stiff peaks form. Fold egg whites into cheese mixture. Dip bread chunks into cheese to coat each piece. Place coated cubes of bread on cookie sheet with wax paper lining, freeze until firm 30-60 minutes. Bake at 400 degrees for about 10 minutes. This recipe takes time to prepare, but is a perfect make ahead dish to pop in oven when guests

157. Feta Bruschetta

Serving: 0 | Prep: | Cook: | Ready in:

Ingredients

- 1/4 cup butter, melted
- 1/4 cup olive oil
- 10 slices French bread (1 inch thick)
- 1 package (4 ounces) crumbled feta cheese
- 2 to 3 garlic cloves, minced
- 1 tablespoon minced fresh basil or 1 teaspoon dried basil
- 1 large tomato, seeded and chopped

Direction

- In a small bowl, combine butter and oil; brush onto both sides of bread. Place on a baking sheet. Bake at 350° for 8-10 minutes or until lightly browned on top.
- Combine the feta cheese, garlic and basil; sprinkle over toast. Top with tomato. Bake 8-10 minutes longer or until heated through. Serve warm.
- Nutrition Facts
- 1 each: 296 calories, 14g fat (5g saturated fat), 18mg cholesterol, 547mg sodium, 35g carbohydrate (1g sugars, 3g fiber), 8g protein.

158. Fig And Ricotta Crostini Recipe

Serving: 12 | Prep: | Cook: 10mins | Ready in:

Ingredients

- 4 fresh figs (not dried)
- fresh basil about 4 leaves
- ricotta cheese 1/2 tub
- Balsamic glaze (also called Balsamic Reduction)
- 1 baguette
- 2 tbsp olive oil

Direction

- First, make the crostini. Slice the baguette into 1/2-3/4 inch thick slices. Then drizzle olive oil onto a cookie sheet. Place baguette slices on cookie sheet. Bake on one side at 400 degrees for about five minutes. Then flip over each piece and bake on other side for five minutes. (This step can be done ahead of time, just store pieces in a plastic bag until you need them)
- Take each fig, give it a little rinse and pat dry with a paper towel. Then carefully cut each fig into four quarters.
- Cut the basil lengthwise into thin strips (best to use a composite or plastic knife for a metal one will make edges go dark)
- Take one piece of crostini, spread an even layer of ricotta cheese on top. Take one fig quarter and place on top, then a few basil strips over fig. Drizzle balsamic glaze over top.
- Makes about 12-15 pieces. So pretty!

159. Fig And Goat Cheese Bruschetta Recipe

Serving: 20 | Prep: | Cook: 2mins | Ready in:

Ingredients

- 1-1/4 cups chopped dried Mission figs
- 1/3 cup sugar
- 1/3 cup coarsely chopped orange sections
- 1 tsp. orange zest
- 1/3 cup fresh orange juice
- 1/2 tsp. chopped fresh rosemary
- 1/4 tsp. freshly ground black pepper
- 40 (1/2" thick) slices French bread baguette, toasted
- 1-1/4 cups crumbled goat cheese
- 5 tsp. finely chopped walnuts

Direction

- 3 days before serving make the fig jam and refrigerate, then bring to room temperature just before serving on toast.
- Combine first 7 ingredients in a small saucepan, bring to a boil.
- Cover and reduce heat and simmer 10 minutes until figs are tender.
- Uncover and cook 5 minutes until mixture thickens.
- Remove from heat and cool completely, refrigerate.
- The Day of serving.
- Preheat oven to 350*F
- Toast the bread until light brown on both sides.
- Preheat oven to broil.
- Top each bread slice with 1-1/2 tsp. of fig mixture and 1-1/2 tsp. goat cheese.
- Arrange bruschetta on a baking sheet.
- Sprinkle evenly with chopped walnuts.
- Broil 2 minutes until nuts begin to turn brown.
- Serve warm.

160. Fontina N Gorgonzola Crostini Recipe

Serving: 8 | Prep: | Cook: 10mins | Ready in:

Ingredients

- Servings: 8
- Ingredients:
- 1 tablespoon extra-virgin olive oil
- 1 tablespoon butter
- 8 ounces fresh exotic mushrooms, (such as shiitake or oyster), sliced
- 8 ounces portobello mushrooms, sliced
- 1 teaspoon mixed fresh herbs, such as thyme, rosemary, basil, minced
- 1 tablespoon flat-leaf parsley, minced
- salt and freshly-ground pepper, to taste
- 8 slices rustic country-style bread, toasted
- 2 garlic cloves, peeled and halved
- 1 cup (4 ounces) Fontina cheese, grated
- 1/2 cup (3 ounces) gorgonzola cheese, crumbled
- juice of 1/2 lemon
- Whole flat-leaf parsley leaves, for garnish
- .

Direction

- Cooking Directions:
- Preheat oven to broil.
- Heat olive oil and butter in large skillet over medium-high heat. Add mushrooms and cook until the liquid has evaporated and mushrooms are dry, about 10 minutes. Add mixed herbs and parsley, and toss to mix. Season with salt and pepper. Remove from heat.
- Rub each side of toasted bread slices lightly with garlic clove. Divide and distribute warm mushrooms on top of bread slices. Combine the cheeses and sprinkle evenly over mushrooms. Place mushroom toasts under hot broiler. Broil until cheese melts, 30 to 60 seconds. Place the toast slices on serving platter and drizzle with lemon juice. Garnish with parsley leaves. Serve immediately.

161. French Bread Dip Recipe

Serving: 8 | Prep: | Cook: 60mins | Ready in:

Ingredients

- 1 loaf Colombo round French bread (round sour dough is great also)
- 1/2 cup chopped green onions
- 1 8 oz package cream cheese
- 1 pint sour cream
- 1 cup chopped ham
- 1 cup shredded cheddar cheese

Direction

- Pre-heat oven to 350 degrees. Cut off top of French bread round. Hollow out bread to form bowl shape. Save leftover bread. Combine onions, cream cheese, sour cream, ham, and cheese. Mix well. Fill bread shell with mixture. Replace top of bread. Bake for 45 minutes. Cut up left over bread into bite size pieces and use for dipping.

- Approximate preparation and baking time: 1 hour

162. Fresh Bruschetta Recipe

Serving: 4 | Prep: | Cook: 20mins | Ready in:

Ingredients

- 1 small loaf french baguette or Italian loaf
- 1 cup cherry tomatoes, chopped
- 4 cloves garlic
- 1 tsp balsamic vinegar
- 2 tbs extra virgin olive oil
- 2 tbs fresh basil, roughly chopped
- 6 oz fresh mozzarella

Direction

- Add tomatoes and vinegar to a small bowl and set aside
- In a non-stick pan, heat olive oil.
- Cook 3 cloves of garlic in 2 Tbsp. olive oil until golden brown, stirring constantly
- Add garlic and oil to tomatoes
- Slice loaf of French or Italian bread on a bias and place on oiled cookie sheet in a single layer;
- Bake at 350 for 5 minutes or less to lightly toast bread. The bread can also be toasted on a grill for a bit more flavour (this goes quickly so be careful not to burn your toast!)
- Immediately rub with a garlic clove and drizzle with extra virgin olive oil.
- Mix basil into tomato mixture
- Top each slice toast with a slice of fresh mozzarella and a heaping spoonful of tomato mixture.
- Serve immediately.

163. Fresh Easy Bruschetta Recipe

Serving: 12 | Prep: | Cook: 5mins | Ready in:

Ingredients

- 1 (32-ounce) can whole tomatoes, drained .
- 1 cup fresh basil leaves.
- 4 tablespoons extra-virgin olive oil
- 6 cloves garlic, peeled.
- kosher salt and freshly ground black pepper .
- 2 French baquettes, sliced 1-inch thick (about 36 slices)
- 1 1/2 pounds fresh mozzarella cheese, sliced 1/4-inch thick.

Direction

- Preheat oven to 375.
- In the bowl of a food processor, add drained tomatoes, 1 cup basil leaves, olive oil and 2 cloves garlic. Pulse until smooth, but somewhat chunky. Season with salt and pepper.
- On a baking sheet, line up baguette slices. Toast in oven for about 3 minutes or until light golden brown.
- Working quickly, rub the remaining garlic cloves on the toasted side of each slice and then lay a piece of mozzarella cheese on top. Place bread back in oven and melt cheese slightly, about 45 seconds.
- Remove from oven and spread one tablespoon of the tomato mixture on each piece.
- Serve, and enjoy

164. Fresh Mozzarella And Tomato Crostini Recipe

Serving: 8 | Prep: | Cook: 18mins | Ready in:

Ingredients

- Ingredients:
- extra-virgin olive oil for brushing, plus 1/4 cup
- 1 baguette, cut crosswise into 1/4-inch-thick slices
- salt and coarsely ground pepper, to taste
- 8 vine-ripened tomatoes, about 1 1/2 lb. total
- 1/2 cup slivered fresh basil leaves
- 2 Tbs. finely minced red onion
- 1/4 tsp. minced garlic
- 1 Tbs. aged balsamic vinegar
- 1 1/2 lb. fresh mozzarella cheese

Direction

- Preheat oven to 350.
- Brush a baking sheet with olive oil and arrange the baguette slices on the sheet in a single layer. Brush the tops with oil, and season with salt and pepper. Bake until crisp and golden, 15 to 18 minutes. If not using immediately, let the crostini cool, then store in an airtight container at room temperature until ready to use.
- Core, seed and dice the tomatoes. In a bowl, stir together the tomatoes, half of the basil, the onion, garlic, vinegar, the 1/4 cup olive oil, salt and pepper.
- Slice the mozzarella into 1/4-inch-thick pieces or into smaller pieces so they fit on the crostini. To assemble, lay a piece of mozzarella on each crostini and spoon 1 to 2 Tbs. of the tomato salad on top. Garnish each with a pinch of the remaining basil. Serve immediately.

165. Fresh Peach Salsa & Brie Bruschetta Recipe

Serving: 6 | Prep: | Cook: | Ready in:

Ingredients

- 2 large peaches (or nectarines), diced
- 1-2 red fresno chilies, minced (or jalapeno)
- 1-2 green onions, chopped
- 2 tablespoons chopped fresh cilantro (or basil)
- 1 tablespoon granulated sugar
- fresh lime juice, to taste
- splash of white peach balsamic
- fresh ground black pepper and sea salt, to taste
- ~
- any kind of brie/creamy cheese (I prefer St. Andre for this!)
- 1 baguette, sliced on a bias, brushed with olive oil, grilled or toasted

Direction

- In a medium bowl, all salsa ingredients. Let chill for at least one hour (or overnight). Serve atop cheese on grilled/toasted bread

166. Friendship Bread Recipe

Serving: 8 | Prep: | Cook: 80mins | Ready in:

Ingredients

- 1 large round loaf Hawaiiam bread
- 4 cups (16 oz) shredded sharp cheddar cheese
- 8 ounces cream cheese, softened
- 8 ounces sour cream
- 1/2 cup finely choped green onions
- 2 (4 ounces) cans chopped green chiles, drained
- 1 to 11/2 cups chopped ham, crumbled crisp cooked bacon, chopped cooked turkey or a combination

Direction

- Cut the top from the bread and scoop out the centre to form a bread bowl, reserving the top and centre. Tear the reserved bread centre into bite size pieces.
- Combine the Cheddar cheese, cream cheese, sour cream, green onions, green chiles and ham in a bowl and mix well. (The mixture will

be stiff) Spoon into the bread bowl. Replace the top and place on a baking sheet. Bake at 350 degrees for 1 hour and 10 minutes. (The outside of the bread may blacken a little, but it won't affect the taste) Serve with the reserved bread pieces or tortilla chips for dipping.

167. Fruit Bruschetta Recipe

Serving: 12 | Prep: | Cook: 30mins | Ready in:

Ingredients

- 6 Rhodes Warm-N-Serv™ Crusty rolls, thawed
- 2 tablespoons butter, melted
- 2 tablespoons sugar
- 1/2 teaspoon cinnamon
- fresh diced, strawberries, pineapple & kiwi
- 1/2 cup sour cream
- 2 tablespoons honey
- 1 teaspoon lemon zest
- 2 teaspoons fresh lemon juice

Direction

- Slice crusty rolls into 1/2-inch thick slices.
- Place on a baking sheet and brush with melted butter.
- Combine sugar and cinnamon and sprinkle over slices.
- Bake at 400°F 5-10 minutes or until edges are toasted.
- Set aside to cool. Place strawberries, pineapple and kiwi in a bowl and toss gently to combine.
- Place about 1 tablespoon fruit mixture on top of each toasted roll slice.
- Combine sour cream, honey, lemon zest, and lemon juice and mix well.
- Drizzle over fruit.

168. GREEK BREAD Recipe

Serving: 6 | Prep: | Cook: 12mins | Ready in:

Ingredients

- 1 small can chopped black olives
- 1/2c mayonnaise
- butter
- 2 green onions, minced
- 12oz grated mozzarella cheese
- 1/4c parmesan cheese
- 1/2t italian seasoning
- dash of Tabasco
- French bread

Direction

- Mix all ingredients but bread, refrigerate overnight. Spread on French bread sliced lengthwise.
- Cook at 400F for 12-15 minutes.

169. Gamberi Aragonati Shrimp With Garlic And Toasted Bread Crumbs Recipe

Serving: 6 | Prep: | Cook: 15mins | Ready in:

Ingredients

- 1 cup fresh bread crumbs, made from Italian or French bread
- 1/3 cup very finely chopped flat-leaf parsley
- 1 large garlic clove, finely chopped
- salt and freshly ground black pepper
- About 1/4 cup extra virgin olive oil
- 1 and 1/2 pounds large shrimp, peeled and deveined
- lemon wedges

Direction

- Preheat the oven to 450° F.
- Lightly oil a large baking pan.

- In a bowl, combine the bread crumbs, parsley, garlic, and salt and pepper to taste.
- Add 3 tablespoons olive oil, or enough to moisten the crumbs.
- Arrange the shrimp in the pan in a single layer, curling each one into a circle.
- Spoon a little of the crumb mixture onto each shrimp.
- Drizzle with a little more olive oil.
- Bake for 10 to 15 minutes, depending on the size of the shrimp, or until the shrimp turn pink and the crumbs are lightly browned.
- Serve piping hot with lemon wedges. .
- That's it! Mangia!

170. Garbanzo Bean Bruschetta Recipe

Serving: 68 | Prep: | Cook: | Ready in:

Ingredients

- 1 can garbanzo beans, rinsed and drained
- ~6 plum tomatoes, rinsed and diced
- 1/2 small red onion chopped
- handful of basil (about 8-10 leaves) chopped
- 2 cloves garlic, chopped
- balsamic vinegar
- olive oil
- Sprinkle of sea salt
- Sprinkle of pepper

Direction

- The bulk of this recipe is prep time. Once everything is washed and chopped, simply toss it together.
- Toss the tomatoes, chickpeas, onion and basil together first.
- Add a light coating of olive oil and balsamic vinegar (~1 tablespoon--I don't measure)
- Toss again
- Serve with sliced Italian bread and/or crostini.

171. Garlic Bread Fantastique Recipe

Serving: 4 | Prep: | Cook: 5mins | Ready in:

Ingredients

- INGREDIENTS
- * 1/2 cup butter, softened
- * 2 tablespoons mayonnaise
- * 1/4 teaspoon sage
- * 1/4 teaspoon sage
- * 1/4 teaspoon rosemary
- * 3 cloves garlic, chopped
- * 2 teaspoons dried oregano
- * salt to taste
- * 1/2 teaspoon black pepper
- * 1 french baguette, halved lengthwise
- * 2 tablespoons grated parmesan cheese, or to taste

Direction

- DIRECTIONS
- 1. Preheat oven to broil.
- 2. In a medium bowl combine butter, mayonnaise, sage, garlic, oregano, salt and pepper. Spread mixture evenly on bread and sprinkle with Parmesan cheese.
- 3. Place bread under broil for 5 minutes, or until lightly toasted.

172. Garlic Bread Recipe

Serving: 6 | Prep: | Cook: 5mins | Ready in:

Ingredients

- 1/2 cup butter (1 stick) room temperature
- 1/4 cup Italian parsley (the flat kind) chopped
- 2 big cloves garlic, crushed
- 1/2 cup parmesan, grated (preferably not the powdered kind)

- 1/2 teaspoon salt
- 1 long French or sour dough loaf, cut lengthwise

Direction

- Preheat Broiler
- Mix all ingredients (except bread obviously) and 1/4 cup parmesan in small bowl
- Spread mixture on each side of cut loaf
- Sprinkle extra parmesan on each loaf
- Place on baking sheet and put under broiler - but not too close
- Cook until the loaves start to get brown, but not too crispy
- Slice into 2 inch pieces and serve

173. Garlic Bread Skewers Recipe

Serving: 6 | Prep: | Cook: 6mins | Ready in:

Ingredients

- 1 baguette(you won't need the whole baguette)
- 24 cherry tomatoes or grape tomatoes
- 1/4c extra virgin olive oil
- 2 garlic cloves (or more) minced
- 1/2tsp sweet paprika
- 1/2tsp dried Italian herb seasoning
- grated romano cheese

Direction

- Cut baguette into 1-2" chunks. Alternately skewer 3 pieces of bread and 2 tomatoes onto each of 12 metal or soaked wooden skewers.
- In a small bowl combine oil, garlic, paprika and herb seasoning; brush over skewers.
- Place skewers on oiled grill over medium heat; close lid and grill turning once until golden and crisp; about 8 mins. Sprinkle with cheese.

174. Garlic Bread With Gorgonzola Sauce Recipe

Serving: 0 | Prep: | Cook: 50mins | Ready in:

Ingredients

- Sauce:
- 1 c low sodium chicken broth
- 1 c milk
- 1/4 c unsalted butter
- 1/2 c all purpose flour
- 1/2 c heavy cream
- 6 oz dolce gorgonzola crumbles
- 3 T fresh grated roman cheese
- salt and pepper to taste
- bread Topping
- 1 large french baguette
- 1/4 c olive oil
- 2 cloves garlic minced
- 3 T chopped parsley or dried parsley
- 1/4 tsp Herbes de Provence

Direction

- Combine milk and chicken broth and place in a small saucepan on medium until it simmers then leave on low.
- In a medium saucepan, melt butter and add flour (best if flour is added while pan is off the heat). The mixture will be very firm almost like cookie dough.
- Drizzle the broth mixture into the flour mixture and continue to incorporate until you can use a whisk.
- Whisk until mixture is smooth and raise the heat to medium until just boiling, continually stirring.
- Add heavy cream and cook until reduced to about 2 1/2 cups. The mixture will have basically no taste at this point. About 8 minutes.
- Add the Gorgonzola and Romano cheese and stir until creamy.

- Add salt and pepper to taste. Begin with pepper. I never add additional salt but all preferences are different :-}
- Bread:
- Cut off ends.
- Slice the loaf in half so that you now have two loaves.
- Cut each loaf in half and lay open on a cookie tray.
- In a small pan, place the olive oil and bring to a low smoke.
- Add the garlic but do not brown. Lower heat if necessary
- Add 2 Tbsp. of parsley and the herbes de Provence.
- Heat for about 3 minutes to incorporate all of the flavours.
- Brush over both sides of the 2 half loaves and place under a broiler for 1 1/2 minutes until golden brown (not black).
- Remove and slice the bread in1 inch slices.
- Have a large heated platter ready (a Pyrex 9X13 lasagne pan will do but DO NOT place Pyrex under a broiler to heat)
- Pour hot sauce into heated platter, add the bread on top, sprinkle with remainder of parsley and serve immediately. I have also surrounded a container of the sauce with the bread available for dipping,

175. Garlic Bread W Cheese Recipe

Serving: 4 | Prep: | Cook: 10mins | Ready in:

Ingredients

- 8 tbps garlic butter
- 4 slices Italian style bread
- 2 Cups Grated Marble cheddar cheese
- parsley flakes

Direction

- Slice bread into 1 inch thick slices

- Spread garlic butter on both sides of the bread
- Layer onto a cookie sheet
- Cover with grated cheese as desired
- Bake under broiler at 400 degrees until cheese is bubbly
- Sprinkle parsley on top and serve.

176. Garlic Tomato Bread Recipe

Serving: 2 | Prep: | Cook: 3mins | Ready in:

Ingredients

- bread
- garlic clove cut in half as many as you need
- tomato cut in half as many as you need cherry work best but you can use any kind as long as there fresh

Direction

- Toast the bread I have used French bread. You can also use plan sandwich bread in a toaster
- Rub the half garlic clove on all over the bread
- Rub the tomato all over the bread
- Top with anything you like

177. Garlic And Onion Bruschetta Recipe

Serving: 6 | Prep: | Cook: 5mins | Ready in:

Ingredients

- * 6 or 7 ripe plum tomatoes (about 1 1/2 lbs)
- * 3 cloves garlic, minced
- * 1/2 medium red onion chopped
- * 1 Tbsp extra virgin olive oil
- * 1 teaspoon balsamic vinegar
- * 7 fresh basil leaves, chopped.
- * salt and freshly ground black pepper to taste

- * 1 baguette of bread (your choice, i like french)
- * 1/4 cup olive oil

Direction

- Preheat oven to 450 degrees
- Peel the tomatoes (you can do this by boiling them for a short time)
- Remove juice and seeds from tomatoes
- Chop tomatoes, and add to a bowl. Combine garlic, 1tbsp of extra virgin olive oil, vinegar and basil.
- Slice baguette into about 1/2 inch thick slices
- Coat each side of bread with olive oil (use a brush)
- Toast break on top rack of oven for about 5 minutes
- Take bread pieces out and put tomato mixture on top

178. Genuine Bruschetta Recipe

Serving: 1 | Prep: | Cook: 5mins | Ready in:

Ingredients

- coarse Italian style country bread, thickish slices, day old
- garlic clove peeled and cut in half
- olive oil, the best you can find
- optional salt

Direction

- Grill or broil day old bread slices-- you can use older, staler bread, but grill only one side then.
- When the bread is grilled to suit you, use the cut side of the garlic clove to gently rub one side of the slice-- be careful not to overdo it, as you can easily melt the whole clove into the bread!
- Drizzle great olive oil over the rubbed and grilled bread.
- Sprinkle with salt if you have used salt-free Tuscan or Umbrian bread.
- That's it, folks. What you put on top is your business, but if you haven't started with this, it isn't bruschetta-- or in Tuscany, it is called fettunta, which means "oiled slice"
- If you plan to use truffles on the bruschetta, skip the garlic and go straight to oil, because garlic cancels out the truffles.

179. Goat Cheese And Chorizo Crostini Recipe

Serving: 0 | Prep: | Cook: 15mins | Ready in:

Ingredients

- french baguette, sliced on the bias (diagonal) in 1/2" widths
- crumbled goat cheese-there are some small-farm sources online where you can buy great quality goat cheese, or you can buy this in 4 ounce containers at grocery stores. You will put about 1 teaspoon on each baguette slice
- Spanish chorizo sausage--the best is from a specialty butcher, but most grocery stores have it as well, you will put one slice on each baguette slice
- 2 TBSP (or more, depending on taste) of finely chopped (mixed) fresh basil, Greek oregano, rosemary, and thyme, divided in half (fresh is best, and makes the best presentation, but dried herbs may be used--just be careful, as dried herbs are more intense--so use less)
- extra virgin olive oil to drizzle

Direction

- Preheat the oven to 400 degrees F
- Chop the fresh herbs very finely, and divide in half
- Slice the baguette, and place the slices flat on a cookie sheet. Make sure there is some room between the slices, but as close together as you can get them without touching.

- Drizzle the EVOO over the slices, and sprinkle 1/2 of the fresh herbs evenly over all the pieces
- Pop those in the oven to get them light brown, and a little crispy--keep an eye on them, so they don't burn--this can happen fast, so be careful!
- Take the casing off the Chorizo and cut the sausage in half, lengthwise, and then thinly slice into half-moon shaped pieces/ it is very easy to slice these thinly if you have a sharp knife, because the chorizo is very dense.
- Take the light brown crostini out of the oven, and then turn the oven to "broil"
- While still on the cooking sheet, spoon about 1 teaspoon of goat cheese onto each slice of baguette, and top with one slice of chorizo and sprinkle the other half of the fresh herbs on top
- Pop them back into the oven and broil for no more than one minute (watch them so they don't burn)
- Remove from oven, place on platter and serve. Enjoy!

180. Goat Cheese And Sun Dried Tomato Profiteroles With Herb Oil Recipe

Serving: 12 | Prep: | Cook: 25mins | Ready in:

Ingredients

- Pate a Choux dough:
- 1 cup water
- 1/2 cup butter (1 stick)
- 1 cup flour
- 1 cup eggs (4 large eggs)
- 2 tablespoons parmigiano-Reggiano, grated
- pinch of kosher salt
- Filling:
- 8 ounces fresh goat cheese, room temperature
- 1/4 cup cream
- 1/2 cup diced sun dried tomatoes (oil drained)
- Pinch salt and freshly ground black pepper
- herb Oil:
- 3/4 cup fresh mint leaves
- 3/4 cup fresh basil leaves
- 1 large clove of garlic
- 1 cup olive oil
- a few squeezes of fresh lemon juice
- Pinch of kosher salt
- Freshly ground black pepper
- 1 cup chopped toasted walnuts, saving some for garnish

Direction

- For the Profiteroles:
- Preheat the oven to 425 degrees F. Line a heavy large baking sheet with a silicon pad or parchment paper. Combine the water, butter, and salt in a heavy medium saucepan over medium heat. Bring to a boil, stirring until the butter melts. Add the flour and stir over medium heat for 1 minute. Cool for 5 minutes. Crack the eggs into a measuring cup. Use a wooden spoon to beat the eggs into the dough, 1 at a time (you get faster and fluffier results if you use a stand mixer with a paddle). Stir in the Parmesan. Pipe or spoon about 20 mounds of dough onto the prepared baking sheet, spacing 2 inches apart. . Bake in a hot oven: 425 for 10 minutes, 350 for another 25 minutes or so, is ideal. Allow the profiteroles to cool completely.
- For the Filling:
- Combine the goat cheese and cream in a medium bowl. Using an electric mixer, whip together the cheese and the cream. Stir in the tomatoes, salt and pepper. Set aside.
- For the Herb Oil:
- Combine the garlic & herbs in a food processor and pulse to chop. With the machine running add the oil, lemon juice, salt, and pepper. Transfer to a small bowl, cover with plastic wrap and set aside.
- To serve:
- Using a serrated knife, cut off the top of the profiteroles. Fill each profiterole with a spoonful of the goat cheese mixture, a few bits

of walnuts and return the top of the pastry. Drizzle serving plate with herb oil and place profiteroles on top. Sprinkle with additional walnuts. Serve. Here is Giada's pic:

181. Goat Cheese Bruschetta With Cherries And Mint Recipe

Serving: 4 | Prep: | Cook: 10mins | Ready in:

Ingredients

- 1/2 pound (about 2 cups) cherries, pitted and halved
- 1/4 cup lightly packed mint leaves, thinly sliced
- 2 tablespoons orange juice
- 4 slices rustic whole wheat bread, toasted
- 4 ounces fresh goat cheese
- .

Direction

- In a medium bowl, toss together cherries, mint and orange juice. Spread bread with goat cheese, spoon cherry mixture over the top and serve

182. Goat Cheese Crostini Recipe

Serving: 8 | Prep: | Cook: 18mins | Ready in:

Ingredients

- 1/2 french baguette, cut into 16 thin slices
- 3 Tbl E.V.O.O
- 1(6 oz.) pkg Chevre (goat) cheese
- 2 Tbl finely chopped sun-dried tomatoes in herbs and oil
- 1 tsp dried basil leaves
- 5 to 6 drops hot pepper sauce or to taste

Direction

- Heat oven to 375
- Arrange bread on cookie sheet and brush with oil
- Bake at 375 for 10 to 15 minutes or until lightly browned
- Meanwhile in a small bowl, combine all remaining ingredients; blend well
- Remove bread slices from oven
- Spread with cheese mixture
- Return to oven; bake an additional 2 to 3 minutes or until heated through
- 16 appetizers

183. Goat Cheese Crostini With Wild Mushrooms Recipe

Serving: 8 | Prep: | Cook: 15mins | Ready in:

Ingredients

- 4 large shallots, thinly sliced
- 2 tablespoons unsalted butter
- 16 oz. mixed wild mushrooms, larger mushrooms coarsely chopped (about 10 crimini mushrooms, coarsely chopped, can be sub'd)
- 2 tablespoon brown sugar
- 1 tablespoon fresh thyme leaves
- 6 tablespoons aged balsamic vinegar
- kosher salt and white pepper taste
- 1 french baguette loaf's worth of fresh homemade crostini (or foccacia bread, as seen in my photo)
- 8 oz fresh goat cheese, room temp
- 4 sprigs fresh parsley, finely chopped
- zest of one lemon

Direction

- Preheat oven to 375 degrees. Spread about a tablespoon of goat cheese on each crostini. Place them on a cookie sheet while you make the reduction.

- Sauté the shallots in the butter for three minutes. Add the mushrooms and brown sugar, stirring for one minute.
- Add the thyme, salt and pepper and the balsamic vinegar. Allow to come to boil, then reduce for about 3 minutes, stirring constantly.
- Top each crostini with about a teaspoon of mushroom-shallot mixture, reserve any extra sauce from pan. Bake for 6-8 minutes or until cheese slightly melts. Drizzle with remaining pan sauce and garnish with chopped parsley and lemon zest.

184. Goat Cheese Stuffed Mushrooms With Bread Crunbs Recipe

Serving: 8 | Prep: | Cook: 30mins | Ready in:

Ingredients

- 24 large cremini mushrooms(1 1/2lbs) stems discarded
- 1/4c plus 2 Tbs extra virgin olive oil
- 1tsp rosemary leaves plus one 3" sprig of rosemary
- kosher salt and pepper
- 3Tbs fine bread crumbs
- 6oz. fresh goat cheese, cut into 24 pieces

Direction

- Preheat oven to 400. In a bowl, toss the mushrooms with 3Tbs oil and rosemary leaves and season with salt and pepper. Transfer mushrooms to baking sheet, rounded side up. Roast about 30 minutes, until tender and browned around the edges. Let cool to room temperature, about 15 mins.
- In skillet, heat remaining 3 Tbs. of oil. Add rosemary sprig and cook over moderately high heat until the leaves are crisp, 30 seconds. Drain on paper towels, then strip off the leaves. Pour off all but 1 tsp. of rosemary oil and reserve for another use.
- Add the bread crumbs to the skillet and toast over moderate heat until golden and crisp, 2 mins. Stir in fried rosemary leaves and season with salt and pepper.
- Gently press a piece of goat cheese into the centre of each mushroom and sprinkle with bread crumbs and serve.
- Make ahead: The goat cheese-filled mushrooms can be refrigerated for up to a day. Bring to room temperature and sprinkle with bread crumbs before serving.

185. Goat Cheese, Fig And Proscuitto Crostini Recipe

Serving: 15 | Prep: | Cook: 25mins | Ready in:

Ingredients

- 1-11 oz. or 2 4 oz logs of Chavrie fresh goat cheese
- 15 biscuit type crackers
- 1 small jar fig jam
- 2 oz. shaved prosciutto
- 1 oz. white peppercorns cracked

Direction

- Pre heat oven to 350 degrees.
- Spread ½ tsp. of fig jam on ea. Cracker.
- Place a small piece of prosciutto on ea. cracker.
- Slice the goat cheese.
- Place 1 slice on each prepared cracker.
- Arrange on sheet trays.
- Bake in oven for 10 -12 minutes until edges of cheese start to brown.
- Remove from oven and top with cracked white pepper

186. Gold Stars Recipe

Serving: 85 | Prep: | Cook: 2hours | Ready in:

Ingredients

- 4 oz shredded cheddar cheese
- 2 oz flour
- 2 1/4 oz spelt flour
- 1 tbsp cheddar cheese powder
- 1 tsp kosher salt
- 1/2 tsp baking powder
- 1/4 tsp onion powder
- pinch black pepper
- 1/4 cup 1% milk
- 1 tbsp canola oil

Direction

- Combine all the ingredients in a bowl until well combined.
- Knead by hand in the bowl until a stiff, slightly dry "doughy" mass forms.
- Wrap in plastic and chill 1 hour, up to 1 day.
- Preheat oven to 375F and line 2 baking sheets with parchment.
- Roll dough out to 1/8" thickness and cut with star-shaped cutters (or your favourite small cutter).
- Bake for 10 minutes. Cool completely on the sheets.
- Transfer to an airtight container and eat within a few days.
- NI is per cracker

187. Gorgonzola Bread Appetizers Recipe

Serving: 10 | Prep: | Cook: 15mins | Ready in:

Ingredients

- 1 french baguette, sliced into 1/4 inch rounds
- 1/4 cup olive oil or melted butter
- 2 pears - peeled, cored and sliced
- 8 ounces crumbled gorgonzola cheese
- 1 cup chopped walnuts

Direction

- Preheat the oven to 350 degrees F (175 degrees C).
- Arrange the baguette slices in a single layer on a baking sheet.
- Brush the top of each one with olive oil or melted butter.
- Place a slice of pear onto each onto each piece of bread, then crumble some of the cheese over the top. Sprinkle with walnuts.
- Bake for 12 to 15 minutes in the preheated oven, or until the pears are browned and the cheese has started to melt.

188. Gorgonzola And White Bean And Honey Crostini Recipe

Serving: 30 | Prep: | Cook: 20mins | Ready in:

Ingredients

- 18 inch baguette cut into 30 slices
- 1/4 cup plus 2 Tbs olive oil
- 3 cloves garlic minced
- 14 oz canelllini beans drained
- 5 1/2 oz gorgonzola cheese crumbled
- 1/4 cup honey
- salt and pepper to taste

Direction

- Line slices of bread on baking sheet.
- Drizzle with the 1/4 cup oil
- Bake 350F 5 to 10 minutes or golden and crisp
- With remaining oil, sauté garlic briefly in pan add beans and season with salt and pepper
- Cook until beans are very soft about 10 to 15 minutes
- Then mash beans and set aside
- Then spread some of mashed beans on each bread slice, top with the cheese and drizzle with the honey
- Perhaps a sprinkle of fresh chopped parsley too!

189. Grape Relish Recipe

Serving: 8 | Prep: | Cook: 15mins | Ready in:

Ingredients

- • 2 cups finely chopped red and green seedless California grapes
- • 2 tablespoons minced shallot
- • 2 teaspoons chopped fresh thyme
- • 1 tablespoon sherry vinegar
- • 1 1/2 teaspoons sugar
- • 1 teaspoon safflower or vegetable oil
- • 1/4 teaspoon each salt and freshly ground pepper
- • 1 baguette, sliced thinly

Direction

- In a medium bowl combine the chopped grapes, shallot, thyme, sherry vinegar, sugar, oil, salt and pepper. Transfer to a small serving bowl and set aside. Makes 2 cups.
- To make the crostini, preheat the oven to 350 F. Spread baguette slices on a baking sheet and toast until crisp, about 10 minutes. Let cool.

190. Greek Flavor Bread Recipe

Serving: 20 | Prep: | Cook: 35mins | Ready in:

Ingredients

- 3 cups Bisquick baking mix
- 3 eggs
- 1 1/2 cup buttermilk
- 3 cups crumbled feta cheese (flavored or reduced fat if you prefer), divided
- 1 cup frozen chopped spinach, thawed and drained
- 1/4 cup butter, melted
- salt to taste

Direction

- Preheat the oven to 350 degrees. Line a jelly roll pan or baking sheet with foil and then grease the foil. Set aside.
- In a medium bowl, mix baking mix, eggs, and buttermilk until combined.
- Mix in 1 cup of feta and all the spinach.
- Spread dough mixture evenly in the foil lined pan. Drizzle melted butter over dough, and then crumble the remaining feta over the mixture. You can sprinkle some salt over the pan as well to add a little more oomph.
- Bake 35-40 minutes, or until golden brown.
- Let cool 10-15 minutes, then pull the entire loaf out and transfer to a cutting board. Remove foil. Using a pizza cutter, cut into bite sized squares.
- Serve with simple marinara sauce.

191. Grilled Avocado Recipe

Serving: 4 | Prep: | Cook: 10mins | Ready in:

Ingredients

- 2 large ripe avocados
- 2 TB fresh lime or lemon juice
- 1-1/2 TBS olive oil
- seasoned salt to taste
- 1/2 c fresh salsa(optional)
- sour cream (optional)
- shredded cheedar cheese(optional

Direction

- Cut avocados in half and remove seeds. Drizzle with fresh lime/lemon juice and brush lightly with olive oil.
- Gently pace cut side down on grill over med-high heat for 2-3 mins. Season with salt to taste
- Optional, fill with salsa sour cream and shredded cheddar cheese.

192. Grilled Eggplant And Pepper Bruschetta Recipe

Serving: 8 | Prep: | Cook: 20mins | Ready in:

Ingredients

- 4 red bell peppers, about 1 1/2 pounds
- 2 large egg plant or 4 small, about 2 to 3 pounds
- 2-3 fresh garlic cloves
- 1/4 cup olive oil
- 2 large red-ripe tomatoes
- 3-4 tablespoons chopped fresh basil leaves
- 1 small red onion
- 1/2 cup shredded mozzarella cheese
- 2-4 tablespoons balsamic or red wine vinegar
- 1-2 teaspoon salt
- 1/2 teaspoon freshly ground pepper
- 1/2 to 1 teaspoon ground chipotle pepper

Direction

- Get the grill ready. Low, even heat is perfect for the eggplant.
- Bell peppers are best cooked over a little higher heat, grill the peppers first, and then move on to the eggplant.
- Wash the peppers and eggplant. Core the peppers, remove the seeds and membrane, and cut into 4-6 large pieces.
- Peel the eggplant, cut off and discard a one-inch slice from the top and bottom, then slice the eggplant into circles, roughly 1 inch thick.
- Place the pepper and eggplant pieces on a baking sheet. Peel and crush up the garlic cloves, mixing them with the olive oil.
- Drizzle or brush the oil onto both sides of the eggplant and the non-skin side of the peppers.
- Grill the peppers for 3-5 minutes per side, and then do the same for the eggplant. It is fine for the skin side of the peppers to blacken and blister, as that makes it easier to remove the skin. Eggplants can be a bit tricky, they go from undercooked to very soft quickly, and they can burn if the coals are too hot. Since they'll be mashed up anyway, how they look coming off the grill isn't important, they just need to be fully cooked.
- Remove from the grill and let cool.
- While cooling, dice the tomato, chop the basil and peel and mince the red onion.
- Place in a large bowl with the mozzarella cheese, drizzle with balsamic vinegar, add 1 tsp. of salt, black pepper and chipotle pepper.
- Cut up the eggplant into small pieces or mash it if it got really soft on the grill, and add to the bowl.
- Peel the skins, at least mostly, off the peppers, using a paring knife. It should be quite easy if the skins blackened during the grilling, running water helps get the skins off if not.
- Mince the peppers, add to the bowl, toss, taste, and adjust seasonings as necessary. Sometimes a bit more olive oil or vinegar and extra salt are nice.
- Serve with dense, crusty French bread to soak up the taste juices.
- NOTES: Roasting bell peppers
- Place a ripe pepper right on the stove top burner over medium-high heat. The pepper will start to blacken after about 1 1/2 minutes. Using tongs, turn the pepper, a quarter at a time, giving each side time to blacken. After all four sides have been done, look at the pepper and time it over the flame so any no blister surfaces get a chance to blacken. The whole job should take about 7 to 8 minutes, and you can do 4 at a time (one on each burner) and save the rest. An electric stove can be used, but the pepper has to be watched more closely so it doesn't get completely burned. After the pepper is fully blackened, remove them from the burner and wrap tightly in plastic wrap. Let steam for 15 minutes. Unwrap the pepper and run under cool water, the skin should come right off, exposing the brilliantly red pepper flesh (peel or pare off any stubborn bits). Core and remove seeds and veins, then mince the flesh into small bits. This is where you will see how remarkably changed the

pepper is-from raw, strong-tasting, acidic and crispy, to meaty, velvety and smoky. This traditionally called pimento, and it will add a wonderful dimension to this dish and many others without an overpowering bell pepper flavour.

193. Grilled Grapefruit And Honey Chili Flatbread Recipe

Serving: 1 | Prep: | Cook: 15mins | Ready in:

Ingredients

- • 1 naan flatbread
- • 2 tbsp olive oil
- • 1 Florida Grapefruit, peeled and sliced into 8 quarters
- • 125g fresh mozzarella, cut into pieces
- • 1/2 cup cooked barbecue chicken, chopped
- • 2 slices of prosciutto, cut into pieces
- • 1/2 an avocado, peeled, pitted and chopped
- • Handful of freshly washed arugula
- • Handful of freshly washed watercress
- • Salt and pepper
- • 2 tbsp honey
- • 1 red chili pepper, finely diced
- • 1 clove of garlic, finely diced

Direction

- 1. Preheat oven to 400°F. Line a baking sheet with parchment paper and set aside.
- 2. In a small bowl, combine honey, chili pepper and garlic and set aside.
- 3. Grill flatbreads four minutes on each side and transfer to lined baking sheet.
- 4. Heat grill pan over high heat. In a medium bowl, toss quartered grapefruit with olive oil.
- 5. Grill grapefruit one minute each side and set aside.
- 6. Evenly distribute mozzarella, grilled grapefruit, chicken, sliced prosciutto and avocado over flatbread and season with salt and pepper.
- 7. Bake flatbread for 6 minutes until cheese is melted.
- 8. Finish with fresh arugula and watercress.
- 9. Drizzle with honey chili sauce. Serve warm.

194. Grilled Tomato And Fresf Mozzarella Bruschetta Recipe

Serving: 6 | Prep: | Cook: 5mins | Ready in:

Ingredients

- 3 beefsteak or heirloom tomatoes
- 1c olive oil
- 1 clove garlic ,chopped
- 1/2 bunch cilantro
- 1/2c basil leaves,roughly torn
- 1 loaf Italian bread sliced
- 1/2lb fresh mozzarella,sliced
- salt and pepper

Direction

- In a mixing bowl, combine 3/4c olive oil, cilantro and garlic
- Coat the tomatoes with the marinade and place on the grill. Grill on all sides for 3-4 mins. Remove tomatoes and dice.
- Slice 1 loaf of Italian bread and brush both sides with olive oil. Place on the grill for approximately 30 seconds. Flip and repeat. Season lightly with salt and pepper. Top with tomato and finish with 1 thin slice of fresh mozzarella. Garnish with torn basil leaves.
- This marinade is also nice for just a tomato or tomato and mozzarella salad (do not dice tomatoes, chunk and chop mozzarella)

195. Halloumi Cheese Bruschetta Wtomato And Olive Tapenade Recipe

Serving: 1 | Prep: | Cook: 5mins | Ready in:

Ingredients

- Sliced crusty bread-French or Italian - cut on the diagonal
- 2 medium thick slices halloumi cheese
- 1 medium thick slice ripe firm tomato
- olive tapenade
- *As with all simple dishes, the quality of the ingredients is key to the success of the recipe. Do get some good bread and ripe tomatoes and you will be halfway there before you even begin! A good storebought tapenade should not be too hard to find either. Then all you have to do is assemble and enjoy!

Direction

- Smear the tapenade lightly on the bread (a little goes a long way-very salty!)
- Place tomato on bread and top with cheese.
- Toast until cheese is melting and starts to brown.
- **if you have a toaster oven this would make an easy, satisfying snack.
- **this would also be very good to serve at an elegant supper as a starter or just with cocktails.

196. Ham And Asparagus Toast Rounds With Creamy Smoked Gouda Drizzle Recipe

Serving: 6 | Prep: | Cook: 5mins | Ready in:

Ingredients

- 6 slices good quality bread
- 5 tablespoons butter, divided (melt 2 tablespoons and set aside)
- 3 slices of good quality baked deli ham, cut in half
- At least 12 stalks thin asparagus (2 or more for each toast)
- 1/4 cup heavy cream
- 3 ounces smoked Gouda
- 1/2 tsp. zatarains garlic and herb seasoning
- Parsley
- Dash pepper and salt
- Optional baby kale or other greens for garnish

Direction

- Cut bread using biscuit cutter or bottom of glass
- Brush both sides of bread rounds with 2 tablespoons melted butter and brown in skillet until lightly browned on each side (about 30 to 40 seconds per side) set bread onto serving plates or a serving tray
- Add 1 tablespoon butter to skillet and heat on med high heat
- Add ham and cook until brown on each side (it only takes a minute or two per side)
- Remove ham and place one serving onto each round (you may need to fold ham if too large)
- Add a drizzle of olive oil plus 1 tablespoon butter to skillet and heat on med high
- Add asparagus and cook until just tender (about 2-3 minutes) season with salt and pepper
- Place a few asparagus on top of each ham toast
- Place remaining tablespoon of butter in small saucepan and melt over med heat
- Stir in garlic and herb spice and heavy cream and allow to cook a minute or two
- Add smoked Gouda and stir until melted
- Remove from heat and drizzle each toast round with cream sauce
- Enjoy!

197. Ham And Cheese Canapes Recipe

Serving: 10 | Prep: | Cook: 10mins | Ready in:

Ingredients

- 1 package party rye bread
- 1/2 lb. cooked ham, diced
- 1 8 oz. can mushrooms, drained and diced
- 1 8 oz. can black olives, drained and diced
- 1/2 c. provolone, cheddar mix, shredded
- 1/4 c. mayonnaise
- 2 T. Dijon mustard

Direction

- Sort out the party rye bread and line them up on a cookie sheet
- Heat oven to 350
- Cut up your ham, mushrooms, and black olives very fine
- Mix all ingredients together except the rye bread
- Top the rye bread with the mixed ingredients
- Bake at 350 for 10 minutes or until the rye bread is crispy.

198. Hearty Double Pesto Crostini Recipe

Serving: 0 | Prep: | Cook: 30mins | Ready in:

Ingredients

- 1lb french baguette, sliced into no more than 1/2in slices
- about 1/2 cup traditional basil pesto
- about 1/4 cup sun dried tomato or roasted red pepper pesto
- 8oz Gouda, fontina, Havarti or Edam, sliced into about 1in square slices
- 1/2lb smoked italian sausage, sliced into no more than 1/2in rounds

Direction

- Spread basil pesto lightly over all bread pieces
- Top with a piece of cheese
- Top with a slice of sausage
- Add a dollop of tomato or pepper pesto
- Bake in a 400 oven for about 10-12 minutes until cheese is melted and sausage is heated through.

199. Herb Baguettes Recipe

Serving: 0 | Prep: | Cook: 35mins | Ready in:

Ingredients

- 1 Loaf Rhodes™ bread dough or 12 Rhodes™ dinner rolls, thawed to room temperature
- 1 tablespoon dried parsley flakes
- 1 1/2 teaspoons dried basil
- 1 1/2 teaspoons dried, crushed, rosemary
- 1/2 teaspoon garlic powder
- 1/2 teaspoon onion powder
- 1/4 teaspoon pepper
- olive oil for brushing

Direction

- Spray counter lightly with non-stick cooking spray. If using rolls, combine them together to make a ball. Flatten dough into a rectangle. In a small bowl, combine parsley, basil, rosemary, garlic powder, onion powder and pepper. Sprinkle over the flattened dough. Fold the rectangle in half enclosing seasonings and knead until evenly mixed throughout the dough. Divide dough in half and roll each half into a baguette shape, about 16 inches long. Place on a sprayed baking sheet. Make 4 or 5 cuts across the top of each one 1/4-inch deep and brush with olive oil. Cover with sprayed plastic wrap and let rise until double in size. Remove wrap and bake at 350°F 10-15 minutes. Cool, slice and enjoy dipped in olive oil and seasoned balsamic vinegar.

200. Herb Dip And Oil For Bread Recipe

Serving: 6 | Prep: | Cook: | Ready in:

Ingredients

- These are all approximate...Use more or less based on your taste. I used fresh herbs (because I had them), but I'm sure dried herbs would be just as delicious!
- All herbs should be finely chopped.
- 1/2 teaspoon crushed red pepper
- 1/2 teaspoon ground black pepper
- 1 teaspoon oregano,
- 1 teaspoon rosemary
- 1 teaspoon basil (I used lemon basil...made it extra tangy!)
- 1 teaspoon parsley
- 1 teaspoon garlic powder
- 1 teaspoon minced fresh garlic
- 1/2 teaspoon salt (I think the restaurant used more)
- 1/4 cup extra virgin olive oil (or as needed)
- bread for dipping

Direction

- Combine all ingredients EXCEPT oil, into a bowl.
- Mix together till it looks nicely blended.
- To serve, scoop whatever amount you'd like onto a dipping dish or plate.
- Pour your desired amount of olive oil over the top of this mixture.
- Dip your bread.
- Eat.
- Enjoy!
- I used individual bread dipping dishes so that everyone could use as much or as little of the dip and oil as they wanted...and double dip with no fear of embarrassment!

201. Herbed Fresh Lobster Bruschetta With Red Pepper Mousseline Recipe

Serving: 68 | Prep: | Cook: 20mins | Ready in:

Ingredients

- 8 ounces fresh Maine lobster meat, large dice (appropriate size for crouton)
- ½ teaspoon fresh minced garlic
- 2-3 Tablespoons dry sherry
- To taste salt and freshly ground pepper
- 3 Tablespoons whole butter
- 12 French bread croutons
- ½ cup red pepper mousseline - recipe follows
- ½ cup chiffonnade fresh basil
- 12 slices fresh mozzarella to fit croutons
- As needed chives
- 1 Tablespoon lemon zest
- As needed melted butter for croutons
- Sauté lobster, garlic, sherry, salt and pepper in whole butter very briefly (just to warm and cook garlic). Set aside.
- Grill croutons, cool to room temperature and brush with melted butter and lemon zest. Spread a little mousseline on each crouton and divide the basil up amongst the croutons. Equally divide the lobster meat over the croutons. Place a slice of fresh mozzarella over the lobster. Sprinkle with chopped chives. Place croutons on a sheet pan and bake briefly or until the mozzarella starts to melt.
- Serve immediately, three to a portion arranged nicely on a plate with lemon wedge or appropriate garnish.

Direction

- Red Pepper Mousseline:
- 1 ounce whole butter
- 2 ounces minced onion
- 1½ pounds diced red pepper
- 1 teaspoon minced garlic
- 4 ounces white wine

- 4 ounces chicken stock
- To taste salt and pepper
- 4-5 ounces cream cheese to tighten
- In a skillet, sauté onion and red pepper till the peppers have started to take on a light brown colour. Add the garlic, cook 30 more seconds, and then add remaining ingredients except the cream cheese. Cook until liquid has reduced to 1/2 volume, Season and place all ingredients into a food processor and process until smooth. Let cool slightly before placing on croutons.

202. Herbed Goat Cheese Crostini Recipe

Serving: 8 | Prep: | Cook: 10mins | Ready in:

Ingredients

- Long Thing baguette
- extra virgin olive oil
- goat cheese
- rosemary
- thyme
- parsley
- lemon zest
- Salt
- Coarsely ground pepper

Direction

- Slice the baguette into thin slices (about 1/2 inch) and place on a baking sheet.
- Drizzle the extra virgin olive oil over the slices suited to your love of olive oil.
- Bake in oven at 425 degrees for 10 minutes, or until golden.
- Coarsely chop the Rosemary, Thyme, and Parsley. Mix together in a small bowl with the lemon zest, salt, and coarsely ground pepper.
- Form the goat cheese into balls of about 1 inch in diameter. Be sure to select a brand of goat cheese that is neither too runny, nor too dry. Also, to make the cheese easier to handle, be sure that you remove it from the fridge only moments before rolling.
- Lightly coat the goat cheese balls in the herb mixture by rolling them in the chopped herbs.
- Arrange the crostini and herb-covered goat cheese balls on a plate and serve.

203. Hogazas Recipe

Serving: 4 | Prep: | Cook: 20mins | Ready in:

Ingredients

- 2 oz. chorizo sausage
- 1/2 jar roasted red peppers (or roast your own)
- 8 2" slices Italian bread
- Extra virgin olive oil for drizzle
- 1 T minced cilantro

Direction

- Peel the papery casing from the chorizo, pierce with a fork simmer in a skillet with water to cover for 15 minutes.
- Transfer to a cutting board and finely chop the sausage and roasted pepper and combine in a small bowl.
- Toast the bread slices until golden.
- Spoon the chopped sausage and pepper mixture on the toasts.
- Drizzle tops with a good extra virgin olive oil.
- Sprinkle with the cilantro.

204. Honey Pear Bruschetta Recipe

Serving: 50 | Prep: | Cook: 20mins | Ready in:

Ingredients

- 6 firm pears, small diced
- 1 clove garlic, minced

- 1 cup honey
- 2 - 3 cups sugar
- 2 sprigs rosemary, minced / or chopped fresh thyme
- 2 teaspoons lemon zest
- freshly ground pepper to taste
- 1 pound brie cheese
- 1 baguette
- 1 cup toasted, chopped pecans

Direction

- Combine pears, garlic, honey, 2 cups sugar, rosemary and lemon zest in a saucepan and cook over medium heat until the mixture becomes thick and syrupy. Adjust sugar and season to taste with freshly ground pepper.
- Cool and reserve. Can be done in advance and frozen for up to one month.
- To assemble canapé
- Thinly slice baguette into 50 pieces. Toast in 350°F oven until golden brown, about 15 minutes. Cool and reserve.
- Remove side rind of the Brie, cut into slices 1/8 - 1/4" thick and cut slices into squares. Reserve.
- Top each slice of bread with a piece of Brie
- Just before serving, heat in 350°F oven until warm, about 10 minutes
- Top with 1 - 1 1/2 teaspoons honey-pear preserves. Garnish with pecans.
- NOTES:
- I use the thyme instead of the rosemary I much prefer the taste. I use all of the honey amount but taste as you go with the sugar, I have never used to total amount.

205. Hong Kong Style Pizza Recipe

Serving: 0 | Prep: | Cook: 15mins | Ready in:

Ingredients

- 1 ball frozen bread dough
- 2 cups chicken
- 2 large shallots
- 1 clove garlic
- 1 green pepper
- 4 table spoons ginger and sesame sauce
- sesame oil to drizzle
- 1/2 cup finely sliced mushrooms, i use shiitake but whatever you lile wil work

Direction

- Do yourself a favour, make it easy, and get some frozen pizza dough at the supermarket. Thaw, divide one ball into two parts and roll out to 12" rounds, let rise 20 minutes
- Meanwhile, marinate shredded cooked chicken in a good, commercial sesame ginger sauce
- Preheat oven to 425, I use a pizza stone but a pan will do fine
- Sauté finely sliced green pepper, shallots, garlic and mushrooms in olive oil
- Divide ingredients in two and top the pizza dough
- Drizzle with sesame oil
- Bake 20 minutes

206. Hot Bruschetta Dip Recipe

Serving: 8 | Prep: | Cook: 2mins | Ready in:

Ingredients

- 2 roma tomatoes, seeded and diced
- 1 small onion, chopped
- 1 clove garlic, peeled and minced
- 1 to 2 tsp chopped fresh basil
- 1 to 2 tsp chopped fresh parsley
- 1/4 cup extra virgin olive oil
- 1 (8 oz) wheel of Brie

Direction

- In a small bowl, mix first 6 ingredients. Cover and refrigerate at least one hour.
- Remove top rind from brie.
- Place brie in the centre of a microwave safe serving dish
- Microwave on high 30 seconds or until cheese begins to soften. (Original recipe said 1 minute, but that melted the cheese in my microwave)
- Spoon the tomato mixture over the cheese and microwave another 30 to 60 seconds, until cheese is slightly melted.
- Serve with a variety of good crackers or crisp toast points

207. Hot Crab Hero Recipe

Serving: 12 | Prep: | Cook: 40mins | Ready in:

Ingredients

- 2 cans (6oz each) lump crabmeat, drained and flaked
- 1/2 cup mayonnaise
- 1/4 cup minced fresh parsley
- 1/4 cup sour cream
- 1 T lemon juice
- 1/2 t garlic powder
- 1/8 t salt
- 1 loaf (8oz) French bread
- 2 T butter
- 4 or more slices swiss cheese

Direction

- In a large bowl, combine the first seven ingredients
- Slice bread horizontally and spread cut sides with butter
- Top with cheese
- Spread with crab mixture
- Place on an ungreased baking sheet and bake at 350 for 20-25 minutes or until lightly browned

208. Hot Italian Bread Dip Recipe

Serving: 12 | Prep: | Cook: 35mins | Ready in:

Ingredients

- 1 cup mayonnaise (no substitute)
- 1 cup sour cream
- 2 (.7 or 1 ounce) packages dry Italian dressing mix (such as Good seasoning)
- ¼ cup finely diced red, orange or green bell pepper
- 1½ cups grated swiss cheese (gruyere is excellent, too)
- sliced Italian, French, Rye, or any hearty bread

Direction

- Mix all ingredients, except bread slices, together in a bowl.
- Pour mixture in a generously buttered shallow casserole.
- Bake at 350 degrees for 30 to 35 minutes, until dip is hot and bubbly.
- Serve with bread slices.

209. Italian Bread Dip Recipe

Serving: 4 | Prep: | Cook: | Ready in:

Ingredients

- 2/3 cup Fig balsamic vinegar (Any flavor is fine)
- 1/3 cup extra-virgin olive oil
- 1 artichoke heart marinated in oil (I bought this in a big jar)
- 1 Loaf of Chewy and crusty bread.

Direction

- Put the Balsamic Vinegar and Olive Oil together in a small bowl and mix thoroughly.

- Chop the artichoke heart into about fingernail sized pieces.
- Add artichoke to the vinegar/oil mixture.
- Enjoy with the bread. I like to use a fresh Kalamata Olive bread.

210. Italian Bread Dipping Oil Recipe

Serving: 6 | Prep: | Cook: | Ready in:

Ingredients

- 1 Cup extra virgin olive oil
- 1 Tablespoon balsamic vinegar (Optional)
- 1 Tablespoon Each: Chopped fresh basil & parsley
- 1 Tablespoon Chopped Dried oregano
- 1 to 2 Minced fresh garlic cloves (Depending On Your Preference)
- 1/2 Teaspoon salt
- 1 Teaspoon Fresh Ground coarse black pepper
- Dash of red pepper flakes (Optional)
- 1 Tablespoon Sundried tomatoes, Finely Chopped (Optional)

Direction

- Mix all the ingredients together and let sit to allow the flavours to meld for at least an hour or two before serving.
- Serve in a shallow bowl with crusty Italian bread cut into thick slices.
- Makes one cup

211. Italian Salad Sandwich Recipe

Serving: 0 | Prep: | Cook: 30mins | Ready in:

Ingredients

- 1lb loaf rustic Italian bread, sliced into 1/2 inch slices
- 1/2 stick butter, melted
- 4 cloves garlic, halved (roasted, if desired)
- 8oz fresh mozzarella, sliced
- about 6oz fresh baby spinach leaves
- 2 fresh tomatoes, sliced thin
- 1 red onion, sliced thin
- 8oz prosciutto, sliced thin
- fine sea or kosher salt and fresh ground pepper
- Italian dressing or vinegar and oil, optional

Direction

- Brush melted butter over one cut side of each slice of bread (12-18 pieces, depending on the size).
- Rub cut side of garlic over the buttered bits of bread.
- Sprinkle with salt and pepper.
- Bake at 400 for about 5 minutes, just until edges are beginning to turn golden.
- Add slices of cheese, spinach leaves, tomato and onion slices and prosciutto and return to oven.
- Bake another 5 minutes or so until cheese is melted and toast edges are crunchy.
- Drizzle with dressing just before serving, if desired.

212. Italian Style Creamy Mushroom Sauce On Sourdough Recipe

Serving: 0 | Prep: | Cook: 35mins | Ready in:

Ingredients

- 1tbsp Extra Virgin Olive Oil
- 15g/½oz butter
- 6 Rashers Pancetta or Streaky bacon
- 1 clove Garlic - very finely chopped
- 1 Onion - finely chopped

- 240g/8oz button mushrooms - cleaned & sliced
- 150ml/5fl oz dry White Wine
- 150ml/5fl oz Crème Fraiche or Sour Cream
- 1tbsp Flat leaf Parsley - chopped
- Salt and freshly ground black pepper
- Slices Sourdough bread - to taste - toasted

Direction

- Heat the oil and butter in a frying pan, add the pancetta and fry until crisp;
- Remove and save on kitchen towel;
- Reduce heat to low, add the onions and cook, stirring occasionally, for some 5 to 7 minutes or so or until softened but not coloured;
- Add the garlic and the mushrooms and cook for some 3 to 4 minutes or until the mushrooms have softened a bit;
- Add the wine, increase the heat to high, and reduce the volume of liquid by half;
- Stir in the crème fraiche or cream and parsley and heat through and season to taste;
- Serve on top of toasted sourdough with slices of crispy pancetta

213. Jarlsberg Onion And Apple Canapes Recipe

Serving: 16 | Prep: | Cook: 25mins | Ready in:

Ingredients

- 1 tablespoon butter
- 1 medium onion, cut into fourths and sliced
- 4 ounces thinly sliced Jarlsberg or swiss cheese
- 16 slices pumpernickel cocktail bread***
- 1 tablespoon Dijon-mayonnaise blend or Dijon mustard
- 1 to 2 tablespoons chopped fresh chives
- 1 medium unpeeled apple, thinly sliced
- *****I would use a good bakery pumpernickel bread cut into cocktail size instead... if it is too soft, lightly toast it first

Direction

- Sauté onion until soft and caramelized
- Cut cheese to fit bread. Spread each bread slice with Dijon-mayonnaise blend. Top each with onion, apple and cheese. Sprinkle with chives.
- Place in ungreased jelly roll pan, 15 1/2x10 1/2x1 inch.
- Bake about 5 minutes or until cheese is melted. Serve warm.

214. Killer Bread Recipe

Serving: 6 | Prep: | Cook: 20mins | Ready in:

Ingredients

- 1 cup real mayonnaise
- 1 cup freshlly grated parmesan cheese
- 2 tbsp. fresh basil chopped (2 tsp. dried)
- 2 minced green onions
- 1 1/2 tsp. minced garlic (or to taste)
- 1 lb. loaf round sourdough bread, halved horizontally
- butter

Direction

- Preheat broiler. Mix mayonnaise, Parmesan cheese, green onion and garlic; set aside.
- Arrange bread, cut side up on cookie sheet. Butter bread. Broil until crisp and brown.
- Spread Parmesan mixture over cut sides of bread.
- Broil until top is puffed and golden brown. Sprinkle with basil.
- Cut into wedges and serve.

215. LUSCIOUS APPETIZER BREAD Recipe

Serving: 12 | Prep: | Cook: 25mins | Ready in:

Ingredients

- 2 c. grated cheddar cheese
- 1 c. mayonnaise
- 1 tsp. Italian herb seasoning
- 1 bunch green onions, finely chopped
- 1 long loaf French bread, halved lengthwise
- parmesan cheese

Direction

- Combine cheddar cheese, mayo, herb seasoning and green onion. Mix thoroughly. Spread mixture evenly on bread halves and sprinkle generously with Parmesan. Place bread on large cookie sheet. Bake, uncovered at 350 degrees for 20 minutes or until bubbly. Remove bread from oven and slice into 2" pieces. Serve immediately.

216. Lavash Cracker Bread Bites Recipe

Serving: 0 | Prep: | Cook: 20mins | Ready in:

Ingredients

- Lavash cracker bread
- fresh basil Pesto
- prosciutto (or Speck)
- Goat's milk creamy cheese
- Blackberry jelly
- balsamic vinegar
- Organic arugula

Direction

- Preheat the oven to 350°. Cut the cracker bread into rectangles (1 inch X 3 inches). Place the pieces on a sheet pan and bake for 5 minutes, or until crisp. (Watch carefully so as not to burn.) When the crackers are cool they can be placed in an airtight container until ready to use.
- Mix jelly with balsamic vinegar, enough to give it a sauce consistency.
- Spread a little pesto on the cracker then top with a roll of prosciutto. (I halved the slice of prosciutto and rolled it.) Add a small dollop of the goat cheese, squirt (or drizzle) some of the blackberry balsamic and top each with an arugula leaf.
- Hecka easy, right? Place on a platter and serve!

217. Little Puff Ball Breads Recipe

Serving: 10 | Prep: | Cook: 35mins | Ready in:

Ingredients

- 250 ml water
- 50 g butter
- 125 g white cornmeal
- 1/2 tsp salt
- ground pepper
- grated nutmeg
- 3 eggs
- 1/2 tsp baking powder
- 100 grated cheese

Direction

- Place butter and water in a small pot and bring to a boil
- Mix the dry ingredients together
- Place the dry ingredients all at once into the hot liquid
- Mix and stir very well for a minute or so into a smooth dough
- Remove from heat and let cool a bit
- Add the eggs one at a time, stirring each into the dough as quickly as possible until each egg is well incorporated
- Lastly stir in the grated cheese along with the baking powder
- Using two tablespoons, scoop out 10 to 12 little dough balls and place on a baking sheet, giving room to spread out
- Bake 180C for 35 minutes or puffed and golden

218. Lump Crab Crostini Recipe

Serving: 15 | Prep: | Cook: 20mins | Ready in:

Ingredients

- 1 lb. Good crab Meat
- 1 Tbsp. scallions, diced
- 10 oz. swiss cheese, shredded
- 1 cup mayonnaise
- 1 tsp. salt
- 1 tsp. fresh lemon juice
- 1 baguette, sliced into about 50 1/4- inch thick rounds

Direction

- Preheat oven to 375 degrees F.
- Gently combine crab meat and Swiss cheese.
- Add remaining ingredients, being careful not to break up crab lumps.
- Spread baguette rounds onto baking pan.
- Top each round with crab meat mixture.
- Bake at 375 degrees F for 15-20 minutes or until golden brown
- Appetizer Serves Up To 20 People

219. Margarita Bread Recipe

Serving: 6 | Prep: | Cook: 30mins | Ready in:

Ingredients

- 1 1/2 Cups lukewarm water
- 2 Tsp granulated yeast (1 1/2 packages)
- 2 Tsp Kosher or other coarse salt
- 3 1/4 Cups unsifted, unbleached, all-purpose white flour, measured with the scoop-and-sweep method.
- If you use bleached flour increase the flour by 1/4 cup.
- 1/2 cup chopped chipotle peppers in adobo sauce

Direction

- Warm the water slightly, should feel a little warmer than body temp - about 100 degrees.
- Add yeast and salt to the water in a 5-quart bowl, or in a resealable, lidded plastic food container.
- Mix in the flour, kneading is unnecessary. Add all the flour at once, measuring it scooping up the flour and sweeping the top level with a knife or spatula. If you are hand mixing and it becomes difficult to incorporate the flour reach in with wet hands and gently mix in the remaining flour. Don't knead. Everything should be uniformly wet without dry patches.
- Allow to rise. - Cover with a lid, not airtight, that fits well. Allow mixture to rise at room temp until it collapses (or at least flattens on top) about 2 hours depending on the room temp. Cover and refrigerate overnight.
- Baking Day
- Prepare a cookie sheet by sprinkling it liberally with cornmeal.
- Sprinkle the surface of the dough lightly with flour to keep the knife from sticking.
- Hold the dough in your hands, add a little flour as needed so it won't stick to your hands. Gently stretch the surface of the dough around to the bottom on all four sides, rotating the ball a quarter turn each time. Most of the flour will fall off, it's not intended to be incorporated into the dough. The bottom of the ball will be a collection of bunched end but it will flatten. The correctly shaped ball will be smooth and cohesive. The whole process should take less than a minute.
- Shape the ball into a cylinder, and roll into a rectangle, about ½" thick.
- Sprinkle the chipotle peppers evenly over the dough.
- Roll the dough back up into a cylinder. (Rolling it up on itself)

- Rest the cylinder and let it rise on the cookie sheet. Allow to rest for 1 hour if it has been refrigerated.
- Heat the oven to 450 degrees 20 minutes before baking. Before the oven is turned on place an empty broiler pan on the lowest rack of the oven, and put a rack above that for baking the bread. You want the broiler pan to be hot when the bread goes in the oven.
- When you are ready to bake, dust the top of the loaf liberally with flour which will allow the slashing knife to pass without sticking. I slash four slashes angled out from the bottom, like a hand, at least 1/4 inch deep to help oven spring. Use a pattern of your own, an X, and tic tac toe square etc.
- Place the bread in the oven and carefully pour a cup of hot or boiling water into the broiler pan and quickly shut the door. Do not open for at least 15 minutes to allow the steam to work. Bake 30-35 minutes until the top is browned and it sounds hollow when tapped, or an instant read thermometer reads at least 190 degrees.

220. Margherita Pizza Recipe

Serving: 0 | Prep: | Cook: 40mins | Ready in:

Ingredients

- 6 Rhodes Texas™ rolls or 12 Rhodes™ dinner rolls, thawed to room temperature
- 2-3 roma tomatoes
- 1 medium ball fresh mozzarella cheese
- fresh basil
- pizza sauce or thick spaghetti sauce
- salt and fresh ground pepper, to taste

Direction

- Spray counter lightly with non-stick cooking spray.
- Flatten one Texas roll or 2 dinner rolls combined into a 6-inch circle.
- Cover with plastic wrap and let rest.
- Slice tomatoes and cheese into 1/8-inch thick slices.
- Cut basil into long strips.
- Remove wrap from dough and place circles on sprayed baking sheets.
- Poke with a fork several times to prevent bubbles from forming and pre-bake at 350°F 5-10 minutes.
- Remove from oven and top each one with sauce, tomatoes and cheese.
- Sprinkle with salt and freshly ground pepper.
- Bake an additional 10-15 minutes.
- Remove from oven and top with fresh basil.

221. Margies Cheese Crusty Canape Recipe

Serving: 18 | Prep: | Cook: 20mins | Ready in:

Ingredients

- 1 stick butter
- 1 cup flour
- 1 3-ounce package cream cheese

Direction

- Preheat oven to 375 degrees F.
- Mix ingredients as for dough.
- Roll thin.
- Cut into circles or squares.
- Place filling in centre.
- Fold over.
- Seal.
- Bake on cookie sheet about 20 minutes.
- Can be kept for several days or frozen indefinitely.
- FILLINGS:
- Cooked sausage, browned ground beef, 1/2 anchovy filets

222. Marinated Peppers With Crusty Grilled Bread Recipe

Serving: 4 | Prep: | Cook: 30mins | Ready in:

Ingredients

- 2 red bell peppers
- 2 green bell peppers
- 2 yellow peppers
- 4 jalapeños
- 3 garlic cloves, chopped
- 2 Tbsp balsamic vinegar
- 1/2 cup extra virgin olive oil
- 2 tsp fresh basil, chopped
- 2 tsp fresh parsley, chopped
- salt to taste
- pepper to taste
- 1 loaf Italian bread, sliced
- extra virgin olive oil to drizzle
- Wedge of gorgonzola cheese

Direction

- Wash and dry peppers.
- Roast whole peppers in oven at 450°F for 10-15 minutes or until skin blisters and blackens.
- Immediately transfer peppers to a holding pan, seal with plastic wrap and cool.
- Remove skins and seeds from cooled peppers.
- Slice peppers into strips.
- Season peppers with extra virgin olive oil, vinegar, basil, parsley, garlic, salt and pepper.
- Marinate peppers for 45 minutes in a covered bowl
- Drizzle both sides of bread with extra virgin olive oil.
- Grill bread on both sides.
- Transfer peppers to serving plates.
- Serve with crusty grilled bread and a glass of red wine and a wedge of Gorgonzola.

223. Marinated Peppers Bruschetta Recipe

Serving: 6 | Prep: | Cook: 5mins | Ready in:

Ingredients

- 1/2 cup each: diced red pepper, yellow pepper, and orange pepper
- 1 clove garlic, minced
- 1 Tbsp olive oil
- 1 tsp dried basil, or 1 Tbsp chopped fresh
- salt and pepper to taste
- parmesan cheese
- french breach

Direction

- In the morning, combine peppers, garlic, oil, basil and salt & pepper. Marinate in the fridge through the day.
- When time to serve: Cut French bread in diagonal slices and lightly toast in hot oven. Spoon 2 Tbsp. over each hot piece and sprinkle with parmesan cheese. YUM

224. Mediterranean Pizza Bites Recipe

Serving: 24 | Prep: | Cook: 2hours | Ready in:

Ingredients

- 1 batch homemade (or already prepared) pizza dough
- Filling:
- 1 cup whole milk mozzarella, shredded
- 1 cup feta cheese, crumbled
- 1 package frozen artichoke hearts, defrosted and chopped
- 1 package frozen spinach, well drained, chopped
- 1/2 cup sun dried tomatoes in olive oil, julienned
- 1/4 cup kalamata olives, chopped

- 1 teaspoon oregano
- freshly ground black pepper, to taste
- Topping:
- 1 clove of garlic, minced
- 1/4 cup fresh parsley, chopped
- 1 teaspoon red chile flakes
- 1/4 cup olive oil
- 1/4 cup freshly grated parmigiano-reggianno

Direction

- Preheat oven to 400 degrees Fahrenheit. If making homemade dough, prepare pizza dough according to directions (I use Wolfgang Puck's pizza dough recipe, always).
- Combine all filling ingredients in large bowl.
- On a lightly floured board, pinch off about 25 (1-inch) balls of dough and flatten slightly, filling the middle with desired amount of filling (be careful to keep a good ratio of filling to dough as you don't want the bites to be too doughy). Wrap dough around filling and roll into a ball, placing in parchment lined, large round pizza pan. Repeat with remaining dough.
- Combine garlic, parsley, and red chile flakes in olive oil and brush or drizzle over the pizza bites. Sprinkle with parmesan cheese.
- Bake in oven for 15 to 20 minutes or until top is nicely browned (they smell AWESOME as they are baking!).
- Notes:
- You can substitute in any type of "toppings" you want instead of the above, like pepperoni/sausage. It might be a good idea if using vegetables like onions, green peppers or mushrooms to sauté them a little before using as the filling.

225. Mediterranean Shrimp Bruschetta Recipe

Serving: 6 | Prep: | Cook: 60mins | Ready in:

Ingredients

- 7-8 assorted, ripe tomatoes (I used red Roma, yellow, and orange tomatoes, any will do)
- 6 fresh basil leaves
- 3oz EVOO
- 2oz red wine vinegar
- 1tsp miced garlic
- 4oz Fresh Mozzerella (pearls, cubed...personal preference)
- salt and pepper to taste
- 20 med sz cooked, deveined, tailess shrimp (opt)
- 1 loaf french baguette bread (or your favorite)

Direction

- Put Basil leaves, EVOO, Red Wine Vinegar, Garlic, and S/P, if desired, into a blender/food processor to make a salad dressing consistency of the ingredients. You don't HAVE to use a food processor, just chop it and stir it up well :)
- Dice tomatoes
- Cut shrimp and mozzarella into bite size pieces
- Add all ingredients to large bowl and stir well
- Let chill in fridge for at least an hour for ingredients to marinate tomatoes
- Slice bread into 1/2in slices and toast in oven
- *If you prefer a tangier dressing, add more Vinegar, I add more to mine, but the family doesn't like it that way

226. Mini Brie And Apple Quiches Recipe

Serving: 30 | Prep: | Cook: 30mins | Ready in:

Ingredients

- 30 min phyllo shells
- 1/2 med. apple, diced
- 5 lg. eggs
- 1 tsp Dijon mustard

- 1/4 tsp salt
- pinc of pepper
- pinch of nutmeg
- 4 oz. Brie cheese (cut into 30 squares)

Direction

- Preheat oven to 350
- Arrange phyllo shells on large, parchment - lined baking sheet.
- Divide apple among the shells. Whisk eggs, Dijon, salt pepper, and nutmeg in large measuring cup.
- Pour egg mixture over apple (do not over fill)
- Place one piece of brie in each shell. Bake till egg is set, Brie melted and phyllo starting to brown, about 15 mins. Let cool slightly before serving.

227. Mini Pepperoni Bread Recipe

Serving: 8 | Prep: | Cook: 10mins | Ready in:

Ingredients

- 1 - 2 cans crescent rolls
- 1/4 lb. pepperoni, sliced thin
- 1/2 lb. thinly sliced Mozzarella

Direction

- Preheat oven to 350 degrees.
- Open and separate crescent rolls.
- Lay 1 piece of cheese on dough.
- Place 1 to 2 pieces of pepperoni on top of cheese, as desired.
- Lay second piece of Mozzarella cheese on top of pepperoni.
- Fold dough into crescent shape, making sure ends are closed.
- Place on ungreased cookie sheet and bake approximately 7 to 10 minutes or until golden brown.

228. Mini Spinachoke Bowls Recipe

Serving: 0 | Prep: | Cook: 45mins | Ready in:

Ingredients

- 2lbs bread dough(can use fresh dough that is at the ready to bake stage or frozen, that's been thawed)
- 8oz cream cheese, softened
- 1/2 cup sour cream
- 6oz jarred artichokes, drained and chopped fine(can use plain or marinated)
- 2 cloves garlic, minced
- 4-5oz fresh spinach, chopped fine
- 1/2 cup fresh parmesan cheese, grated, plus 2-3T
- 1/4 cup fresh mozzarella, shredded
- 2 green onions, chopped
- dash of hot sauce
- fresh ground black pepper

Direction

- Combine all ingredients except bread dough and 2-3T grated Parmesan.
- Lightly spray mini muffin tins and, using walnut sized pieces of bread dough, spread out circles to form into bottom, and up sides, of the muffin tins. Make sure dough comes up the sides of the cups.
- Fill each with a rounded spoonful of the spinach dip mix. Don't be afraid to fill them full. The bread will rise over the sides a bit and should contain the dip.
- Sprinkle with remaining Parmesan cheese.
- Bake at 350 for about 15-20 minutes until edges are lightly golden brown and dough is done.

229. Mixed Olive Crostini

Serving: 16 | Prep: | Cook: 60mins | Ready in:

Ingredients

- 1 can (4-1/4 ounces) chopped ripe olives
- 1/2 cup pimiento-stuffed olives, finely chopped
- 1/2 cup grated Parmesan cheese
- 1/4 cup butter, softened
- 1 tablespoon olive oil
- 2 garlic cloves, minced
- 3/4 cup shredded part-skim mozzarella cheese
- 1/4 cup minced fresh parsley
- 1 French bread baguette (10-1/2 ounces)

Direction

- In a small bowl, combine the first six ingredients; stir in mozzarella cheese and parsley. Cut baguette into 24 slices; place on an ungreased baking sheet. Spread with olive mixture.
- Broil 3-4 in. from the heat for 2-3 minutes or until edges are lightly browned and cheese is melted.
- Nutrition Facts
- 1 each: 102 calories, 6g fat (2g saturated fat), 9mg cholesterol, 221mg sodium, 10g carbohydrate (0 sugars, 1g fiber), 3g protein.

230. Monkey Bread Recipe

Serving: 6 | Prep: | Cook: 20mins | Ready in:

Ingredients

- 1/2 cup nuts, chopped
- 2 cans biscuits cut into 1/4
- 1/2 cup sugar
- 1Tbsp cinnamon
- 1/4 cup butter
- Glze
- 1/4 cup butter
- 1 cup brown sugar

Direction

- Pour the chopped nuts into the bottom of a well-greased Bundt pan
- Mix 1/2 cup sugar and 1 Tbsp. cinnamon and coat the biscuit and place in the pan
- Melt 1/4 cup butter with the brown sugar and cinnamon. Boil two minutes and pour over the biscuits
- Bake at 350 degrees for 20 minutes
- Glaze
- Melt 1/4 cup butter to 1 cup brown sugar and drizzle over biscuits

231. Mozzarella Impanata Breaded And Fried Mozzarella Recipe

Serving: 4 | Prep: | Cook: 5mins | Ready in:

Ingredients

- 10 ounces fresh mozzarella, cut in four 1 inch thick slices
- 2 large eggs, lightly beaten with a pinch of salt
- 1 cup plain or seasoned bread crumbs, spread evenly over a sheet of foil
- vegetable oil for frying
- 8 leaves fresh basil, finely shredded by hand

Direction

- Dip Mozzarella slices into egg, shake off excess, and dredge completely in bread crumbs, pressing crumbs in with the palms of your hands.
- Heat one inch of oil in medium skillet over high heat.
- When oil is very hot, lower slices of mozzarella into oil with slotted spoon - do not crowd. When slices are golden brown, (less than one minute) turn and fry other side,

- With slotted spoon, transfer to paper towel-lined plate to drain.
- Serve piping hot, topped with shredded basil.

232. Mozzarella Pepperoni Bread Recipe

Serving: 24 | Prep: | Cook: 15mins | Ready in:

Ingredients

- 1 loaf (1 pound) French bread
- 3 tablespoons butter, melted
- 3 ounces sliced turkey pepperoni
- 1-1/2 cups (6 ounces) shredded part-skim mozzarella cheese
- 3 tablespoons minced fresh parsley

Direction

- Cut loaf of bread in half width wise; cut into 1-in. slices, leaving slices attached at bottom. Brush butter on both sides of each slice. Arrange pepperoni between slices; sprinkle with cheese and parsley.
- Place on an ungreased baking sheet. Bake at 350° for 12-15 minutes or until cheese is melted.
- Yield: 24 slices.
- We just use plain pepperoni.

233. Mozzarella And Tomato Crostini Recipe

Serving: 8 | Prep: | Cook: 18mins | Ready in:

Ingredients

- 1/4c. + more for baking extra virgin olive oil
- 1 baguette, cut into 1/4" slices
- salt and coarse ground black pepper
- 8 vine ripened tomatoes
- 1/2c. slivered fresh basil leaves
- 1/4T. minced garlic
- 1T. aged balsamic vinegar
- 1-1/2 lbs. fresh mozzarella cheese

Direction

- Preheat an oven to 350ºF.
- Brush a baking sheet with olive oil and arrange the baguette slices on the sheet in a single layer.
- Brush the tops with oil, and season with salt and pepper.
- Bake until crisp and golden, 15 to 18 minutes.
- Let cool, then store the crostini in an airtight container at room temperature until ready to use.
- Core and seed the tomatoes and slice lengthwise into 1/4-inch-thick slices.
- In a mixing bowl, combine the tomatoes, half of the basil, garlic, vinegar, the remaining 1/4 cup olive oil, salt and pepper and mix well.
- Slice the mozzarella into 1/4-inch-thick pieces or into smaller pieces so they fit on the crostini.
- To assemble, lay a piece of mozzarella on each crostini and spoon 1 to 2 Tbs. of the tomato salad on top.
- Garnish each with a pinch of the remaining basil.
- Serve immediately.

234. Muffaletta Bites Recipe

Serving: 0 | Prep: | Cook: 15mins | Ready in:

Ingredients

- 1 large loaf french baguette, baked.
- 1 jar undrained Olive Antipasto with pepperoncinis, olives, garlic, onion, red pepper, etc...OR, make your own, tapenade style with the above ingredients. You want a touch of heat, but it's basically an olive spread.
- 6oz sandwich sliced provolone cheese

- 1/2lb thinly sliced salami

Direction

- Slice bread on a bias into about 1/2 inch slices.
- Slice salami pieces in half.
- Slice cheese pieces in half.
- Drain the olive mix, reserving liquid, and pulse in food processor for a couple minutes to chop.
- Using pastry brush, brush on a fair bit of the reserved liquid onto one side of each slice. This will help give that yummy soaked taste that is so indicative of a muffuletta!
- Top each with several pieces of salami (I used 8 halves on each, I think)
- Top with a slice of provolone cheese
- Spoon on about 1T of olive mix over the top.
- *you can use a spicy ham in addition to the salami, if you'd like....my deli just didn't have anything appropriate, or I would have! :)
- **these are fine at room temperature

235. Muffuletta Appetizer Recipe

Serving: 16 | Prep: | Cook: 1hours20mins | Ready in:

Ingredients

- 1 jar (12 ounces) pickled mixed vegetables, drained
- 1/4 cup pimiento stuffed olives, chopped
- 2 ounces ham or salami slices, finely chopped
- 1 tablespoon finely minced garlic
- 1 tablespoon olive oil
- 2 cans (10 ounces each) refrigerated flaky biscuits
- 1/2 cup provolone cheese or Mozzarella, finely shredded

Direction

- Finely chop the drained pickled vegetables. Combine with olives, ham or salami, garlic, and olive oil. Chill for at least 1 hour. Bake biscuits according to package directions; cool slightly. Scoop out centre of 16 biscuits (reserve remaining biscuits for another use). Stir cheese into the vegetable mixture and spoon 1 heaping tablespoon into each hollowed out biscuit.
- Bake filled biscuits at 400° for 8 to 10 minutes, or until heated through. Serve warm.
- Makes 16.

236. Mushroom Bread Recipe

Serving: 12 | Prep: | Cook: 15mins | Ready in:

Ingredients

- 1 loaf Italian bread
- 1/2 cup butter, softened
- 1 pound sliced, fresh mushrooms
- 2 cups shredded mozzarella cheese
- 6 green onions, chopped
- 3 cloves garlic, minced

Direction

- Preheat oven to 400
- Slice bread in half horizontally and scoop out most of the bread to form a shell
- Save bread for some other use, like fresh breadcrumbs
- Sauté the mushrooms in a small amount of olive oil until slightly softened
- Mix butter, mushrooms, cheese, green onions and garlic
- Spread the mixture on both shells of bread
- Place bread on baking sheet
- Bake until cheese has melted about 10 to 15 minutes
- Cut into wedges and serve

237. Mushroom Canapes Recipe

Serving: 30 | Prep: | Cook: 15mins | Ready in:

Ingredients

- 1/4c butter
- 2 Tbs fine chopped onion
- 1/2lb mushrooms,fine chopped
- 2Tbs flour
- 1Tbs salt
- 2Tbs cream
- 2Tbs sherry
- 30 2" circles of bread,toasted on 1 side
- 1/2c grated parmesan cheese
- 5 slices lean bacon,cut into 30 squares

Direction

- Sauté onion and mushrooms in butter 5 mins. Add flour and salt and blend. Add cream and cook, stirring constantly for 5 mins. Stir in sherry.
- Spread on untoasted side of bread. Sprinkle with cheese and top with a square of bacon. Broil till bubbly and bacon is crisp. Serve immediately.

238. Mushroom Garlic Crostini For The Slow Cooker Recipe

Serving: 28 | Prep: | Cook: 240mins | Ready in:

Ingredients

- 8 cloves of garlic, roasted
- 1 lb small white mushrooms cleaned and trimmed
- 2 large shallots, finely chopped
- 2 Tbl EVOO
- 1/4 C dry white wine
- 2 Tbl chopped fresh parsley
- 2 Tbl heavy cream
- 2 Tsp balsamic vinegar
- salt and freshly ground pepper
- 28 crostini
- Crumbled soft goat cheese

Direction

- Combine garlic, mushrooms, shallots, olive oil and wine in a slow cooker.
- Cover and cook on high 4 hours or on low about 8 or until mushrooms are soft.
- Drain off liquid and refrigerate, for use in soups, sauces or gravies later.
- Place mushroom mixture in a food processor
- Add parsley and pulse until finely chopped, but not pureed.
- Add cream, vinegar, salt and pepper to taste and pulse two or three times to combine.
- Heat oven to 375.
- Spread mushroom mixture over crostini
- Sprinkle with goat cheese
- Place on baking sheet and bake until cheese just start to brown and melt
- Serve hot
- Notes: These two steps can be done ahead
- To roast several garlic cloves at a time, peel and place on foil, drizzle with olive oil wrap tightly and bake at 400 for 20 minutes
- To make crostini: preheat broiler, brush slices of baguette on both sides with olive oil and toast under broiler turning once until crisp and lightly browned

239. Mushroom Strudel Recipe

Serving: 0 | Prep: | Cook: 1hours | Ready in:

Ingredients

- 1 pound assorted mushrooms, chopped
- 2 shallots, minced
- 8 oz cream cheese or crumbled goat cheese (this dish also works with cottage cheese)
- 1 cup sour cream, yogurt, or a combination

- 1 tsp salt
- freshly grated black pepper
- 1 tsp dill, minced
- 1 cup bread crumbs
- 2 scallions, finely minced
- ¼ cup parsley, minced
- 3 Tbsp lemon juice
- 10 sheets phyllo pastry
- 3-4 Tbsp olive oil or melted unsalted butter
- ½ c poppy or sesame seeds (optional)

Direction

- Preheat the oven to 375°. Oil a sheet pan or cover it with a Silpat baking non-stick baking sheet.
- In a medium skillet, sprinkle minced shallots with a generous pinch of salt and pepper and sauté until soft. Add chopped mushrooms and continue cooking over medium heat for about 10 minutes. Drain mixture and squeeze out all the liquid. Place in bowl.
- Add crumbled goat cheese or cream cheese and mix well; then add other filling ingredients.
- Place a sheet of phyllo pastry clean, dry surface. Brush with oil or melted unsalted butter; layer another sheet on top and repeat until you have 5 sheets layered with oil or melted butter.
- Place half of the filling along one long side, fold in the ends, and roll (being extremely careful not to break the fragile phyllo pastry). Carefully transfer roll to baking sheet and brush top with oil or melted unsalted butter.
- Repeat with remaining phyllo and filling, so that you end up with two rolls. Sprinkle top with optional seeds.
- Bake 25-30 minutes, until golden brown and very crispy.
- Cut with serrated knife and serve hot or warm.

240. Mushrooms/ Smoked Salmon Bruschetta Recipe

Serving: 0 | Prep: | Cook: 30mins | Ready in:

Ingredients

- Mushroom paste
- 1 tbsp lemon
- 1 cup sauteed wild mushrooms (quick sautee in 1 tbsp olive oil, salt, pepper and 3 tbsp white wine)
- 4 tbsp cream cheese
- 1 tbsp parmesan cheese, grated
- smoked salmon spread
- 1/2 cup smoked salmon
- 1/4 cup cream cheese
- 1/2 tsp lemon zest
- 1 tbsp lemon
- white pepper to taste
- 1 loaf of good Italian bread
- olive oil

Direction

- Slice the bread and drizzle with olive oil.
- Put the slices in the oven and broil until toasted with a golden colour, this should take about 5 minutes in a hot oven, keep an eye on them so they won't burn.
- Make the pastes by mixing the ingredients of each one in a food processor. (1st make the mushroom paste, wash the container and then 2nd the salmon paste)
- Spread an even amount of paste on each slice.
- Arrange the slices in plates and serve.

241. My Favorite Bruschetta Recipe

Serving: 8 | Prep: | Cook: 15mins | Ready in:

Ingredients

- 8 slices artisan sourdough bread

- ~1/4 cup extra virgin olive oil
- 1 garlic clove, peeled and cut in half
- ~4 ripe tomatoes, thinly sliced
- ~4 basil leaves - stacked, rolled, then thinly sliced
- salt
- parmesan cheese (optional)
- capers, chopped (optional)

Direction

- Prepare a hot grill. A charcoal fire is the best!
- Lightly brush the bread with the olive oil. Place the bread slices on the grill and toast until you have grill marks on each side. (You can use a broiler if it's not grilling weather - put a rack on the top shelf and broil the bread for 2-3 minutes.)
- Remove the bread from the grill/broiler. Rub one side of the bread with the cut side of the garlic clove.
- Arrange the tomato slices on the top of the bread, overlapping them slightly. Sprinkle to taste with salt.
- Put the tomato-topped bread slices back on the grill / under the broiler briefly to warm everything up again.
- Remove the bread slices, and top with the basil chiffonade. Add parmesan cheese and capers, if using. Buon Appetito!

242. Olive & Roasted Pepper Bruschetta

Serving: 4 | Prep: | Cook: 40mins | Ready in:

Ingredients

- 1/2 cup grated Romano cheese
- 1/2 cup chopped pitted green olives
- 1/2 cup chopped roasted sweet red peppers
- 2 teaspoons olive oil
- 1/2 teaspoon dried basil
- 16 slices French bread baguette (1/2 inch thick), toasted

Direction

- In a small bowl, combine the first five ingredients. Top each bread slice with 1 tablespoon olive mixture.
- Nutrition Facts
- 1 piece: 62 calories, 3g fat (1g saturated fat), 4mg cholesterol, 251mg sodium, 7g carbohydrate (0 sugars, 0 fiber), 3g protein. Diabetic Exchanges: 1/2 starch, 1/2 fat.

243. Olive Cheese Bread Recipe

Serving: 12 | Prep: | Cook: 30mins | Ready in:

Ingredients

- One 12 oz -14-oz jar pimiento-stuffed olives (can use combo of these and black olives if you like), drained well and roughly chopped
- 6 scallions (diced)
- ¾ pound shredded cheese (I like the Mexican blends)
- 8 oz. cream cheese, softened
- ½ cup real mayonnaise
- 1 stick butter, softened
- 1/2 teaspoon black pepper
- 2 cloves of garlic, minced
- Optional: 1 jalapeno (remove seeds and ribs to decrease heat, if desired), minced
- 1 to 1 1/2 loaves baguettes, ciabatta, French bread (your choice)

Direction

- Combine olives, scallions, shredded cheese, softened cream cheese, mayonnaise, softened butter, black pepper, garlic and jalapeno pepper. Mix well.
- Slice bread in half lengthwise.
- Spread mixture evenly over the halves.
- Bake at 325 degrees for 30-35 minutes, or until topping is melted and starting to turn light brown.

- Cut into diagonal slices and enjoy.
- NOTE: When I make this with my homemade baguettes, it easily covers three halves without skimping.
- It's very delicious and addictive.

244. Olive Pesto And Bruschetta Cheese Torta Recipe

Serving: 16 | Prep: | Cook: 360mins | Ready in:

Ingredients

- 1/3 cup BUITONI Refrigerated Pesto with basil
- 1 container (10.5 ounces) BUITONI Refrigerated Classic Bruschetta
- 1 can (4 1/2 ounces) chopped black olives, drained
- 1 clove garlic, finely chopped
- 2 packages (8 ounces each) cream cheese, at room temperature
- 1 package (5.5 ounces) soft goat cheese, at room temperature
- Shredded fresh basil
- crackers

Direction

- PLACE pesto in a strainer set over a bowl. Let oil drain for 15 minutes; discard oil. Place bruschetta in a strainer set over a bowl. Let juice drain for 15 minutes. Using back of spoon, gently press tomatoes to remove any remaining juice; discard juice.
- COMBINE olives and garlic in small bowl. Place cream cheese and goat cheese in large mixer bowl. Beat until fluffy.
- LINE 1-quart bowl with 2 sheets of plastic wrap that are large enough to allow a generous overhang on all sides of the bowl and covers all of the inside surface of the bowl.
- SPREAD about 1/3 cup cheese mixture evenly over bottom of prepared bowl. Top with all of olive mixture, spreading evenly. Drop 1/2 cup cheese mixture by spoonfuls over olive mixture and spread gently to cover olives. Top with pesto, spreading evenly. Drop 1/2 cup cheese mixture by spoonfuls over pesto and spread gently to cover pesto. Top with bruschetta, spreading evenly. Drop remaining cheese mixture over bruschetta and spread gently to cover bruschetta. Cover with plastic wrap; refrigerate for at least 6 hours before serving.
- To serve: Remove plastic wrap from top of bowl and invert serving plate over bowl. Turnover and remove bowl; peel off remaining plastic wrap. Top may be smoothed with a knife before serving. Top with basil. Serve with crackers.
- Tip: For easier assembly, each layer may be chilled for about 15 minutes before adding next layer.
- NOTE: Try substituting BUITONI Refrigerated Pesto with Sun Dried Tomatoes for the Pesto with Basil.

245. Olive Goat Cheese Bruschetta Recipe

Serving: 16 | Prep: | Cook: 10mins | Ready in:

Ingredients

- 1 cup diced seeded plum tomato
- 1/4 cup chopped pitted olives
- 2 tablespoons chopped fresh basil
- 1 teaspoon sherry vinegar
- 1/8 teaspoon salt
- 1/8 teaspoon freshly ground black pepper
- 16 (1/4-inch-thick) slices French bread baguette (about 4 ounces)
- 1 garlic clove, peeled
- 1/4 cup mild goat cheese, at room temperature

Direction

- Preheat oven to 400°.

- Combine first 6 ingredients in a small bowl, and set aside.
- Arrange bread on a baking sheet; bake at 400° for 8 minutes or until lightly browned and crisp. Remove toast slices from oven, and cool 2 minutes.
- Rub both sides of each toast slice with garlic clove. Spread goat cheese thinly on 1 side of each toast, and top with the olive mixture.

246. Onion Bread Recipe

Serving: 6 | Prep: | Cook: 10mins | Ready in:

Ingredients

- crusty Italian bread
- 3 tablespoons of grated onion
- 2 cups of mayo
- 8 tablespoons of grated parm cheese

Direction

- Mix together the mayo, cheese, and onion
- Slice the bread in half-length wise
- Spread the mixture over the bread
- Broil until bubbly (I like it almost brown)

247. Onions Au Gratin With Parmesan And Sherry Recipe

Serving: 4 | Prep: | Cook: 50mins | Ready in:

Ingredients

- 2 T. unsalted butter
- 8 c. sliced sweet onions
- 1/2 c. dry sherry or chicken broth
- 2 sprigs fresh thyme
- 2 bay leaves
- 1/2 c. shredded Parmigiano-Reggiano cheese (4 oz.)
- 1/2 c. shredded Gruyere cheese

Direction

- Preheat oven to 400 degrees F.
- Melt butter in a large cast-iron or other ovenproof skillet over medium heat. Add onions, stirring until slightly softened to make room in the pan; cover and cook until completely softened, 10 minutes.
- Add sherry, thyme, and bay leaves; increase the heat to medium-high. Sauté, uncovered, until the liquid evaporates and onions are browning, stirring occasionally, 10-15 minutes.
- Combine cheeses, the stir 1/2 cup of cheese mixture into onion mixture. Top with remaining 1/2 cup cheese and bake until cheese is bubbly and browned, about 20 minutes.
- Remove thyme sprigs and bay leaves. Let stand to cool slightly before serving.

248. Pan Grilled Bruschetta Pomodoro Recipe

Serving: 4 | Prep: | Cook: 2mins | Ready in:

Ingredients

- 1 large tomato, seeded and diced fine
- ¼ tsp lemon juice
- ½ tsp fresh thyme
- salt and pepper, to taste
- 4 small or 2 large bias-cut slices baguette bread
- 2 tsp olive oil
- 1 large clove garlic, halved

Direction

- Preheat a grill pan over high heat.
- Combine chopped tomato, lemon juice, thyme and seasoning in a small bowl, set aside.
- Lightly brush each side of the baguette slices with olive oil.
- Place slices on the grill pan and cook without moving 1 minute.

- Flip slices and cook one minute further, until toasty brown.
- Immediately rub one side of each slice with the cut side of garlic.
- Top each slice with equal amounts of the tomato mixture and serve immediately.

249. Pancetta Ricotta Roll Crostini Recipe

Serving: 12 | Prep: | Cook: 10mins | Ready in:

Ingredients

- 1 baguette (12 half inch slices)
- 1/4 cup fresh grated parmesan cheese
- 12 slices pancetta
- olive oil
- 1 large yellow onion (sliced)
- 1/2 lb ricotta
- 10 leafs fresh basil (chopped)
- 1 tbsp. unsalted butter
- salt
- pepper

Direction

- In a large skillet over medium low heat, add the butter and the onion. Salt the onions liberally. Let cook for 30 min or until the onions are a golden colour. Once they turn golden, remove the onions from heat and let cool briefly. Dice them until smaller pieces.
- While the onions are cooking, you can make the crostini. Set your broiler to high. Slice the baguette into 1/2 inch slices. Lay them out on a cookie sheet and light drizzle with olive oil. Salt, pepper and grate on the cheese. Run under your broiler for about two minutes or until the cheese is melted and the bread is golden brown. In the alternative, if you have a toaster oven you can toast them in batches.
- It's time to make the filling. In a bowl, mix together the ricotta, caramelized onion, and basil. It's important to taste. You will want to season the filling with salt and pepper, but you don't want to over salt. The key is to remember it's going to be wrapped in pancetta, which has a nice salty flavour; over salting will be like doubling the saltiness of each bite.
- Set out your pancetta. Place about a tablespoon of filling in the centre of each slice. Fold up two sides until they are about a quarter of the way in. Roll the remaining portion careful to keep the ends inside the roll. This is roughly like folding up a small burrito. Place on a plate or cookie sheet with seam side down until you are ready to cook.
- Place a large non-stick pan over medium heat. Let the pan heat up for about 1 minute. Add the rolls to the pan seam-side down. There is no need for oil because the pancetta will give off its own fat. Cook for about 2 min or until they are crisp. Using a pair of tongs to gently turn over. If they open up, don't worry. Cook on the other side for another 2 minutes or until crisp. Once cooked, remove the pan from the heat.
- The trick is transferring them now to the crostini. If the rolls didn't open, you can simply use a spatula and place them seam-side down on the crostini. If they did open, an easy technique is to press the crostino (the singular form of crostini) against the top of the roll, and then roll them over using a spatula to apply upward pressure. Once completed, serve warm. Enjoy!

250. Papas Trashy Fish Bread Recipe

Serving: 6 | Prep: | Cook: 10mins | Ready in:

Ingredients

- loaf of crusty artisian bread (we use sesame semolina)
- 1/2 stick butter
- 1 can salmon, drained

- maybe a bit of fresh ground pepper
- wedge of lemon

Direction

- Cut slits in bread.
- Insert pats of butter.
- The more butter, the merrier.
- Empty a can or two of drained salmon on top of bread.
- Heat in oven 10-15 minutes, or until the smell is really quite enough.
- Take it out!
- Serve with fresh ground pepper and a squeeze of lemon.
- And I always need extra butter.

251. Parmesan Aioli On Grilled Country Bread Recipe

Serving: 6 | Prep: | Cook: 10mins | Ready in:

Ingredients

- 3 lrg. garlic cloves
- pinch of salt
- 1 lrg. egg
- 2T. champagne vinegar
- 1c. corn oil
- 6-oz. parmigiano-Reggiano
- 2T. fresh parsley; finely chopped
- 1T. black pepper; freshly ground
- 1 loaf country bread (white & peasanty); not pre-sliced

Direction

- PREP TIME: (at least 24 hours prior to serving)
- Mince garlic cloves in a food processor.
- Add egg, salt & vinegar.
- Process mixture for a few seconds; then add oil in a very, very slow stream.
- Process until the mixture thickens to the consistency of mayonnaise.
- Transfer the aioli to a bowl & stir in the cheese, parsley & pepper.
- Cover the aioli & refrigerate for 24 hours to marry the flavours & soften the impact of the garlic.
- ASSEMBLY:
- Preheat the broiler.
- Slice bread into the piece size that you wish to serve.
- Toast or grill bread briefly on both sides.
- Slather the aioli on the grilled bread & broil until golden & bubbly. Serve immediately.

252. Pastel Recipe

Serving: 10 | Prep: | Cook: 30mins | Ready in:

Ingredients

- PASTRY
- 300 G flour
- 5 ML salt
- 30 ML VEG oil
- 15 ML CACHACA OR vodka (OPTIONAL - BUT I LIKE IT hehehehe)
- 15 ML white wine vinegar
- 125 ML water
- FILLING
- 205 G tomato & onion MIX (CAN)
- 15 ML brown sugar
- 15 ML balsamic vinegar
- 15 ML oregano, CHOPPED
- 10 ML CRUSHED garlic (DRIED) OR 1-2 cloves garlic CRUSHED
- 250 ML GRATED CHEDDAR (I USE MOZZARELLA INSTEAD)

Direction

- Mix all the pastry ingredients together
- Knewad for a minute then set aside to rest for 10 minutes
- Roll small pieces of dough into 10x10cm sized squares
- Mix all the filling ingredients together

- Top one half of each square of dough with a generous dollop of filling
- Brush edges of dough with water and fold to enclose filling
- Crimp with a fork to seal
- Heat 2cm oil in a pan and fry pastries until golden all over
- Drain on kitchen paper and serve warm
- I serve it with sweet chilli sauce most of the time
- Enjoy :)
-

253. Peach Bread Pudding Recipe

Serving: 6 | Prep: | Cook: 60mins | Ready in:

Ingredients

- 9 Rhodes Warm-N-Serv™ Soft White dinner rolls, baked and day old
- 3 eggs
- 1 1/2 cups milk
- 1/3 cup sugar
- 1 teaspoon almond extract
- 21 ounce can peach pie filling

Direction

- Cut rolls into 1/2 inch cubes.
- Place cubes in a sprayed 8-inch square baking pan.
- In a bowl, combine eggs, milk, sugar, almond extract and 1 cup peach pie filling.
- Mix well.
- Pour over roll cubes.
- Press down with a spoon to make sure all of the roll cubes are covered with egg mixture.
- If time permits, let soak for 30 minutes.
- Bake at 350°F 30-40 minutes.
- Heat remaining pie filling and serve over warm pudding.

254. Pear Walnut And Gorgonzola Bruschetta Recipe

Serving: 6 | Prep: | Cook: 15mins | Ready in:

Ingredients

- 6 slices rustic Italian bread
- 12 walnuts, finely chopped
- 6 ounces gorgonzola OR other meltable blue cheese
- 2 bosc pears
- olive oil

Direction

- Preheat oven to 425 degrees F.
- Slice the bread thinly into 1/2" thicknesses.
- Brush bread slices with olive oil.
- Place bread on a rack in a hot oven and toast until browned.
- Reduce oven temperature to 325 degrees F.
- Remove the rind from the cheese.
- Lay the toasted bread in an ovenproof dish.
- Cover bread with thinly sliced cheese.
- Garnish with walnuts.
- Put bread back into a medium hot oven until cheese melts.
- Core and cut the pears into small cubes.
- Garnish the bruschetta with pear cubes as soon as it comes from the oven.
- Serve.

255. Pecorino Romano Crostini With Apples And Fig Jam Recipe

Serving: 6 | Prep: | Cook: 15mins | Ready in:

Ingredients

- 6 dried figs, halved
- 1/2 cup simple syrup, recipe follows

- 2 tablespoons brandy
- 1/4 cup chopped toasted hazelnuts
- 24 baguette slices
- olive oil, for drizzling
- 1/2 cup grated Pecorino Romano
- 1 large apple (Granny Smith or Braeburn), thinly sliced into 24 slices
- 1/4 pound chunk Pecorino Romano, for shaving 24 pieces
- Simple syrup:
- 1/2 cup water
- 1 cup sugar

Direction

- For simple syrup: In a saucepan combine water and sugar over medium heat. Bring to a boil, reduce heat and simmer for 5 minutes, until the sugar has dissolved. Take pan off heat and cool the syrup. Any extra cooled syrup can be saved in an airtight container in the refrigerator.
- Preheat the oven to 375 degrees F.
- Place a small saucepan over medium heat. Add the figs, simple syrup, and brandy. Bring the mixture up to a simmer. Turn off the heat and let sit for 10 minutes. Place the fig mixture and the hazelnuts in a food processor and blend, pulsing a few times, until pureed. Set aside.
- Place the baguette slices on a heavy baking sheet. Drizzle with olive oil. Top each slice with 1 teaspoon grated Pecorino Romano. Bake until the bread is toasted and the cheese is melted and golden, about 7 minutes.
- Top each slice of toast with 2 teaspoons of fig jam, a slice of apple and a piece of shaved Pecorino Romano. Transfer the toasts to a serving platter and serve.

256. Pepper Crostini Recipe

Serving: 6 | Prep: | Cook: 30mins | Ready in:

Ingredients

- 1 large red pepper
- 1 large orange pepper
- 1 large yellow pepper
- 1 large green pepper
- 1 large red onion minced
- 2 large cloves of garlic minced
- 2 tsp balsamic vinegar
- salt and pepper to taste
- olive oil
- 1 large handful of fresh basil. chopped fine
- 1 day old baguette (I used ciabatta)
- fresh (very thin) sliced parmesean

Direction

- Chop peppers into small cubes
- In fry pan over medium heat fry onion in olive oil, add garlic.
- Add peppers, salt and pepper and balsamic. Stir fry till peppers are almost soft. Remove from heat and toss with basil.
- Cut baguette lengthwise.....layer pepper mixture on top and bake 10 minutes at 325 degrees... Remove from oven
- Top with shaved parmesan. Cut into slices.
- This is my youngest daughter's favourite crostini!

257. Pepperonata Sweet And Sour Peppers On Bruschetta Recipe

Serving: 8 | Prep: | Cook: 30mins | Ready in:

Ingredients

- 4 red bell peppers,seeded and small diced
- 3 Tbs EVOO
- 2 tsp salt
- 2 Tbs sugar
- 1/4 c red wine vinegar
- 1 large garlic clove,peeled
- 1 loaf rustic crusty bread

Direction

- Heat med. sized saucepan over med. heat. Add oil, peppers and salt to pan. Allow to simmer with lid for 30 mins. stirring occasionally.
- Remove lid, turn heat to high. Add sugar and vinegar and cook another 5 minutes, stirring often. Remove the peppers from heat; set aside.
- Slice bread 1/2" thick and grill or toast. While the bread is still hot, gently rub the whole peeled garlic on 1 side. Top the same side with the peperonata and its juices and serve.

258. Pepperoni Bread Recipe

Serving: 4 | Prep: | Cook: 20mins | Ready in:

Ingredients

- 1 loaf frozen bread dough
- 1 1/2 Cups mozzarella cheese (or whatever you have in the fridge)
- pepperoni
- pizza sauce
- garlic powder
- parmesan cheese
- 1 Stick butter
- *This is NOT one of those recipes that requires exact amounts of everything! Use the amount of cheese, pepperoni, etc. that you would like. It can be made with sauce or without...if making it without, use sauce for dipping. I have made it with a butter mixture instead of sauce and think it turns out better.

Direction

- Thaw and raise dough according to package directions.
- Preheat oven to 400 degrees.
- For butter mixture: melt butter in microwavable bowl, mix in desired amount of garlic powder and parmesan cheese...set aside for later.
- When dough has risen, roll in to rectangle approximately 8 x 15. This does not have to be exact - you just don't want it too thin.
- If using sauce, spread a THIN layer of sauce across the dough, keeping it away from the edges. Sprinkle small amount of garlic powder and parmesan cheese on top. OR...
- If using butter mixture, spread a THIN layer across the dough, keeping it away from the edges.
- Place pepperoni on top of sauce or butter mixture, again keeping it from the edges.
- Spread mozzarella evenly on top.
- Roll like a jelly roll: this should look like a loaf of French bread when you get done, long and skinny.
- Pinch ends and openings together so there is no way for any of the mixture to escape.
- Place on baking sheet to rise for 15-20 minutes.
- Bake on 400 degrees for 18-22 minutes or until golden brown.
- Brush with butter mixture when the bread comes out of the oven.
- Place on cooling rack to cool; it is easier to cut if it's cooled a bit.
- Cut with serrated bread knife and enjoy!

259. Perfect Bruschetta Recipe

Serving: 46 | Prep: | Cook: 30mins | Ready in:

Ingredients

- 6 roma tomatoes, seeds removed and diced
- 1 medium shallot, diced
- 10 fresh basil leaves, thinly sliced
- 1 1/8 cup balsamic vinegar
- 1 tbsp garlic salt
- 1/8 cup olive oil

Direction

- Combine all ingredients in a bowl and allow to marinade for at least 30 minutes in the refrigerator.

260. Pesto Bruschetta

Serving: 100 | Prep: | Cook: 1mins | Ready in:

Ingredients

- 1 loaf (1 pound) French bread, cut into slices
- 1 jar (7 ounces) prepared pesto
- 2 medium tomatoes, seeded and finely chopped
- 1 package (4 ounces) crumbled feta cheese

Direction

- Arrange bread slices on an ungreased baking sheet. Spread with pesto; top with tomatoes and cheese. Broil 4 in. from the heat for 3-5 minutes or until edges are lightly browned.
- Nutrition Facts
- 1 each: 93 calories, 4g fat (1g saturated fat), 4mg cholesterol, 196mg sodium, 10g carbohydrate (1g sugars, 1g fiber), 4g protein. Diabetic Exchanges: 1 fat, 1/2 starch.

261. Pita Bread With Baked Spinach Dip Recipe

Serving: 10 | Prep: | Cook: 15mins | Ready in:

Ingredients

- 12 ounces fresh spinach
- 1 tablespoon butter, Melted
- 1 clove Garlic, chopped
- 8 ounces cream cheese
- 14 0z artichoke hearts, drained and chopped
- 1/2 cup sour cream
- 1/2 cup mozzarella cheese, shredded & divided
- 1/2 teaspoon salt
- 1 package pita bread

Direction

- Wash the spinach in a large bowl or colander. Microwave on HIGH for 3 minutes or until wilted. Drain well, press between paper towels to dry. Chop spinach into medium pieces.
- Drain the artichoke hearts, chop and remove the tougher parts that don't cut up well.
- Cut the Pita Bread into small triangles. About 2 inches wide by 2 inches long.
- Melt butter in a non-stick skillet over medium-high heat. Add cream cheese and garlic, cook 3-4 minutes, stirring constantly, until cream cheese melts.
- Fold in spinach, artichokes, sour cream and 1/4 cup mozzarella cheese. Stir until cheese melts.
- Transfer mixture to a 1 qt. shallow baking dish. Sprinkle with the remaining 1/4 cup of mozzarella cheese.
- Bake at 350 degrees for 15 minutes or until hot and bubbly. Serve hot.

262. Pizza Bread Sticks Recipe

Serving: 12 | Prep: | Cook: 5mins | Ready in:

Ingredients

- 12 plain prepared bdreadsticks
- extra virgin olive oil
- Freshly shredded mozzarella cheese
- Ragu Pizza Quick (traditional)
- freshly ground black pepper
- Pam

Direction

- Arrange bread sticks on prepared baking sheet about 1-inch apart and set aside.

- Brush the tops of the breadsticks with the olive oil and the pizza sauce.
- Grind black pepper over all to taste.
- Sprinkle with mozzarella and bake about 5 minutes.
- Serve with extra sauce for dipping.
- -Susana

263. Pizza Style Cheese On Toast Recipe

Serving: 2 | Prep: | Cook: 20mins | Ready in:

Ingredients

- 120g/4oz Cheddar/Parmesan cheese mix - grated
- 1 clove Garlic - finely chopped
- ½ Onion - finely chopped
- 1 Tomato - finely chopped
- 30g/1oz cooked Ham and/or cooked crispy bacon rasher(s) - shredded
- Knob butter
- 1½tbsp medley of fresh herbs - Oregano/basil/Parsley/Thyme Leaves - finely chopped
- 2 slices Ciabatta/Chapata bread

Direction

- Mix all ingredients together in a bowl;
- Toast bread on both sides;
- Spread cheese/ham/bacon mixture on toasted slices, making sure toast is completely covered;
- Place under grill until cheese bubbles and browns slightly;
- Serve.

264. Pizza Whirls Recipe

Serving: 0 | Prep: | Cook: 40mins | Ready in:

Ingredients

- 2 packets of pizza base mix
- Tomato puree
- Mixed herbs
- Toppings of your choice
- Grated cheese

Direction

- Make up the pizza base mix (or use half a small packet of bread mix) to make a firm dough which is not sticky, or make a bread dough using around 250g of flour.
- Knead and leave to rise for around 30-60 minutes.
- Roll out onto a floured board until you have a rectangle of around 20cm by 30cm.
- Spread 2-3 tbsp of tomato puree over the dough (but leaving the top and bottom 2cm free of toppings)
- Sprinkle with mixed herbs and add toppings of your choice (chopped mushrooms, onion, peppers, ham, salami, sweetcorn etc.) and then top with grated cheese.
- Roll the pizza up tightly (long ways), to make a sort of pizza Swiss roll!
- Stick the outside edge down with a little water if needed.
- Cut with a sharp knife into 2cm slices and place on a greased baking tray, leaving a 1-2cm gap between each one.
- Leave to rise for a further 10 minutes.
- Cook at 200 C/Gas 6 for around 10-15 mins, or until they are lightly browned.

265. Polenta Bruschetta With Tomato Caper Sauce Recipe

Serving: 6 | Prep: | Cook: 15mins | Ready in:

Ingredients

- 1/3 cup chopped onion
- 1 clove minced garlic

- 1 tablespoon olive oil
- one 14-ounce can Italian-type tomatoes, finely cut up
- 2 tablespoons tomato paste
- 1 tablespoon snipped fresh basil
- 1 tablespoon drained capers
- 1 tube prepared polenta
- italian seasoning, grated parmesan or romano cheese to taste (optional)

Direction

- For the TOMATO-CAPER SAUCE: Cook the chopped onion and minced garlic in hot olive oil in a medium saucepan. Carefully stir in the tomatoes and the tomato paste. Bring mixture to a boil. Reduce heat; simmer, uncovered, about 10 minutes or until desired consistency. Stir in 1 tablespoon snipped fresh basil and 1 tablespoon drained capers. This can be done up to 2 days ahead; prepare sauce, cover, and chill. To serve, reheat in a saucepan.
- Slice polenta (not too thin or it will fall apart). Place on baking sheet and bake in 350 degree oven for 5 minutes. Turnover and sprinkle with some Italian seasoning, garlic salt and parmesan or Romano cheese, as desired. Bake for 5-10 minutes more or until golden. (You can run it under the broiler for a minute or two if you want/need to.)
- Arrange on platter and put warm tomato-caper sauce in the middle so people can help themselves just like a bruschetta.

266. Pomegranate Pistachio Crostini

Serving: 4 | Prep: | Cook: 10mins | Ready in:

Ingredients

- 36 slices French bread baguette (1/4 inch thick)
- 1 tablespoon butter, melted
- 4 ounces cream cheese, softened
- 2 tablespoons orange juice
- 1 tablespoon honey
- 1 cup pomegranate seeds
- 1/2 cup finely chopped pistachios
- 2 ounces dark chocolate candy bar, grated

Direction

- Preheat oven to 400°. Arrange bread slices on an ungreased baking sheet; brush tops with butter. Bake until lightly toasted, 4-6 minutes. Remove from pan to a wire rack to cool.
- Beat cream cheese, orange juice and honey until blended; spread over toasts. Top with remaining ingredients.
- Nutrition Facts
- 1 appetizer: 44 calories, 3g fat (1g saturated fat), 5mg cholesterol, 46mg sodium, 5g carbohydrate (2g sugars, 0 fiber), 1g protein.

267. Pomodoro Fresco Sourdough Bruschetta Recipe

Serving: 4 | Prep: | Cook: | Ready in:

Ingredients

- Ingredients
- 1 (12 to 16-inch) sourdough baguette
- 2 garlic cloves, halved plus 1 tablespoon minced garlic
- 5 tablespoons extra-virgin olive oil
- 1/4 cup grated parmigiano-Reggiano, plus more for garnish
- 2 cups diced roma tomatoes
- 1/3 cup thinly sliced fresh basil leaves, plus more for garnish
- 2 tablespoons balsamic vinegar
- 1/2 teaspoon sea salt
- 1 teaspoon freshly ground black pepper

Direction

- Directions
- Preheat the oven to 350 degrees F.

- Cut the baguette in half lengthwise, place on a sheet tray and bake in the oven until lightly brown. Rub with the garlic cloves. Drizzle with 2 ounces of the olive oil and sprinkle with the Parmigiano-Reggiano. Return to oven to melt cheese.
- In a medium mixing bowl, add the tomatoes, minced garlic, basil, vinegar, remaining olive oil, salt and pepper. Mix thoroughly and let sit for 5 minutes at room temperature.
- Remove baguette from oven and top with the tomato mixture. Garnish with basil and Parmigiano-Reggiano.

268. Poor Mans Crab Canapes Recipe

Serving: 6 | Prep: | Cook: 5mins | Ready in:

Ingredients

- 1/4 lb. bacon, cooked and chopped
- 5 oz. jar of Old English cheese spread
- 1/2 t garlic powder
- 1/2 t Lawry's seasoning salt
- 1/2 t Miracle Whip
- 6 oz. canned crab meat
- 6 English muffins, halved

Direction

- Mix all ingredients together and spread on English muffin halves. Place muffins and spread in the freezer for one half hour. Place on broiling pan/baking sheet and broil to desired doneness, about 5 minutes. Cut into wedges and serve.
- You can also toast the English muffin halves in the toaster on the "bagel" setting, then spread on the mixture and bake in a 400 degree oven for about 12 minutes. Be careful; topping is really hot.

269. Pork Tenderloin And Goat Cheese Crostini Recipe

Serving: 24 | Prep: | Cook: 5mins | Ready in:

Ingredients

- 1 loaf french baguette, sliced 1/4 inch thick
- extra virgin olive oil
- 2 cloves garlic, cut in half
- 1 package herbed goat cheese
- 24 thinly sliced pieces of roasted pork tenderloin

Direction

- Preheat broiler and position top rack on second highest height.
- Evenly arrange slices of bread on a cookie sheet.
- Drizzle olive oil on each slice.
- Place bread under broiler, and keep watch for them to turn golden brown, 3-4 minutes.
- Remove, flip pieces, drizzle with olive oil again, and place back under broiler for about 2 minutes. Watch carefully so they don't burn.
- Remove, and rub each piece of bread with the cut side of the garlic. Allow bread to cool for about 10 minutes.
- Spread goat cheese on each slice of bread and top with pork tenderloin. Serve immediately.

270. Port Wine And Sesame Biscuits Recipe

Serving: 24 | Prep: | Cook: 2hours | Ready in:

Ingredients

- 1/2 cup port wine
- 1/3 cup fruity, rich olive oil
- 1/2 cup sugar
- 2 tsp lemon zest
- 1/2 tsp anise or fennel seed
- 1 1/4 cups flour

- 1/2 tsp baking soda
- 1/4 tsp salt
- 2/3 cup sesame seeds

Direction

- In a bowl, combine wine, oil, sugar, lemon zest and anise, mixing well.
- Stir in the flour, baking soda, salt and sesame seeds.
- Cover and chill for at least 1 hour.
- Preheat the oven to 350F and line two sheets with parchment.
- Scoop tablespoons of dough onto the sheets and bake the cookies (while the dough is still cold) for 13-14 minutes, rotating the sheets halfway through baking.

271. Portobello Mushroom And Bread Appetizer Recipe

Serving: 2 | Prep: | Cook: 5mins | Ready in:

Ingredients

- 1 10-ounce pkg of baby mushrooms
- Extra virgin olive to taste
- Dijon mustard to taste
- Fresh minced garlic to taste
- salt and pepper to taste
- 2 large slices from a round rustic white bread toasted
- extra virgin olive oil
- fresh chopped parsley for garnish

Direction

- In a large skillet with a few tbsp. of extra virgin olive oil, sauté sliced Portobello mushrooms until tender.
- Add the garlic and a few tbsp. of Dijon mustard to taste.
- Season with a bit of salt (mustard is salty too) and fresh grated black pepper.
- Cover and set aside.
- Take two long slices of fresh homemade white bread and toast slices in toaster oven or oven.
- Liberally cover with the mushrooms and any liquid.
- Drizzle over the olive oil and add some chopped parsley.
- Cut each piece of bread into two so you will have 4 appetizer pieces.
- Garnish with fresh chopped parsley.
- Serve immediately.
- Serves 2 to 4.
- If desired one may sprinkle on some fresh grated Romano cheese.
- Note: I like to use a Rosemary White bread as the bread for this recipe

272. Primanti Brothers Sliders Recipe

Serving: 0 | Prep: | Cook: 15mins | Ready in:

Ingredients

- 1 1lb loaf handmade Italian bread, sliced into about 1/2 inch slices(YOU don't have to make it, but you'll find this in a bakery section, not the Wonder Bread section)
- 1 1/2lb deli pastrami or corned beef
- 6oz sandwich sliced provolone cheese
- about 1/2pt cherry(not grape) tomatoes
- about 1/2 bag Waffle style french fries(pieces are okay, but you just need the equivalent of 1 fry per sandwich :), baked per package directions
- Your favorite cole slaw...but not overly sweet. My quick version follows!
- mayo
- For Cole Slaw
- 1 bag preshredded cole slaw mix
- 1/2 bottle Poppyseed dressing
- about an extra t or 2 of red wine vinegar
- dash of cayenne
- dash of celery powder(crushed seed)
- fresh ground black pepper

- *you will have left over cole slaw

Direction

- Prepare coleslaw by combining all ingredients and let rest in fridge while preparing the rest of the ingredients, then assemble shortly before serving.
- Slice bread through the middle of the all of the slices.
- If needed, slice meat pieces in half so that they create about a 3X1 piece.
- Cut cheese slices into 4 equal pieces (I used round, and they sat so perfectly on the bread. The nearly OCD portion of my brain LOVED this fact. ;)
- Slice tomatoes into adorable slices. I got 3 out of each tomato, I think . :)
- To Stack Sandwiches
- I suggest using bread pieces on the SAME side of the loaf as each other. In other words, don't use it's "mate" on the opposite side of the cut, because they may not be as symmetrical, since this should be a hand shaped loaf.
- Now, lay what will be your bottom pieces down on a large surface, then take its "top" and lay it down in front of its matching piece.
- Assemble by folding a piece of meat to fit the bread.
- Top with a piece of cheese.
- Add a piece, or pieces of waffle fry
- Top with a drained T full of coleslaw
- Top with a couple adorable slices of tomato
- Spread about 1t mayo on the inside of the upper piece of bread, and add it to the top!
- You can serve with toothpicks down the middle, if you want, but I didn't bother. They actually held together much better than I anticipated. They aren't difficult to eat, but you still get the threat, and occasional drip of coleslaw dressing....so, a perfect mini version of the original! :)
- Serve with dill pickles.
- *these are fine at room temperature!

273. Pro Bowl Bread Recipe

Serving: 0 | Prep: | Cook: 20mins | Ready in:

Ingredients

- 1 1lb loaf Italian bread, sliced in half, then each piece horizontally
- 8oz cream cheese, softened
- 2-4T butter, softened
- 1/4 cup mayonnaise
- 2t dried dill weed
- dash of hot sauce
- 2t Dijon or brown mustard
- 1/4 cup chopped green olives
- 1 clove garlic, minced fine
- 1lb boneless ham steaks, cubed in 1/2 inch cubes
- 6oz sliced muenster cheese
- 2 medium tomatoes, sliced
- 1/2 can pineapple tidbits, drained well
- 1 large red onion, sliced thin
- 1/2 cup shredded cheese(I used pepperjack and cojack)

Direction

- In medium bowl, combine cream cheese, butter, mayo, dill, hot sauce, mustard, green olives and garlic.
- Spread evenly over cut sides of all pieces of bread.
- Top with slices of cheese.
- Add ham and pineapple pieces, then onion slices and tomato slices.
- Sprinkle with shredded cheese.
- Bake at 400 for about 12-15 min until edges of bread are crusty and golden brown and cheese is melted.

274. Proscuitto Balsamic Crostini Appetizer Recipe

Serving: 2 | Prep: | Cook: 10mins | Ready in:

Ingredients

- Stick bread or Baguette
- Fig Jam
- Goat cheese (soft)
- Prosciutto - thin sliced
- Balsamic Glaze
- Fresh basil leaves

Direction

- Slice bread on an angle. Can be lightly toasted or not.
- Let cool if toasting.
- Spread bread with Fig Jam, then some sliced Goat Cheese, a piece of Prosciutto, drizzle with Balsamic Glaze, then top with a fresh Basil leaf.
- Enjoy!

275. Provolone Tomato Bruschetta Recipe

Serving: 6 | Prep: | Cook: 10mins | Ready in:

Ingredients

- 12 pieces of bread, sliced into bite size pieces.
- 2 tomatoes, sliced
- 1/3 cup of olive oil
- seasonings-I use oregano, italian seasoning, garden mix
- 12 slices provolone cheese
- 6 sage leaves, optional

Direction

- Preheat oven to 350
- Mix seasonings with olive oil
- Place bread onto pan and lightly cover with oil mixture
- Top with slice of cheese and tomato
- Lightly cover with more oil
- If want to sprinkle chopped sage leaves on top
- Bake for about 10 minutes, or until cheese melts

276. Pull Apart Cheese Bubble Bread Recipe

Serving: 20 | Prep: | Cook: 30mins | Ready in:

Ingredients

- 2 loaves (or bags) frozen bread dough, thawed
- 32 (half-inch) cubes mild cheddar cheese
- 1 stick butter, melted (can substitute margarine)
- 1/2 cup parmesan
- 1 tsp oregano
- 1/2 tsp garlic salt
- 1 tsp parsley flakes

Direction

- Melt a stick of butter in a small bowl, add parmesan, oregano, garlic salt, and parsley.
- Cut thawed bread dough into 32 equal pieces
- Wrap each piece of dough around 1 cube of cheese, dip in butter mixture.
- Place in a greased Bundt pan.
- Let rise 1 1/2 hours
- Bake at 350 for 30 minutes.

277. Pumpernickel Bread Dip Recipe

Serving: 10 | Prep: | Cook: 10mins | Ready in:

Ingredients

- 1 cup mayo
- 2 cups sour cream
- 1 envelope vegetable soup mix
- 1 teaspoon tarragon
- 1 teaspoon fresh chopped dill weed (optional)

- 2 tablespoons, pickle juice
- 1 can water chestnuts, chopped
- 1 1/2 packages of frozen spinach (drained and chopped)
- 3 green onions, chopped
- 1/2 cup chopped red peppers
- 2 loaves pumpernickel bread

Direction

- Mix mayo, sour cream, tarragon, pickle juice, dill weed (optional) and soup mix.
- Stir in water chestnuts, onions and red peppers.
- Squeeze extra water out of spinach (note: since the recipe calls for 1 1/2 packages of frozen spinach, cut through the second package while still frozen with a serrated knife, so you can put it back in the freezer to save for something else). Stir spinach into mixture.
- Cut the top off one loaf of bread, and slice down around the edge (almost to the bottom) scoop out the middle to form a big bowl. Place the dip in the bowl and cut the remaining bread into cubes for dipping.

278. Pumpernickle Bread Dip Recipe

Serving: 10 | Prep: | Cook: | Ready in:

Ingredients

- 1 whole round unsliced soft bread such as pumpernickle, corn rye, rye etc.
- 1 pint sour cream
- 1 pint mayonaisse
- 3 tsp dried dill weed
- 3 tsp beau monde seasoning (try not to substitute for best results)
- 3 tbs chopped parsley
- 6 tbs diced sweet onion (red or white)

Direction

- Mix dip ingredients together and let chill several hours to blend flavours.
- When ready to serve cut out top of bread and hollow out insides
- .Place dip inside of bread bowl.
- Place on platter surrounded by pieces of the soft torn bread.

279. Put The Shamalama In Your Ding Dong Bruschetta Recipe

Serving: 6 | Prep: | Cook: | Ready in:

Ingredients

- 6 med sized tomatoes
- 1 sweet onion
- 1 bunch fresh oregano
- 1 bunch fresh basil
- 1 lemon
- 1 heaping tablespoon of minced garlic
- 1 1/2 cups crumbled feta cheese
- 3-4 tablespoons of extra virgin olive oil
- pepper

Direction

- Finely dice tomatoes and onions and put in bowl
- Add minced garlic
- Finely chop basil and oregano
- Add to tomatoes and onions mix well
- Add Olive oil and the juice of the lemon and mix well
- Add crumbled Feta and pepper to taste
- Let stand for 10 minutes
- Serve on crusty baguette or toasted garlic bread
- Enjoy!
- To kick it up a notch add hot sauce

280. Quick Fix Focaccia Wedges Recipe

Serving: 0 | Prep: | Cook: 1hours | Ready in:

Ingredients

- 2 small onions, thinly sliced
- 1/4 tsp coarsely ground pepper
- 1 Tbs olive oil
- 3/4 cup rinsed and drained canned white beans
- 1/2 cup dry white wine or reduced-sodium chicken broth
- 1 tsp dried thyme, crushed
- 4 pieces focaccia, each about 4"X6"
- red sweet pepper (optional)
- fresh marjoram (optional)

Direction

- Cook and stir onion and pepper in hot oil in a skillet over medium-high heat, uncovered, for 7 minutes or until onion turns brown. Remove from heat; set aside.
- Add beans to skillet; cook 2 minutes, swirling the skillet to brown the beans.
- Add wine or broth and thyme; reduce heat and simmer, uncovered, 3 to 4 minutes or until liquid is reduced by half. Mash beans slightly. Set aside.
- Cut each piece of focaccia in half horizontally; for 8 pieces. Spread bread with bean mixture; top with onion; place on a baking sheet.
- Bake in a 450°F oven for 8 to 10 minutes.
- Cut each piece of bread into triangles; making 16 portions. Garnish with red pepper and marjoram, if desired.
- Wine to go with: Gewurztraminer, Pinot Grigio, Riesling, or surprisingly, a 14 Hands 'Hot to Trot'

281. Rainbow Tomato Bruschetta Recipe

Serving: 4 | Prep: | Cook: 5mins | Ready in:

Ingredients

- Red cherry tomatoes
- orange cherry tomatoes
- Yellow cherry tomatoes
- basil
- salt
- pepper
- 1 clove garlic, cut
- 4 slices French bread
- olive oil
- parmesan cheese

Direction

- Quarter the cherry tomatoes.
- Throw them in a bowl with the basil (chiffonade if fresh).
- Salt and pepper to taste.
- Let the tomatoes sit for about 10 minutes.
- Meanwhile, drizzle olive oil on the bread, then toast.
- Cut the garlic clove in half, and rub the bread with it.
- Spread the tomato mixture on the bread, making sure that the juice from the bottom of the bowl makes it onto the bread.
- Top with a bit of grated parmesan.
- Broil for about 3-5 minutes.
- Devour.

282. Raspberry Pistachio Blossoms Recipe

Serving: 6 | Prep: | Cook: 35mins | Ready in:

Ingredients

- 6 Rhodes Texas™ rolls or 12 Rhodes™ dinner rolls, thawed but still cold

- 1 egg white, lightly beaten
- 1/2 cup finely chopped pistachios
- 6 tablespoons raspberry preserves
- 1 cup powdered sugar
- 2-3 tablespoons orange juice
- 1 tablespoon butter, melted
- 1/2 teaspoon vanilla extract

Direction

- Spray counter lightly with non-stick cooking spray.
- Flatten each Texas roll or 2 dinner rolls combined into a 3-inch circle.
- Place on a large sprayed baking sheet and brush tops of rolls with egg white.
- Cover with sprayed plastic wrap and let rise until double in size.
- Place pistachios on a plate.
- Remove wrap and dip rolls, top side down in pistachios, patting gently to adhere.
- Return rolls to baking sheet.
- With scissors or knife, make 5, 3/4-inch deep, cuts evenly around outside edge of each roll to resemble flower petals.
- With fingertips, make indentation in centre of each roll.
- Spoon 1 tablespoon preserves into each indentation.
- Bake at 350°F 18-20 minutes.
- Remove from baking sheet and cool completely on wire rack.
- Combine all remaining ingredients until smooth and drizzle over cooled rolls.

283. Red Bell Pepper Crostini Recipe

Serving: 4 | Prep: | Cook: 5mins | Ready in:

Ingredients

- Recipe from executive chef David Holben
- olive oil for brushing on peppers
- 2 red bell peppers
- 1 teaspoon fresh chopped thyme
- 2 tablespoons pure olive oil
- salt and pepper to taste
- 8 slices French bread, 1/2 inch thick
- 1 clove garlic, peeled
- 6 sprigs fresh thyme

Direction

- Brush olive oil on peppers and place on a sheet pan under broiler and cook for a few minutes, until somewhat black and blistered, turning frequently. Put in a bowl and cover with plastic wrap for 10 minutes. Uncover and remove skin, core, and seeds. Cut into strips 1/4 inch wide and toss with chopped thyme, olive oil, and salt and pepper.
- While shrimp and zucchini are broiling, rub slices of French bread with garlic clove and toast until crisp. To serve, place 2 pieces of bread on a plate, top with peppers, and arrange a skewer of shrimp alongside. Garnish with sprigs of thyme. Serves 4.

284. Red And Yellow Tomato Crostini With Baby Greens Recipe

Serving: 4 | Prep: | Cook: 20mins | Ready in:

Ingredients

- # 2 Yellow vine ripe tomatoes - thinly sliced
- # 4 bocconcini - thinly sliced
- # 2 oz tapenade 4 nice slices of baguette
- # 2 tablespoons olive oil
- # baby greens
- # balsamic vinaigrette

Direction

- 1. Pat olive oil evenly on the bread slices and toast in oven or under broiler until golden brown.
- 2. Spread tapenade on top of toasted bread.

3. Alternate layers of bocconcini and tomato on each toast piece starting with the red tomatoes, then bocconcini, then yellow tomatoes and finish with a layer of bocconcini.
4. Place the completed toasts on a baking sheet and warm in a pre-heated 350 degree oven.
5. Serve crostini with greens dressed with vinaigrette.

285. Ricotta And Roasted Tomato Crostini Recipe

Serving: 24 | Prep: | Cook: 25mins | Ready in:

Ingredients

- 7-8 plum tomatoes
- 2 tbsp olive oil
- ½ tsp ground black pepper
- ¼ tsp salt
- 1-2 baguettes
- 2 cups ricotta
- 3 tsp balsamic vinegar
- 1/3 cup chopped fresh basil

Direction

- Preheat oven to 400°F. Line baking sheets with parchment paper, or lightly grease.
- Slice tomatoes crosswise into ¼" rounds.
- In bowl, toss together tomatoes, oil, pepper and salt.
- Place in single layer on prepared baking sheets. Bake in centre of oven for 15 minutes. Set aside.
- Turn oven to BROIL.
- Cut baguettes into ½" slices, cutting at an angle.
- Place on a wire rack set over a baking sheet. Broil 6-7 minutes, flipping slices ½ way through.
- Spread each toast with some ricotta. Top with a tomato slice, a drizzle of vinegar, and a pinch of basil.

286. Ricotta Pea Crostini Recipe

Serving: 2 | Prep: | Cook: 2mins | Ready in:

Ingredients

- 1 cup petit pois/peas (defrosted if frozen)
- 3 tablespoons ricotta cheese
- lemon zest (see note)
- 1-2 teaspoons olive oil
- salt and pepper
- toasted slices of baguette
- Parmesan shavings or shards

Direction

- In a small pot of boiling salted water, blanch the peas. Cook until tender, approximately 1 to 2 minutes (depending on their size). Once cooked, remove peas to a bowl of ice water to stop the cooking process and set their colour.
- In a mortar and pestle, or a small food processor, mash the peas to form a coarse paste. Stir in the ricotta and lemon zest and enough olive oil to reach the desired consistency. Season to taste with salt and freshly ground black pepper.
- To serve, mound purée onto slices of freshly toasted baguette and garnish with parmesan cheese.

287. Roasted Pepper Tomato Crostini Recipe

Serving: 0 | Prep: | Cook: 12mins | Ready in:

Ingredients

- 18 slices Italian bread,1/2 inch thick
- 2 large tomatoes,diced(2 cups)
- 1 jar roasted red bell peppers, drained and chopped

- 1/4 cup chopped fresh basil leaves
- 1 tablespoon balsamic vinegar
- 1/4 teaspoon salt
- 1/3 cup shredded mozzarella cheese

Direction

- Heat oven to 375
- Place bread on cookie sheet bake for 5 min or until toasted
- Mix tomatoes, bell peppers, basil, vinegar and salt
- Spread tomato mix on bread
- Top each slice with about 1 teaspoon cheese
- Bake for 5 min or until cheese is melted...serve hot.

288. Roasted Red Pepper And Bocconcini Bruschetta Recipe

Serving: 6 | Prep: | Cook: 30mins | Ready in:

Ingredients

- Topping:
- 3 large sweet red peppers
- 1/4 cup chopped fresh basil
- 1 tbsp. olive oil
- 1 tsp. balsamic vinegar
- 1 large clove garlic, minced
- 2 tsp. dry leaf oregano
- 1/2 tsp. salt
- 1/4 tsp. fresh ground pepper
- 5 oz. bocconcini cheese
- 2 tbsp. toasted pine nuts
- Bruschetta:
- 12 slices Focaccia
- 2 tbsp. olive oil

Direction

- Halve peppers, seed and grill (tastes best grilled on the BBQ) until tender and juicy. Slice into strips and place in bowl. Stir in basil, oil, vinegar, garlic, oregano, salt and pepper until well mixed.
- Dice cheese, (there should be about 1 cup). Stir cheese and pine nuts into red pepper mixture.
- When ready to serve, preheat broiler. Rub Focaccia on both cut sides with olive oil. Toast each side 2-3 minutes or until browned. Top each slice with some of the pepper mixture, pressing gently to secure atop the focaccia.
- Return to broiler for 2-3 minutes or until topping is hot and cheese is melted. Transfer to a platter and serve immediately. Enjoy!

289. Roasted Red Pepper Bruschetta Recipe

Serving: 5 | Prep: | Cook: 30mins | Ready in:

Ingredients

- 1 large can roasted red peppers, diced very small (can add hot roasted red peppers)
- 1/8 cup water from can, reserved
- garlic, chopped
- salt to taste
- Italian herbs
- Crushed red pepper
- olive oil

Direction

- Mix ingredients into an oven-safe bowl (I use Pyrex)
- Put into fridge overnight, to help constitute flavours
- Bake for 30 minutes at about 350 F
- Enjoy with Pita, Pita chips, homemade bread, semolina, or fresh veggies!

290. Rob And Ninas Ultimate Bruschetta Recipe

Serving: 4 | Prep: | Cook: 10mins | Ready in:

Ingredients

- 6 beefsteak tomatoes
- 1/3 plus 1/4 cup extra virgin olive oil
- 1/4 cup balsamic vinegar
- 1/4 cup red wine vinegar
- 2 plus 1 teaspoon chopped garlic
- 2 tablespoons chopped fresh basil
- salt & pepper
- 1 (12-inch) loaf crusty Italian bread, cut into 3/4 inch slices
- 1/2 cup julienned roasted red peppers
- 6 kalamata olives
- 1/4 cup shaved parmigiano-reggiano cheese

Direction

- Prepare the tomatoes by coring them and scoring the top with an X. To blanch the tomatoes, place them in boiling water for 1 minute and then immediately transferring them to an ice bath.
- Peel off the skins of the tomatoes, remove the seeds and dice them into 3/4 inch pieces.
- In a medium bowl, toss the tomatoes, 1/3 cup olive oil, balsamic vinegar, red wine vinegar, 1 tablespoon garlic, basil and salt and pepper to taste.
- Marinate in the refrigerator for 1/2 an hour.
- In a small bowl, combine the remaining olive oil and garlic. Brush the slices of bread with this mixture and toast or grill them. Just prior to serving, warm the bread slices in the oven.
- Place the tomato mixture in the centre of a large round platter. Arrange the bread slices around the tomatoes and garnish with roasted red peppers and olives. Sprinkle the Parmigiano-Reggiano on top of the tomatoes and serve.

291. Rye Bread Bowl Dip Recipe

Serving: 6 | Prep: | Cook: | Ready in:

Ingredients

- 1 Can ripe pitted olives
- 1 1/3 cups sour cream
- 1 1/3 cups mayonnaise
- 2 tablespoons onion flakes
- 2 tablespoons parsley flakes
- 2 teaspoons dill weed
- 1 round loaf rye bread (or marble or pumpernickel)

Direction

- Put olives through a blender and strain
- In a mixing bowl, combine sour cream, mayonnaise, onion flakes, parsley flakes, and dill.
- Mix together until blended
- Add drained olives.
- Mix together
- Refrigerate, covered, at least 24 hours before serving
- Pour mixture into a hollowed out loaf of round rye bread and surround with cut bread cubes from loaf (top and centre of).
- Can also serve with carrot and celery sticks

292. Salmon And Cous Cous Rolls With A Spicy Cream Cheese Dip. Recipe

Serving: 6 | Prep: | Cook: 10mins | Ready in:

Ingredients

- salmon rolls
- 2 cup of soaked cous cous
- 80g chopped walnuts
- juice of a lemon
- 1 red pepper

- 1 onion
- Some ginger
- 2 cloves of garlic
- 6 strips of smoked salmon
- Dip
- 3 tbsp of low fat Philadelphia cream cheese
- 1 tsp of crushed ginger
- 1 tsp of garlic powder
- 2 tsp of chilli powder
- 2 tbsp of lemon juice
- 1 tbsp of balsamic vinegar
- 1 tbsp of ground black pepper
- Pinch of salt.

Direction

- Salmon rolls
- Soak the couscous as directed on packet.
- Chop onions, garlic, peppers, walnuts, and ginger finely.
- Mix chopped vegetables and walnuts into couscous.
- Place a spoonful of mix into each of the salmon strips.
- Roll the salmon up and keep in place with a cocktail stick
- Drizzle with lemon juice.
- Dip
- Put all ingredients in a bowl and mix until combined

293. Salsa Dip In Bread Bowl Recipe

Serving: 6 | Prep: | Cook: 75mins | Ready in:

Ingredients

- 4 oz sour cream
- 8 oz cream cheese, softened
- 12 oz cheddar cheese
- 16 oz salsa (medium)
- bread bowl -- i get a large sourdough or pumpernickel, leave out the day before to get a little stale, and it softens in the oven while baking
- Tostitos or favorite brand of scoops or gold chips

Direction

- Preheat oven to 350 degrees
- Mix with mixer the sour cream and cream cheese.
- Hand mix in the cheddar and salsa
- Hollow out bread bowl well -- it fills to top
- Bake 1 hour uncovered -- it gets a crusty top -- mix up a bit then put back in oven for 15 more minutes
- Good out of oven or at room temperature

294. Sausage Bread Recipe

Serving: 6 | Prep: | Cook: 40mins | Ready in:

Ingredients

- 12 oz. bulk pork sausage
- 1/2 c chopped green pepper
- 1/2 c chopped celery
- 1 garlic clove,minced
- 1 pkg (3oz) cream cheese,cubed
- 2 Tbs chopped scallion tops(optional)
- 2 Tbs miced,fresh parsley
- 2 tubes (8oz) refrigerated crescent rolls
- 1 egg,slightly beaten

Direction

- In skillet, cook sausage, green pepper, celery, and garlic till meat is no longer pink and vegetables are tender. Drain juices, add cream cheese, green onion tops and parsley. Cook and stir over low heat until cream cheese is melted. Set aside.
- Unroll crescent dough on greased baking sheet. Press perforations together. Roll into a 12" by 10" rectangle. Spoon sausage mixture to

within 3" of the long side and 1" of top and bottom.
- Starting at one end, fold alternating strips at an angle, forming a braid. Brush dough with egg.
- Bake at 350 degrees for 20-25 mins or till golden brown. Refrigerate leftovers.
- You can do a vegetarian one with broccoli, mushroom or asparagus.

295. Sausage Bruschetta Recipe

Serving: 25 | Prep: | Cook: 15mins | Ready in:

Ingredients

- 6 hot sausage, raw, diced as small as you can cut, Buy your favourite sausage.
- 1 large baguette, cut in rounds
- 3 cloves of roasted garlic, mashed or diced
- 1/2 bunch green onion, finely diced
- 2 tbsp olive oil
- 1 roasted red pepper, finely diced
- 1 tbsp red wine vinegar
- salt and pepper to taste
- 1 sprig Fresh thyme
- 2 tomato, large, finely diced
- 1 cup red wine
- 1 pint fresh or frozen raspberries
- 1 tsp Chipotle paste
- Fresh Parmesan or pecorino cheese

Direction

- Dice all your vegetables and sausage.
- Heat a pot with oil at medium high temperature,
- Add sausage and brown, always stirring the meat for about 5 minutes.
- Add garlic and all veg. Sautee for 2 minutes.
- Add vinegar, chipotle, red wine, thyme, salt and pepper, raspberries, reduce the heat and simmer for 5 minutes.

- Add tomatoes and simmer for another 2 minutes.
- Brush your cut baguette rounds with oil, flavoured oil if you have any and place in the oven till they are toasted golden brown.
- Once the baguette is toasted, top them liberally with the mix and then grate fresh cheese on top.
- BON APPETIT!

296. Savory Bruschetta Tart Recipe

Serving: 12 | Prep: | Cook: 120mins | Ready in:

Ingredients

- For the tart:
- ¼ cup olive oil
- peanut oil for deep-frying
- 2 cups peeled egglant, cut into ¾" dice (about 1 medium)
- Finely ground sea salt
- 1 cup all-purpose flour
- 8 ¼"-thick round slices of country bread (my no-knead bread works well for this, or if you're in Anchorage, Europa Bakery's Spent Grain Bread is good too)
- 8 cups cubed bread (½" cubes)
- 1 cup zucchini, cut into ½" dice (about 2 small)
- ½ cup fresh parmesan cheese, grated
- 1 tablespoon chopped basil
- 1 tablespoon chopped oregano
- 1½ teaspoons minced garlic
- 1 teaspoon red pepper flakes
- 3 cups marinara sauce (recipe follows)
- 2 large egg yolks, beaten
- 1 cup heavy cream
- For the marinara:
- 3 tablespoons olive oil
- ¾ cup minced onion
- 1½ tablespoons minced parsley
- 2 cloves minced garlic

- 2-28oz cans of whole tomatoes or 4½lbs fresh peeled and seeded roma tomatoes, ground or pureed
- 2 large basil sprigs, leaves removed (reserve for another use)
- 1½ teaspoons salt
- A pinch of sugar or baking soda

Direction

- For the marinara:
- In a large pan, heat the olive oil over medium heat. Add the onion and sauté until translucent, about 8 minutes. Add the parsley and garlic and cook briefly to release their fragrance.
- Add the tomato puree, basil stem, and salt and simmer briskly, stirring occasionally so nothing sticks, until the mixture reaches a sauce like consistency. If the sauce thickens before the flavours develop, add a little water and keep cooking.
- Taste and adjust the seasonings. If the sauce taste too acidic, add the baking soda and cook for 5 minutes more. If it needs a touch of sweetness, add the sugar and cook for five minutes longer. Remove the basil stem before serving.
- For the tart:
- Preheat the oven to 300°F. Brush two 9-10" round cake pans or springform pans with 2 tablespoons olive oil each.
- Pour the peanut oil to a depth of at least 3 inches into a deep fryer or a heavy 8" deep stockpot. While the oil is heating toss the eggplant with a little salt in a bowl. Then add the flour to the eggplant and toss to coat evenly. Remove the eggplant from the bowl, lightly patting off the excess flour.
- Working in 2 batches, add the eggplant to the hot oil and fry until light brown, about 2 minutes. Use a slotted spoon to transfer to paper towels to drain.
- Cover the bottom of each prepared cake pan with 4 bread slices. It is okay if there are spaces between the slices. In a large bowl, combine the eggplant, cubed bread, zucchini, cheese, basil, oregano, garlic, red pepper flakes, 1 cup of the marinara, egg yolks, and cream and mix well. Add 1 teaspoon salt and ¼ teaspoon pepper and mix again. Divide the mixture evenly between the 2 pans, packing it lightly and making sure there are no large gaps in the pan.
- Cover the pans with aluminum foil and bake for 1 hour. Raise the oven temperature to 375°F, remove the foil, and continue baking until the top is medium brown, about 15-20 minutes longer. Remove from the oven, place on racks, and let rest for 15 minutes. While the tarts are resting, gently heat the remaining 2 cups marinara until hot.
- Run a knife around the inside edge of 1 pan to loosen the sides of the tart, invert a serving plate over the pan, invert the pan and plate together, and lift off the pan. Repeat with the second tart. Cut into wedges with a serrated knife and serve immediately. Pass the hot tomato sauce at the table.

297. Savoury Parmesan Shortbread Snacks Recipe

Serving: 10 | Prep: | Cook: 30mins | Ready in:

Ingredients

- • 1/2 cup (125 mL) butter, softened
- • 3 tbsp (45 mL) Club House Parmesan & Herbs One Step Seasoning
- • 2 tsp (10 mL) granulated sugar
- • 1 1/2 cups (375 mL) all-purpose flour

Direction

- 1. Combine all ingredients in mixing bowl with wooden spoon then mix with hands to form a smooth dough. Shape into ¾" (2cm) balls. Place on ungreased baking sheet. Press down with a floured fork.
- 2. Bake at 375°F (190°C) for 12 to 18 minutes or until golden around edges. Cool completely.

- Tips
- • Store in an airtight container for up to 5 days or freeze for up to a month.
- • These can also be served warm. To reheat, warm in a 350°F (180°C) oven for about 5 minutes.
- More recipes are available online at flavour.ca.

298. Seafood Bread Bowl Dip Recipe

Serving: 16 | Prep: | Cook: 120mins | Ready in:

Ingredients

- 32 ounces cream cheese, softened
- 1 pound small cooked salad shrimp
- 4 green onions, thinly sliced
- 1 teaspoon garlic salt
- 1 teaspoon ground black pepper
- cayenne pepper to taste
- 1/4 cup sweet onion, minced
- 1/3 cup mayonnaise
- 1 tablespoon lemon juice
- 1 (10 to 12 inch) round loaf crusty bread, unsliced
- 1 egg, beaten

Direction

- Cut a 2 inch slice from top of bread.
- Hallow out bread, leaving a 1/2 inch thick shell.
- Brush inside of bread with beaten egg.
- Bake at 300 degrees until dry.
- Combine remaining ingredients.
- Fill bread shell with cream cheese mixture.
- Replace top and wrap in a double layer of foil. Place on rimmed baking sheet.
- Bake at 300 degrees for 2 hours.
- Unwrap, place on serving platter and surround with bread cubes for dipping.

299. Serrano Ham With Crusty Bread And Tomatoes Recipe

Serving: 12 | Prep: | Cook: 120mins | Ready in:

Ingredients

- 12 plum tomatoes
- 4 tablespoons garlic oil, divided
- 2 teaspoons dried oregano
- 3/4 teaspoon kosher salt
- 1 whole-grain baguette, cut into 24 slices, or 12 pieces whole-grain bread, cut in half
- 6 ounces thinly sliced Serrano ham (about 24 slices; see Note)
- note
- Serrano ham is full-flavored, savory dry-cured ham made from specific breeds of white pigs. It is traditionally enjoyed very thinly sliced, like its Italian cousin prosciutto
- Notes: garlic oil is oil that has been infused with fresh garlic. We like to use it for salad dressings, as dipping oil with crusty bread, in marinades or to simply drizzle over steamed vegetables

Direction

- 1. To prepare tomatoes: Preheat oven to 300°F. Coat a large rimmed baking sheet with cooking spray.
- 2. Cut tomatoes in half lengthwise and place on the prepared baking sheet. Sprinkle each half with some oil, some oregano and salt. Roast for 2 hours. When cool enough to handle, coarsely chop the tomatoes and transfer (with juices) to a serving bowl.
- 3. To serve tapas: Shortly before serving, preheat oven to 350°F.
- 4. Place bread on a baking sheet and brush with some of the remaining garlic oil. Bake until slightly crispy, but not hard, 2 to 4 minutes per side. Let cool slightly. To serve, arrange the bread on a large platter with ham and the bowl of tomato mixture for spreading.

300. Sheepherders Bread Dip Recipe

Serving: 1012 | Prep: | Cook: 60mins | Ready in:

Ingredients

- 8oz package cream cheese
- 16 oz sour cream
- 1 cup grated cheddar cheese
- 4 chopped green onions
- 1-2 tbsp worchestershire sauce
- 2.5 oz chopped dried beef
- 1/4 to 1/2 tsp garlic powder
- dash cayenne pepper
- loaf of unsliced sheepherders bread

Direction

- Combine all ingredients except bread in a bowl and mix well
- Hollow out bread to make a bowl
- Transfer dip into bread bowl
- Cover bread bowl with foil
- Bake in pre-heated 300 degree oven for 1 hour
- Serve with cubed sheepherder's bread

301. Shiitake Ragout On Chevre Crostini Recipe

Serving: 8 | Prep: | Cook: 20mins | Ready in:

Ingredients

- For the Crostini: ----------
- 8 thin slices baguette
- 1 Tbsp butter, melted
- sea salt, to taste
- 4 ounces soft chèvre
- For the Ragout: ----------
- 2 Tbsp extra virgin olive oil
- 1 tsp finely chopped garlic
- 1 Tbsp finely chopped shallots
- 4 tsp chopped fresh thyme, divided
- 2 cups shiitake mushrooms, julienned
- sea salt, to taste
- ground pepper, to taste
- 1Tbsp sherry vinegar
- 1/4 cup sherry wine
- 1/2 tsp cornstarch
- 1Tbsp crème fraiche

Direction

- For the Crostini: ----------
- Preheat oven to 350°F.
- Brush baguette slices lightly with butter.
- Bake until toasted and lightly browned, 4 to 5 minutes per side.
- Lightly season with salt and spread with chevre.
- For the Ragout: ------------
- Heat olive oil in a sauté pan over medium heat. Add garlic and shallot and cook until translucent, 1 to 2 minutes. Do not let the garlic brown.
- Add half the thyme and all of the mushrooms.
- Season with salt and pepper.
- Let the mushrooms cook over medium-high heat without excessive stirring so they will brown.
- Once mushrooms are browned and tender, 5 to 7 minutes, add sherry vinegar and reduce until the pan is dry.
- Combine the cornstarch in the sherry wine until dissolved and add to the pan.
- Cook until reduced and there is almost no liquid left in the pan. Remove from heat and stir in crème fraiche.
- Taste and adjust seasoning with salt and pepper.
- Place a tablespoon of ragout on each crostini and spread to cover the entire toast.
- Garnish with remaining chopped thyme and serve warm.

302. Shrimp Bread Recipe

Serving: 24 | Prep: | Cook: 12mins |Ready in:

Ingredients

- 8 oz sour cream
- 1 pkg. ranch dressing mix
- 1/2 cup parmesan cheese
- 3 tablespoons mayo
- diced jalapeno (as many as you would like)
- 1 can tiny shrimp (can use fresh crabmeat also)
- shredded mozzarella cheese
- French bread

Direction

- Slice bread, I use the small loaves if they have it, if not I cut the big slices in half. Mix all ingredients except mozzarella cheese. Spoon mixture on bread then bake 350 until bread has browned. Then add mozzarella to top and broil until cheese has melted. Watch carefully & enjoy.

303. Shrimp Canapes Recipe

Serving: 20 | Prep: | Cook: 10mins |Ready in:

Ingredients

- 10 slices white or wheat bread
- 2 tblsp. butter, melted
- 1/2 tsp. dried thyme leaves
- 12 oz. cooked shrimp,chopped, or minis from a can are cute
- 1/2 c. cojack cheese, finely shredded
- 1/3 c. real mayo
- salt to taste

Direction

- Preheat the broiler
- Trim the crusts from the bread, then cut into 20 shapes, 2 in. round cookie cutter, triangles, etc...
- Tear enough of the bread trimmings into fine crumbs to measure 1/2 c., set aside
- Mix butter and thyme, brush evenly onto the bread cut-outs, place in a single layer on an ungreased baking sheet
- Broil about 2 min. or until golden brown
- Mix together bread crumbs, shrimp, cheese, mayo and salt
- Spoon onto toasted cut-outs
- Broil another 8-10 minutes or until hot and bubbly

304. Skinny Minis Bruschetta Recipe

Serving: 8 | Prep: | Cook: 10mins |Ready in:

Ingredients

- • 16 Piller's Skinny Bites Minis, halved lengthwise
- • 3 ripe tomatoes, diced
- • 60 ml (1/3 cup) red onion, finely chopped
- • 30 ml (1 Tbs.) olive oil
- • 6 basil leaves, chopped
- • salt and pepper to taste
- • 16 crostini toasts
- • 60 ml (1/3 cup) shaved Parmesan, if desired

Direction

- In a medium bowl mix the tomatoes, garlic, onion, and olive oil. Season to taste with salt and pepper. Gently stir in basil leaves. Arrange crostini toasts on a platter. Use a slotted spoon to evenly divide tomato mixture on each toast. Top each with two halves of Minis. If desired, top with shaved Parmesan. Serve immediately.

305. Spam Melt With French Turkish Bread Recipe

Serving: 8 | Prep: | Cook: 15mins | Ready in:

Ingredients

- 3 egg yolks
- 1 tsp Dijon mustard
- 1 tbsp lemon juice
- freshly ground (!) white pepper and salt to taste
- 1 c olive oil
- 1 tbsp white sine vinegar
- 1/2 c grated (white) cheddar cheese
- 60g Spam, chopped
- French bread sliced

Direction

- First, make the topping: beat the egg yolks, mustard, lemon juice, pepper and salt until mixture begins to thicken. Add olive oil gradually, drizzles at a time, while stirring to let the mixture emulsify. After all the oil is added in the mixture, fold in vinegar. Blend grated cheese and SPAM into the mixture.
- Spread evenly on French bread slice, toast until cheese melts. Serve hot.

306. Spanish Crostini Recipe

Serving: 20 | Prep: | Cook: 5mins | Ready in:

Ingredients

- 1 baguette, sliced thin 1/8 in, on the bias
- 5-10 plum tomato caviar, depending on quality and size
- 1/2 lb manchego cheese
- 1 head garlic
- A Bottle of good quality spanish olive oil

Direction

- Preheat oven to 300 degrees.
- Place each crostini on a sheet pan and dehydrate in the oven, do not toast.
- Lay crostini out to cool.
- Take a clove of garlic and rub it all over each piece of crostini.
- Lightly drizzle with olive oil...Spanish.
- Lay the caviar onto the crostini.
- Microplane enough Manchego to lightly coat the crostini.
- Consume and Experience the flavours and textures.

307. Spanish Olive And Cream Cheese Canapes Recipe

Serving: 40 | Prep: | Cook: 10mins | Ready in:

Ingredients

- 10 slices firm white sandwich bread
- 1 1/2 tablespoons unsalted butter, melted (I like olive oil or a combo of the two)
- 1 oz parmigiano-Reggiano
- 6 oz cream cheese, softened (3/4 cup)
- 1/3 cup pimiento-stuffed green Spanish olives (3 oz), rinsed, drained, and finely chopped
- 1/4 cup finely chopped scallion
- 1/4 cup finely chopped red bell pepper (I like to sub in a chile with heat...jalapenos, serranos...whatever suits you)
- 1/4 teaspoon sweet paprika
- 2 teaspoons medium-dry sherry
- ~~~~
- Optional:
- This recipe works great as written. However, you can play with ingredient list in a number of ways. I have added chicken, crabmeat, shrimp...switched up the cheeses and breads...have fun with it!

Direction

- Put oven rack in middle position and preheat oven to 375°F.

- Cut 40 rounds from bread slices with cutter, then brush 1 side of each round with butter/olive oil and bake on a large baking sheet until pale golden, about 8 minutes. (Leave toasts on baking sheet.)
- Preheat broiler.
- Finely grate (I use a microplane) the Parmigiano-Reggiano (you will have about 1 cup).
- Mash together cream cheese, olives, scallion, bell pepper, paprika, and Sherry until combined well, then top each toast with 1 teaspoon cream cheese mixture and sprinkle with Parmigiano-Reggiano.
- Broil canapés about 4 inches from heat until Parmigiano-Reggiano begins to turn golden, about 1 minute.
- ~~~~
- ~ Toasts can be made 1 day ahead and cooled completely, then kept in an airtight container at room temperature.
- ~ Cream cheese mixture can be made 1 day ahead and chilled, covered. Bring to room temperature before using.

308. Spanner Crab And Corn Quesadilla Recipe

Serving: 8 | Prep: | Cook: 45mins | Ready in:

Ingredients

- 1/4 long red chilli, finely chopped
- 1/4 garlic clove, finely chopped
- 80g spanner crab meat
- 40g corn kernels
- 2 tbs baby coriander sprigs
- 2 flour tortillas
- 1/2 cup manchego cheese, coarsely grated
- For the tomato sauce :
- 1/4 cup extra virgin olive oil
- 1 clove garlic, thinly sliced
- 6 peeled roma tomatoes
- 1/4 cup basil leaves
- For the Salad :
- 6 cherry tomatoes, halved
- 1/4 red onion, diced
- 2 tbs baby coriander sprigs
- 1 tbs extra virgin olive oil
- 1/2 lemon, juiced

Direction

- Preheat oven to 220C.
- For the tomato sauce, heat oil in a saucepan over medium heat. Add garlic and sauté until golden. Add the tomatoes and cook for 2-3 minutes, breaking tomatoes up with a spoon. Add the basil and season to taste. Pulse the mixture in a food processor until coarsely pureed. Set aside.
- Combine the chilli, garlic, crab, corn and baby coriander in a bowl. Season to taste. Place the tortillas on a clean work surface and spread lightly with some tomato sauce. Top one of the tortillas with the crab mixture, cheese, and then remaining tortilla.
- Heat a large, non-stick, oven-proof frying pan over medium heat. Carefully slide the quesadilla into the hot pan and fry for 2 minutes each side. Transfer the pan to the oven for 4-5 minutes.
- For the salad, combine the cherry tomatoes, red onion and baby coriander in a bowl. Drizzle with olive oil, squeeze over lemon juice, and season well with salt and pepper. Toss to combine.
- Slice the quesadilla into 8 wedges and serve with the salad.

309. Spice And Garlic Bread Recipe

Serving: 8 | Prep: | Cook: 12mins | Ready in:

Ingredients

- 1 cup olive oil (or extra-virgin)
- 3 garlic cloves, diced

- 1 large loaf Italian/French bread
- dried oregano
- dried basil

Direction

- Obtain a cookie sheet or a baking dish that is large enough to house the bread. Lay a sheet of aluminum foil large enough to wrap around the bread after prep is done.
- Prepare the bread by cutting 1-inch thick pieces but do not cut to the very end. Place the bread to the center of the aluminum sheet.
- Dice your garlic cloves and place into bowl filled with the cup of olive oil. Using a typical spoon, spoon some of this garlic-oil mixture and pour it in between the spaces of the bread pieces. Make sure to coat the side of each piece. Coat all around the bread, too, making sure to get the sides and especially top (DON'T worry about the bottom!). Preheat your oven to 350°F.
- Sprinkle the dried oregano and dried basil over the loaf. You may use any of your favorite dry spices on the loaf, or a specific spice you think may complement your main course. Wrap the aluminum foil around the loaf. Place into the oven for 10-12 minutes. Enjoy!

310. Spicy Caprese Toasts Recipe

Serving: 0 | Prep: | Cook: 20mins | Ready in:

Ingredients

- 1lb loaf French bread cut into 12 "rounds"
- 12 fresh mozzarella medalions
- 12 medium fresh basil leaves
- 12 slices smallish tomatoes
- 1 red onion sliced thinnly into half or quarter rings to fit the bread rounds
- chili infused olive oil
- balsamic vinegar

Direction

- Drizzle bread rounds with olive oil.
- Toast in a 400 oven for about 5 minutes until just starting to dry.
- Remove from oven and add a medallion of cheese, top with a basil leave, a slice of tomato and a couple slices of red onion.
- Drizzle with balsamic vinegar and return to oven for another 5-7 minutes or so, until cheese is starting to melt.

311. Spinach Artichoke Crab Dip Served In A Bread Bowl Recipe

Serving: 8 | Prep: | Cook: 20mins | Ready in:

Ingredients

- 1 10oz package frozen spinach, thawed and chopped fine
- 1 8oz package cream cheese, softened
- 1 6 to 7oz jar marinated artichoke hearts, chopped fine
- 1/2 lb backfin lump blue crab meat, picked thru for shells and broken up into smaller bits
- 1/2 teaspoon Green Tobasco sauce
- 1/2 teaspoon Old Bay Seasoning
- 1 6 to 8" sized round loaf of bread
- 1/4 cup shredded mozzarella cheese
- 2 tbsp. extra virgin olive oil

Direction

- Preheat oven to 350F
- Toss artichoke hearts, spinach and crab meat in a mixing bowl.
- Fold in cream cheese, Old Bay and Green Tabasco
- Cut round loaf of bread into a bowl large enough to fit 3/4 of the dip into it, by cutting a "lid" from the top.
- With a pastry brush, spread the olive oil all over the inside and outside of the bowl and

- place in the over on a cookie sheet for 5 minutes until the inside gets a little crusty.
- Remove from oven and fill with the crab dip, letting it pile up over the top of the bowl.
- Place back in oven and cook for 10 minutes, then sprinkle the shredded Mozzarella on top and put back in oven until melted, but not browned (if you want it browned, add the mozzarella before baking the crab dip, otherwise the bread will end up too hard)
- Remove from oven, place on serving plate.

- Spoon mixture evenly on both halves of bread
- Sprinkle with cheddar cheese and place in oven
- Bake at 350 for 10 minutes or until cheese is melted and lightly brown.
- *you can place under broiler if you want a darker brown bread.
- Remove from heat and allow to set 1 to 2 minutes.
- Cut into serving slices or wedges

312. Spinach Bread Recipe

Serving: 8 | Prep: | Cook: 10mins | Ready in:

Ingredients

- 1 loaf French bread or Italian bread, cut in half lengthwise
- 1 lb spinach, fresh is best but if your using frozen, defrost under cold water and drain well (remove all moisture)
- 1 onion, chopped
- 1 pound mushrooms, sliced
- 1 stick butter
- 8 oz. cream cheese
- 4 to 5 cloves garlic, minced
- 1 tablespoon creole spice
- salt and cracked black pepper to taste
- dash of hot sauce
- 8 oz. Italian blend shredded cheese
- shredded cheddar cheese (optional)

Direction

- Preheat oven to 350 degrees.
- Place bread on baking pan,
- In large skillet, cook onions, garlic, and mushrooms in butter until tender (about 3 minutes)
- Add spinach, cream cheese and spices including hot sauce and continue to cook for 2 minutes.
- Stir in Italian cheese

313. Spinach French Bread Dip Recipe

Serving: 12 | Prep: | Cook: | Ready in:

Ingredients

- 1 Large Loaf French bread
- 1 Package Chopped frozen spinach
- 1 1/2 Cups sour cream
- 1 Cup mayonnaise
- 1 Package Knorr vegetable soup mix (Knorr is the best soup mix for this recipe)
- 1 Can water chestnuts
- 3 green onions

Direction

- Slice French bread
- Drain Spinach well and Chop
- Slice chestnuts
- Slice Green Onions, using both the white and green parts
- Mix all ingredients together
- Refrigerate at least 12 hours
- Serve with sliced French bread

314. Spinach Shrimp Bread Recipe

Serving: 4 | Prep: | Cook: 15mins | Ready in:

Ingredients

- 1 Box of frozen chopped spinach
- 3-4 artichoke hearts, chopped
- 1 cup of Shredded Mozzarella
- Shredded Parmesan
- 1 lb cooked shrimp, peeled, deveined
- salt, pepper and garlic powder to taste
- Loaf of French bread, split, buttered and seasoned with garlic (sometimes you can find this prepared in the bakery/deli at the grocery store)

Direction

- Preheat oven to about 400 degrees. This could vary, if using prepared garlic bread then you may want to follow the directions on the bag. No need to over think this, it's basically toast!
- Thaw frozen spinach by running cold water over in in a colander. Break it up with your hands while it thaws. Squeeze the water out of the spinach and put in a large mixing bowl. Add artichoke, half of each of the cheeses, shrimp and seasonings. Stir ingredients together.
- Open up the bread onto a cookie sheet or heavy foil. Top with spinach mixture. Top with the remaining cheeses. Bake till the cheese starts to get toasty around the edges.

315. Spinach And Feta Bruschetta Recipe

Serving: 8 | Prep: | Cook: 5mins | Ready in:

Ingredients

- 1 1/2 cups crumbled feta cheese
- 2 10 oz. pkgs. frozen chopped spinach, thawed, drained and squeezed dry
- 1/2 onion, finely chopped
- 1 clove garlic, finely chopped
- 4 roma tomatoes, chopped
- 1/2 cup mayonnaise
- 1/2 cup sour cream
- 1 loaf French bread, sliced diagonally into 3/4 inch thick slices

Direction

- In mixing bowl, combine all ingredients except bread
- Spoon onto bread and broil until crispy and browned

316. Stuffed Bread Italian Appetizer Recipe

Serving: 16 | Prep: | Cook: 25mins | Ready in:

Ingredients

- 1 tablespoon butter, melted
- 1 teaspoon finely chopped fresh garlic
- 1 (1-pound) loaf frozen bread dough, thawed
- 1/4 pound thinly sliced deli genoa salami
- 6 (1-ounce) slices provolone cheese, cut into strips
- 1/4 cup sliced stuffed green olives
- 2 green onions, sliced
- 1 egg, beaten
- 1 teaspoon water
- Poppy seed, if desired

Direction

- Stir together butter and garlic in small bowl.
- Roll out bread dough on lightly floured surface to 12-inch square. Place on lightly greased baking sheet; brush with butter mixture.
- Layer salami, cheese, olives and onions in 3-inch strip down centre of dough to within 1/2-inch of top and bottom, leaving 4 1/2 inches of dough on each side of filling.
- Cut twelve 3-inch long strips, 1-inch apart, along both sides of filling. Fold strips across filling at an angle, alternating sides to give a braided effect.

- Pinch dough at bottom and top to seal.
- Cover; let rise in warm place until almost double in size (30 to 45 minutes).
- Combine egg and water in small bowl; brush over braid.
- Sprinkle with poppy seed, if desired.
- Heat oven to 350°F. Bake for 25 to 35 minutes or until golden brown. Remove from baking sheet; cool 10 minutes.
- Cut into slices.

317. Stuffed Bread Jalapeno, Cheese And Bacon Recipe

Serving: 0 | Prep: | Cook: 30mins | Ready in:

Ingredients

- 2 1lb balls of bread dough(or use 2 frozen or "tubed" versions of a loaf style bread)
- 8oz-12oz colby, cheddar or pepper jack cheese, shredded
- 1/2lb bacon cooked crisp and crumbled
- 2-6 jalapeno peppers, sliced(seeded, if desired, OR, you can use the jarred variety)

Direction

- Roll bread dough to form 2 rectangles, about 16X12 (this is approx. :)
- Place them on large sheet pans (sprayed with no cook spray) or baking stones
- On one half (a short half) of each of the dough rectangles, add cheese, peppers and bacon, evenly between the two. Reserve a little of the bacon and cheese, if desired, to sprinkle over the top.
- Carefully fold the dough over the goodies on the other side and pinch edges together well, to seal.
- Add the extra cheese and bacon over the top.
- Bake at about 400 for 20 minutes or so (follow instructions on packaging if using a purchased dough) until golden brown and heated through.

- Let cool briefly.
- Using a sharp knife, cut into the dough to create "strips"

318. Stuffed French Bread Recipe

Serving: 6 | Prep: | Cook: 25mins | Ready in:

Ingredients

- 1 loaf French bread
- 2 cups diced cooked chicken
- 1 cup mayonaise
- 2 cups grated Jack cheese
- 1/2 cup onion, chopped
- 1/2 cup mushrooms, chopped
- 1/2 cup green pepper
- 1 tsp. garlic powder
- 1 tsp. pepper

Direction

- Preheat oven to 350 degrees.
- Slice bread lengthwise.
- Hollow out.
- Combine chicken, 1 1/2 cups cheese, mayonnaise, mushrooms, onion, green pepper, garlic and pepper.
- Stuff bread.
- Sprinkle with remaining cheese on top.
- Bake for 25 minutes.

319. Stuffed Mexi Pizza Towers W.avocado Jalapeno Crema Recipe

Serving: 0 | Prep: | Cook: 30mins | Ready in:

Ingredients

- 3-4 large flour tortillas

- 1 large white onion- finely diced
- 1-2 (depending on size) red/green bell peppers- finely diced
- 2-3 cloves garlic- crushed and minced
- * 1 tbsp cumin seeds
- * 2 tbsp fresh lemon juice
- * 1 tbsp (or to taste) cayenne pepper
- * coarse black pepper- few grinds (be generous)
- * salt- to taste
- * 1/2 tbsp onion powder
- * 1/2 tbsp garlic powder
- * 1/2 tbsp paprika
- * 2 roma tomatos- seeded and finely diced
- * 1 bunch cilantro- washed and finely chopped
- * 1/2 tbsp extra virgin olive oil
- * PAM olive oil Flavor
- * 1 cup reduced-fat shredded mexican cheese
- * avocado-Jalepeno Crema (RECIPE BELOW)
- * Smokey refried beans (RECIPE BELOW)
- * curled lemon peels- garnishing (optional)
- For remaining: Click Here: http://wp.me/p15gh6-dJ

Direction

- 1. In a medium-sized skillet spray with a little PAM and pour olive oil and set over medium-high flame. Add cumin seeds and toast for 30 seconds or so then add onions and garlic. Sauté for about 2 minutes, then add the bell peppers. Add all the seasonings, including salt and pepper. Sauté for about 5-6 minutes because the vegetables should be soft and flavored well. Taste for salt and seasonings.
- 2. While the vegetables are cooking, use the cookie cutter to cut out round tortilla disks. 3-4 large tortillas should make about 30-32 disks. Place on a baking sheet in a toaster oven, and toast for about 5 minutes, just until they're slightly golden colour and crispy.
- 3. To assemble, place a layer of crispy tortilla disks on a serving dish and pile about 1-2 tbsp. of bean mixture. Spread evenly, but not too much near the edge of the disk. Top with about 1 tbsp. vegetable mixture and cheese (more or less depending on how much you like!).
- Place another disk on top and press down slightly- you don't want the mixture to be oozing out! Drizzle on avocado-jalapeno crema and garnish with chopped tomatoes, cilantro and lemon peel. To add a festive and greener touch, I sliced fresh jalapenos and layered them on the serving dish- just in case anyone wants an extra spicy kick!

320. Summer Bruschetta Recipe

Serving: 2030 | Prep: | Cook: 10mins | Ready in:

Ingredients

- 1 French bread baguette
- 6 roma tomatoes
- 2 TBSP. minced red onion
- ½ - 1 tsp. minced garlic, to taste (if you can find minced roasted garlic, it is delicious)
- 1 tsp. dried minced basil, or if using fresh, use 1 TBSP.
- Dash salt
- Dash black pepper
- 1 TBSP. balsamic vinegar
- 2 TBSP. extra-virgin olive oil, plus more for brushing bread slices
- parmesan cheese, optional

Direction

- Set oven to broil.
- Slice bread into ¼ inch thick rounds. Brush each side lightly with olive oil and place on cookie sheet. Broil until golden brown, turn slices over and brown on opposite side. Remove from oven and cool.
- Chop tomatoes into a ¼ inch dice, add onion, garlic, basil, salt, and pepper. Toss together, add vinegar and oil and stir.
- Top cooled bread slices with tomato mixture. Top bruschetta with a few pieces of grated

parmesan or a parmesan curl, if using. Serve immediately.

- *These are delicious served at room-temperature, but the tomato mixture is equally good chilled before being placed on the bread. Great with good wine (or a cold beer!)

321. Summer Brushcetta Bread Recipe

Serving: 0 | Prep: | Cook: 2hours | Ready in:

Ingredients

- 12 heirloom tomatoes (any nice ripe ones will do)
- 1 clove garlic (minced)
- sea salt
- fresh black pepper
- high quality olive oil
- 1 whole wheat baguette (day old) sliced length wise
- as much fresh basil as you like (I like lots)
- fresh parmigiano Regiano

Direction

- Slice tomatoes in half then the halves in quarters
- Add garlic, salt and pepper to taste and drizzle with olive oil
- Mix to coat and spread on a large cookie sheet
- Cook in oven at 225 degrees for 2 hours or until caramelized
- Remove from oven
- Take baguette lengths and spread basil on top (I love basil so I use a lot)
- Layer still warm tomatoes on top of basil leaves
- Heat in low oven …about 225 for 20 minutes
- Remove from oven
- Take a potato peeler and grate cheese in slices (again be generous)
- Drizzle with olive oil
- Salt and pepper to taste.

- Cut into fairly thick pieces
- I sometimes grill the bread first if we are barbecuing….adds a nice flavour!

322. Summer Heirloom Tomato Bruschetta Recipe

Serving: 8 | Prep: | Cook: 10mins | Ready in:

Ingredients

- assorted heirloom tomatoes, chopped
- green bell pepper, peeled and diced
- fresh basil, hand torn
- quality extra virgin olive oil
- quality balsamic vinegar
- kosher salt and fresh ground black pepper
- 1 fresh baguette

Direction

- 1. Brush bread slices with olive oil. Toast the slices of bread on both sides under the broiler or on a barbecue. Rub them all over with the garlic while they are still hot.
- 2. Mix tomatoes with bell pepper and basil. Season with salt and pepper, and drizzle with olive oil and balsamic. Let them marinate in the fridge for a while.
- 3. Top grilled bread with tomato mixture and serve the bruschetta immediately.

323. Sweet Bacon Crackers Recipe

Serving: 0 | Prep: | Cook: 1hours5mins | Ready in:

Ingredients

- 36 buttery crackers
- 12 slices bacon, cut into thirds
- 12 tablespoons light brown sugar

Direction

- 1. Preheat the oven to 120 degrees C. Line two rimmed cookie sheets with aluminum foil.
- 2. Arrange crackers on the prepared cookie sheets in a single layer. Place a piece of bacon on top of each cracker, then put about a teaspoon of brown sugar on top of the bacon.
- 3. Bake in the preheated oven until bacon is browned and crackers and bacon are glazed, about 45 minutes. Drain on paper towels before serving.

324. Sweet Grape Bruschetta Recipe

Serving: 0 | Prep: | Cook: 30mins | Ready in:

Ingredients

- 1 loaf French bread or baguette
- 1 cup red grapes, quartered
- 1 small yellow onion, diced
- 1 handful raw almonds, chopped
- 1/2 cup fresh parmesan
- olive oil
- salt & pepper
- fresh parsley, chopped

Direction

- Preheat oven to 475 degrees Fahrenheit. Line baking sheets with aluminum foil, set aside.
- Slice baguette thinly, and arrange on baking sheets. Brush liberally with olive oil, and bake for 6 minutes. Remove from oven and set aside.
- In a sauté pan, heat olive oil. When hot, add onion, grapes, and almonds. Season with salt & pepper.
- Spoon a small amount of the grape mixture onto each piece of bread. Sprinkle with parmesan. Bake for 7-10 more minutes, until bread is golden and crispy.
- Serve garnished with fresh parsley.

325. Taste Of Italy Bread Dip Recipe

Serving: 8 | Prep: | Cook: 5mins | Ready in:

Ingredients

- 1 tablespoon dried oregano
- 1 tablespoon dried basil
- 1 tablespoon dried rosemary
- 1/2 teaspoon dried thyme
- 1 tablespoon cracked red pepper
- 1 tablespoon granulated garlic or garlic powder
- 1 tablespoon fresh ground black pepper
- 1 teaspoon salt
- 1 cup + 2 tablespoons extra virgin olive oil
- 3 medium or large cloves garlic, minced
- Crusty Italian or French bread

Direction

- Mix all the herbs together and grind. Use a mortar and pestle for best results.
- For individual servings, divide the herb mixture between 8 shallow dipping bowls.
- In a small skillet, add the oil and heat. Add the garlic and stir, heating for 30 seconds to 1 minute. You don't want the garlic browned, you just want to flavour the oil.
- Remove from heat.
- Ladle 2-3 tablespoons over each individual serving bowl with the herbs. Give a quick stir.
- Serve with crusty Italian or French bread.
- If making one dish for dipping, just put the herbs in the dish and pour the oil over top the herbs.

326. Thai Curry Chicken Salad In Phyllo Cups Recipe

Serving: 0 | Prep: | Cook: 17mins | Ready in:

Ingredients

- 3 boxes purchased mini phyllo cups (45 cups)
- 1/4 cup mayonnaise
- 2 Tbs plain yogurt
- 2 Tbs honey
- juice of 1/2 a lime
- 8 ounces cooked chicken, diced
- 1/2 cup red bell pepper seeded and diced
- 1/4 cup fresh pineapple, diced
- 2 Tbs red onion, diced
- 1 Tbs cilantro, minced
- 2 Tbs slivered almonds
- 2 tsp vegetable oil
- 1 Tbs fresh ginger, minced
- 1/2 tsp Thai red curry paste or chili garlic sauce
- fresh cilantro leaves for garnish

Direction

- Preheat oven to 350°; arrange phyllo cups on a baking sheet. Toast cups in oven until golden, 5 to 8 minutes; set aside to cool.
- Combine mayonnaise, yogurt, honey, and lime juice in a bowl. Add the chicken, bell pepper, pineapple, onion, and cilantro; set aside.
- Sauté almonds in oil in a non-stick skillet over medium heat until golden, stirring often. Add ginger and curry paste and cook until fragrant, about 30 seconds; stir almond mixture into chicken salad until blended. Fill each cup with chicken salad and garnish with a leaf of cilantro.

327. Thick, Buttery Soft Pretzels Recipe

Serving: 10 | Prep: | Cook: 90mins | Ready in:

Ingredients

- 4 teaspoons active dry yeast
- 1 teaspoon white sugar
- 1 1/4 cups warm water
- 5 cups all-purpose flour
- 1/2 cup white sugar
- 1 1/2 teaspoons salt
- 1 tablespoon vegetable oil
- 3 tbs warm water
- 1/2 cup baking soda
- 4 cups hot water
- kosher salt, for topping
- melted butter

Direction

- - In a small bowl, dissolve yeast and 1 teaspoon sugar in warm water. Let stand about 10 minutes.
- - In a large bowl, mix together flour, 1/2 cup sugar, and salt. Make a well in the centre; add the oil and yeast mixture. Mix and form into a dough.
- All the remaining 3 tbsp. warm water and knead the dough until smooth, about 7 to 8 minutes.
- Lightly oil a large bowl, place the dough in the bowl and turn to coat with oil. Cover with plastic wrap and let rise in a warm place until doubled in size, about 1 hour. -- I think it works best to cover the bowl was a wet, warm dish towel and place the bowl in the over (off) with only the light on to keep it warm.
- Preheat oven to 450 degrees F.
- Dissolve baking soda in water over very low heat in a large pot.
- When risen, turn dough out onto a lightly floured surface and divide into 10-12 equal pieces.
- Roll each piece into a rope and twist into a pretzel shape.

- Once all of the dough is all shaped, dip each pretzel into the baking soda solution and place on a greased baking sheet. Sprinkle with kosher salt.
- Bake in preheated oven for 8 minutes, until browned.
- While pretzels are baking melt 1/4 c butter.
- As soon as pretzels are done- brush generously with melted butter and sprinkle with salt.
- Best eating right away!

328. Tia Rosies Football Bread Recipe

Serving: 610 | Prep: | Cook: 20mins | Ready in:

Ingredients

- 1 large soft French bread loaf
- 1 whole pack of bacon, chopped cooked and drained on paper towels
- 2 green onions chopped(about 2 heaping handfulls
- 3 cups of shredded cheese (cheddar/monterey)
- 1 cup of mayo
- pepper to taste
- softened butter

Direction

- Preheat oven to 375 degrees
- Cut French bread in half lengthwise. Spread lightly with softened butter, (lightly), when bacon has cooled completely add all ingredients to bowl except mayo. Toss together, add enough mayo to bring all ingredients together. Add pepper. Pile on the cut side of French bread. Place in oven and bake until top is melted and bubbly and bread has crisped a bit. Serve hot or at room temp

329. Toasted Mushroom Bread Recipe

Serving: 6 | Prep: | Cook: 25mins | Ready in:

Ingredients

- 1 large round loaf bread (Sourdough/Pumpernickel,etc.)
- 1/2 cup margarine
- 5 cups thinly sliced mushrooms
- 2 cups shredded mozzarella cheese
- 8 green onions, finely chopped
- 3 cloves garlic, minced

Direction

- Slice bread in half horizontally. With fingers, pull out about one-third of the soft bread, reserving for another use if you wish.
- In bowl mix margarine together with the mushrooms, cheese, onions and garlic.
- Spread on both cut sides of bread and place, cut side up, on baking sheet.
- Bake in a 400F oven for 20-30 minutes or until crisp on the outside and the cheese is hot and melted.
- Cut each piece of bread into 6 wedges.
- Enjoy!

330. Toasted Seasoned French Bread For Appetizers Recipe

Serving: 10 | Prep: | Cook: 20mins | Ready in:

Ingredients

- 1 loaf day-old Fench bread or baguette (if you live somewhere you can get good puffy, airy, po-boy bread, use that)
- olive oil
- garlic powder
- 2 cookie sheets

Direction

- Cut the bread into 1/2 inch slices and lay out in a single layer on cookie sheets. (If using wider French bread, cut the slices in half to make smaller pieces.)
- Preheat the oven to 350 degrees.
- Using a brush or oil mister, lightly coat both aides of the bread with olive oil. Do not saturate the bread, it just need to be a little damp.
- Lightly sprinkle garlic powder on both sides of the bread.
- Bake for 5 to 10 minutes, or until lightly browned,
- Serve fresh, or place in an airtight container/bag overnight.

331. Tomato And Ricotta Bruschetta Recipe

Serving: 0 | Prep: | Cook: 17mins | Ready in:

Ingredients

- French bread
- tomato, diced
- garlic, diced
- ricotta cheese
- olive oil
- parsley
- Ground peppercorns

Direction

- Preheat the oven to 425 degrees F
- Slice the French bread at an angle. I make 3 or 4 slices per person.
- Prepare the garlic and tomato.
- Arrange the slices on a baking sheet or pizza pan and drizzle with olive oil.
- Coat each slice with diced garlic, and then diced tomato.
- Add a spoonful of ricotta cheese to the top of each of those delicious looking piles :)
- Sprinkle parsley and ground peppercorns over each slice.
- Bake on the top rack of the oven for about 10 minutes.
- Mangia!

332. Tomato Bread Pudding Recipe

Serving: 8 | Prep: | Cook: 45mins | Ready in:

Ingredients

- 1-1/2 C heavy cream
- 1 C canned whole tomatoes, cut up
- 1/2 C juice from canned tomatoes
- 6 oz can tomato paste
- 1 large egg
- 2 egg yolks
- 1 day-old french baguette (about 7 oz)
- 1 tomato, sliced in 6 slices
- 1 medium onion, chopped
- 1 T butter
- 2 T fresh oregano, minced
- 2 T fresh thyme, minced
- 1 T fresh sage, minced
- 1 clove garlic, minced
- salt, hot sauce, to taste
- olive oil

Direction

- Using a 7" diameter deep tart pan to measure, cut pieces of crust from the bread about 1/2'" thick, as wide as the loaf and about 2/3 as long as the pan is tall.
- Butter the pan and stand these pieces in sort of a fence around the perimeter of the pan, with the cut sides facing inward.
- Cut the rest of the bread in 1/2" cubes and place them in the well created by the bread "fence."
- Compress the cubes into the pan with your fingers.
- The bread cubes when compressed should be about even with the top of the bread fence pieces.

- Sauté the onion in 1 T butter slowly, about 8 minutes, stirring occasionally, until translucent.
- Mix herbs together.
- Beat the egg and yolks briefly with a fork and then mix well with the cream, cooked onions, canned tomatoes, tomato juice, tomato paste, garlic and 3/4 of the herbs. Correct seasoning.
- Pour cream / tomato mixture over the bread, to cover the bread.
- (There may be some left over, depending on the size of the pan and how tightly packed the bread is.
- Any leftover custard can be cooked as directed below with or without bread in buttered ramekins, if you like, or used as an enrichment for a soup.)
- Allow pudding to sit for 30 minutes, then set in a pan of boiling water that reaches halfway up the sides of the tart pan and bake in a preheated 350º oven 45 minutes.
- After the first 20 minutes, lay the tomato slices over the top of the pudding and sprinkle with the remaining herbs.
- Paint tomato slices with olive oil when the pudding comes out of the oven and then allow pudding to rest about 30 minutes before unmoulding.
- **Serve with my recipe for Sticky Chicken and a fresh salad...Excellent! **

333. Tomato Bruschetta Recipe

Serving: 8 | Prep: | Cook: 3mins | Ready in:

Ingredients

- 8 roma tomatoes, seeded and chopped
- 1/3 c. red onion, chopped
- 1 c. fresh basil, shredded
- 1/4 c. extra virgin olive oil + a extra for baguette
- 1 T. red wine vinegar
- salt and pepper
- 1 baguette
- 2 garlic cloves, peeled and cut in half (for rubbing on baguette)

Direction

- Combine tomatoes, red onion, basil, olive oil and vinegar.
- Season with salt and pepper to taste.
- Let rest at room temperature for 30-40 minutes.
- Turn on broiler and slice baguette diagonally into 1/2 in. pieces.
- Broil until tops are lightly toasted.
- Take the bread out of the broiler and brush each top with a bit of olive oil.
- Rub each piece with garlic.
- Top baguette slices with tomato mixture and serve.

334. Tomato Crostini Recipe

Serving: 4 | Prep: | Cook: 8mins | Ready in:

Ingredients

- 1 cup chopped fresh plum tomatoes
- 2 Tbsp. fresh basil, chopped
- 2 Tbsp. pitted green olives, finely chopped
- 2 tsp. capers
- 1 tsp. balsamic vnegar
- 1 tsp. olive oil
- 1/2 tsp. sea salt
- dash of freshly ground pepper
- 2 garlic cloves, minced
- 8 (1-inch thick) slices French bread baguette
- cooking spray
- 2 garlic cloves, halved

Direction

- Preheat oven to 375 degrees.
- Combine first 9 ingredients. Lightly coat both sides of bread slices with cooking spray;

- arrange bread slices in a single layer on a baking sheet.
- Bake at 375 degrees for 4 minutes on each side or until lightly toasted.
- Rub one side of bread slices with garlic.
- Top each slice evenly with tomato mixture and serve.

335. Tomato Garlic Bruschetta Recipe

Serving: 0 | Prep: | Cook: 30mins | Ready in:

Ingredients

- 7 Ripe Plum Tomatoes - seeded and sliced
- 2 large garlic cloves - minced real fine
- 1 T Olive Oil plus extra for bread
- 1 large clove, sliced in half
- black pepper to taste (if you have access to Watkins pepper, try it)
- 6 large, fresh basil leaves
- Salt to taste
- 3 tsp balsamic vinegar
- Italian or French baguette (2 if you are feeding more than 4}

Direction

- In a large serving bowl, place diced tomatoes, minced garlic
- Season with salt and pepper (light on the salt until you taste)
- Roll the 6 basil leaves, length-wise.
- Cut down the middle with a sharp knife, holding the two pieces together and then slice thinly.
- Add 1/2 of the basil, olive oil, and vinegar.
- Mix thoroughly, cover and let sit.
- Slice the baguette, lengthwise and open.
- Drizzle oil on both open sides of the bread.
- Close bread and slice about 1/4 inch
- Place bread slices on a cookie sheet and bake until golden brown, flip and do the same.

- Rub garlic halves on toasted bread and serve with tomato mix.

336. Tomato Topped Onion Bread Recipe

Serving: 6 | Prep: | Cook: 35mins | Ready in:

Ingredients

- Salad
- 1 tbls. olive oil
- 2 tomatoes, chopped
- 1 red bell pepper, chopped
- 1 tbls. parsley, chopped
- 1 tbls. tarragon vinegar
- 1/2 tsp. basil
- 1/2 tsp. oregano
- salt and pepper to taste
- bread
- 1/3 cup olive oil
- 1/3 cup onion, finely chopped
- 1 garlic clove, minced
- 1 can refrigerated pizza crust
- 1/4 cup parmesan cheese, grated

Direction

- Preheat oven to 400
- Salad
- Heat oil in skillet
- Add tomato and pepper and cook until liquid evaporates, about 10 minutes
- Stir in remaining ingredients
- Set aside and cool
- Bread
- Heat oil in skillet over medium heat
- Add onion and garlic and cook until tender
- Drain, reserving oil
- Grease round 9 inch cake pan with reserved oil
- Unroll dough and roll into 10 inch circle
- Put dough in pan pressing onto bottom and 1/2 inch up sides

- Using tip of knife, poke holes in dough every 2 inches or so
- Pour remaining reserved oil onto dough and spread evenly
- Sprinkle with onion mixture and cheese
- Bake 18-20 minutes or until golden brown
- Cool a minute or 2 and remove from pan
- Put on serving dish and top warm bread with salad

337. Tomato And Avocado Bruschetta Recipe

Serving: 68 | Prep: | Cook: | Ready in:

Ingredients

- 4-6 roma tomatoes or plum tomatoes, seeded
- 1 avocado--the riper, the more creamy
- 2 green onions, chopped
- 1 small minced garlic clove
- 2 Tbsp fresh basil, or dried to taste
- 2 Tbsp freshly grated parmesan
- 2 tsp freshly squeezed lime or lemon juice
- 1 1/2 tsp olive oil
- 1/2 tsp salt
- pepper to taste

Direction

- Seed and coarsely chop tomatoes.
- Peel and cut avocado into 1/4 inch cubes. Add to tomatoes in small bowl
- Stir in onions, garlic, basil, Parmesan cheese, lime or lemon juice, olive oil, salt and pepper.
- Serve on sliced French bread or crackers.
- Makes about 2 3/4 cups
- Per 1/4 cup: 1.1 gr protein, 3.8g fat, 2.7g carb, 0.3 mg iron, 23 mg calcium, 46 calories

338. Tomato And Avocado Goat Cheese Crostini Recipe

Serving: 6 | Prep: | Cook: 15mins | Ready in:

Ingredients

- 1 loaf french baguette bread
- 3 cloves garlic, minced
- 1/3 cup olive oil
- 2 ripe avocados
- 4 ounces mild goat cheese
- 1/4 teaspoon salt
- Freshly squeezed lemon juice
- 1 1/2 cups tomatoes, seeded, diced 1/4 "
- 2 tablespoons extra-virgin olive oil
- 1/2 teaspoon salt
- 1/4 teaspoon ground black pepper
- 1/4 cup fresh basil, chopped
- Small basil leaves for garnish

Direction

- Pre-heat oven to 350 degrees.
- Slice bread into 1/4 " thick diagonal slices. If you're working with a large loaf, you'll then want to halve each slice again.
- In small bowl, combine garlic and olive oil. Brush bread slices lightly with garlic oil mixture. Arrange on sheet pans in a single layer. Bake crostini for 10-15 minutes until golden brown and crisp. Remove from oven and let cool. You can make these ahead of time and store in an airtight container. Be sure to let cool completely before storing.
- In medium-sized bowl combine avocados, goat cheese and 1/4 teaspoon salt. Mix until smooth. If you add a little fresh lemon juice it will prevent the avocado from browning.
- In separate bowl, combine tomatoes, olive oil, 1/2 teaspoon salt, pepper, and basil.
- To serve, spread each crostini with approximately 1 tablespoon of avocado mixture, then top with tomato-basil mixture. Garnish with small basil leaves if desired. Place on a large serving plate.

- Try not to assemble too far ahead of serving, as the bread can get soggy.

339. Tomato And Olive Bruschetta Recipe

Serving: 10 | Prep: | Cook: 20mins | Ready in:

Ingredients

- 1 teaspoon(s) extra-virgin olive oil
- 1/2 medium. red onion, thinly sliced
- 1/3 cup(s) Niçoise olives, pitted and chopped
- 1/3 cup(s) chopped yellow bell pepper
- 2 cup(s) cherry tomatoes, halved
- 1 teaspoon(s) Maldon sea salt
- 1/8 teaspoon(s) ground black pepper

Direction

- DIRECTIONS
- Heat the oil in a medium skillet over medium-low heat. Add the onion and cook until lightly browned -- about 10 minutes. Transfer to medium bowl and add the olives and yellow pepper. Increase heat to high, add the tomatoes, and sear until heated through.
- Toss the charred tomatoes with the onion mixture. Serve over toasted bread slices. Sprinkle with Maldon sea salt and black pepper.

340. Tony Merlino's Pizza Dough Recipe

Serving: 8 | Prep: | Cook: 1hours | Ready in:

Ingredients

- 3 cups bread flour (high gluten)
- 1/2 cup semolina flour
- 1 package yeast (2 t)
- 2 T sugar
- 1 T salt
- 1 T oregano
- olive oil
- 1 1/2 cups hot water (bottled if you have funky water)

Direction

- * I use a food processor for easiest work. If you don't have one just need the hell out of the dough. You really can't over knead the dough. But you can dry out the dough. You will knead for about 10-15 minutes, but the dough must be moist so use flour carefully!
- In food processor, add hot water. Pulse with sugar.
- Wait 1 minute and add yeast, pulse once.
- Now, add all additional ingredients.
- Turn food processor on for about 4 minutes.
- You will now carefully add just enough flour to allow the dough to form a wet ball. I add 1 T extra flour then turn food processor on for a 30 seconds and reevaluate
- Coat a decent sized bowl with small amount of olive oil.
- Let dough ball rest in bowl with a damp towel over until doubles in size. Punch down and place in fridge til ready to use.
- *To Cook*
- Turn over to 425
- I like to spread my dough out on a sheet pan, use whatever floats you boat.
- There is no perfect pizza, MAKE IT YOUR OWN

341. Tuscan Tuna Bruschetta Recipe

Serving: 10 | Prep: | Cook: 5mins | Ready in:

Ingredients

- 1 can (6 ounce) water-packed tuna, drained
- 1/3 cup minced red onion

- 3 tablespoons chopped fresh Italian parsley
- 2 tablespoons fresh lemon juice
- 1 tablespoon olive oil
- 1 teaspoon chopped fresh thyme leaves, or
- 1/4 teaspoon dried thyme
- 1/8 teaspoon ground black pepper
- 1 container (16 ounces) hummus or other bean puree
- 1/4 cup finely chopped drained oil-packed sun-dried tomatoes
- 20 thin diagonal slices crusty Italian or French bread

Direction

- Flake the tuna with a fork into a bowl, and stir in the onion, parsley, lemon juice, olive oil, thyme and pepper. In a separate bowl mix the hummus and sun-dried tomatoes together. Heat the broiler. Arrange the bread slices in a single layer on a cookie sheets. Broil 1 to 3 minutes on each side, or until lightly toasted. Top each toast with a layer of the hummus mixture and a small mound of the tuna mixture.
- Nutritional Information Per Serving: Calories 170; Total fat 7g; Saturated fat 1g; Cholesterol 5mg; Sodium 360mg; Carbohydrate 18g; Fibre 4g; Protein 10g; Vitamin A 4%DV*; Vitamin C 10%DV; Calcium 4%DV; Iron 10%DV
- *Daily Value

342. Upsydaisy Canape Recipe

Serving: 24 | Prep: | Cook: |Ready in:

Ingredients

- 1 small package of cream cheese at room temperature
- 1 container of oven-baked potato sticks
- (straight pretzels can also be used)
- 2 tbs chopped/crushed salted peanuts
- 8 drops green food coloring
- 4 drops yellow food coloring
- 4 drops red food coloring

Direction

- Mix the softened cream cheese, the peanuts, and the green food colouring.
- Add the yellow and red food colouring and mix leaving streaks.
- Form into small balls and stick a potato stick in them *giggle*
- Place on a wax paper sheet on a plate and refrigerate to firm up.
- Serve with drinks!

343. Very Berry Bruschetta Recipe

Serving: 6 | Prep: | Cook: 4mins |Ready in:

Ingredients

- 12 slices French bread (1/2 inch thick)
- 5 teaspoons sugar, divided
- 8 oz light cream cheese
- 1/2 teaspoon almond extract
- 3/4 cup fresh blackberries
- 3/4 cup fresh raspberries
- 1/4 cup slivered almonds, toasted
- 2 teaspoons confectioners' sugar

Direction

- Place bread on an ungreased baking sheet; lightly coat with cooking spray. Sprinkle with 2 teaspoons sugar. Broil 3-4 in. from the heat for 1-2 minutes or until lightly browned.
- In a small bowl, combine the cream cheese, almond extract and remaining sugar. Spread over toasted bread. Top with berries and almonds; dust with confectioners' sugar. Yield: 12 pieces.

344. Vidalia Onion And Ham Bruschetta Recipe

Serving: 4 | Prep: | Cook: 10mins | Ready in:

Ingredients

- 4 ounces sliced low-fat ham, cut into 1-inch pieces about 1 cup
- 1 vidalia onion, chopped, should have about 1 cup
- 1 cup chopped plum tomatoes
- 2 tablespoons reduced-fat mayonnaise
- 1 tablespoon yellow or Dijon mustard
- 8 large slices of thick Italian bread, toastd

Direction

- Pre-heat oven to 400°.
- In a bowl, combine ham, Vidalia onion, tomatoes, mayonnaise and mustard.
- Arrange bread on a large baking sheet.
- Top with ham mixture.
- Bake until heated through, about 10-15 minutes.
- Serve at room temperature.
- Again, this can be served cold in hollowed-out roll or in pita bread.

345. Vidalia Pitza Recipe

Serving: 0 | Prep: | Cook: 20mins | Ready in:

Ingredients

- 6 pita flatbreads(about 5-6 inches diameter)
- 3 large vidalias, sliced thin
- 1/2 stick butter
- 3 cloves garlic, minced
- about 1/4 cup fresh basil, minced
- 1/4 cup white wine
- 4oz sun dried tomato goat cheese, spreadable or crumbles
- 2T olive tapenade
- 2T roasted red pepper tapenade
- 1/2 cup fresh Parmesan, grated
- fresh ground black pepper

Direction

- In heavy skillet, melt butter over low heat.
- Add onions and garlic and stir to coat well
- Cook until onions are very soft, about 10 minutes.(you can certainly cook these for longer and get a genuine caramelization going, but, I don't think Vidalia need that, as they are SO sweet, already :)
- Meanwhile, heat flatbreads in a 400 oven for a couple of minutes to just begin to crisp up around the edges.
- When onions are done, add wine, basil and a healthy dose of black pepper and continue to cook until all liquid is absorbed.
- Divide goat cheese up between all the flat breads and either crumble or spread cheese over each piece.
- Top each with and equal portion of the onion mixture.
- Drop several 1/2t dots of both of the tapenades around the onion mixture on each bread.
- Sprinkle with Parmesan cheese.
- Bake in 400 oven for about 5 minutes until cheese is melted and edges are crisp. Cut into triangles to serve.
- This was also good room temp! :)

346. Walnut Gougeres Recipe

Serving: 24 | Prep: | Cook: 1hours | Ready in:

Ingredients

- ½ cup water
- 3 tbsp butter, salted
- ½ cup all purpose flour, sifted
- Pinch dry mustard
- Pinch nutmeg
- Pinch chipotle chili pepper
- 2 large eggs

- 75 g California walnut crumbs
- 2 tbsp minced chives
- 200 g Extra-old Cheddar, finely grated

Direction

- Preheat oven to 400°F.
- In a medium sized saucepan over medium-high heat, add cup of water and butter and bring to a boil.
- Reduce heat to low and add flour, mustard, nutmeg, and cayenne, stirring constantly to cook the paste, about 3 minutes.
- Remove paste from heat and transfer mixture into a stand mixer fitted with the paddle attachment.
- Mixing on medium-low speed, add eggs, one at a time, ensuring each one is fully incorporated before adding the next.
- Gently fold in walnuts, chives and cheese by hand.
- Scoop mixture into a piping bag with a large star tip and pipe small bite sized mounds 1-inch apart on a parchment lined baking sheet.
- Optional:
- At this point, you can freeze gougères, transfer to a zip-top bag and bake as needed
- Preheat your oven to 400°F degrees, place frozen gougères 2" apart on lines sheets.
- Bake for 15 minutes, then reduce heat to 350°F and bake for 15 minutes.
- If baking from fresh:
- Bake in the centre oven rack for 10 minutes, then reduce heat to 350°F and bake a further 12 minutes, until golden brown.

347. Walnut Spread Recipe

Serving: 0 | Prep: | Cook: 15mins | Ready in:

Ingredients

- 1 (15-ounce) can garbanzo beans, drained and rinsed
- 1 cup toasted walnuts, chopped
- 1 cup lightly packed fresh basil leaves
- 1/4 cup extra virgin olive oil
- 4 to 6 teaspoons lemon juice
- 1 large clove garlic, cut into pieces
- 1/4 to 1/2 teaspoon sea salt
- Freshly ground black pepper
- Thinly sliced fresh basil
- Thinly sliced radishes

Direction

- Place garbanzo beans, walnuts, basil, olive oil, lemon juice and garlic in the bowl of a food processor. Puree until smooth, adding a little more olive oil or lemon juice if needed to obtain smooth consistency. Add salt and pepper and process again to combine well. Spoon into a serving bowl and garnish with basil and radish.

348. Warm Butter Bean And Sage Bruschetta Recipe

Serving: 4 | Prep: | Cook: 10mins | Ready in:

Ingredients

- Bruschetta:
- French bread- Sliced thick
- 2 cloves garlic
- extra virgin olive oil
- Spread:
- 4 tablespoons extra virgin olive oil
- 1/2 small onion, finely chopped
- 1 tablespoon fresh sage
- 1 teaspoon grated lemon peel
- 1 14 oz can butter beans (can substitute canned lima or fava beans)
- 6 tablespoons of juice from can of butter beans
- 1 teaspoon lemon juice
- pinch cayenne pepper

Direction

- Bruschetta

- Toast bread on both sides under a broiler.
- While still hot rub both sides of bread all over with garlic.
- Drizzle with small amount of olive oil.
- Spread
- Heat oil in a skillet and fry the onion, garlic, sage, and lemon peel for 5 minutes until soft but not golden.
- Add the beans, with about 6 tablespoons of their liquid, the lemon juice, and cayenne.
- Cover and simmer gently for 5 minutes.
- Mash the beans with a potato masher to form a rough paste.
- Season to taste.
- Spread on warm bruschetta and serve immediately.

349. Warm Tomato And Feta Bruschetta Recipe

Serving: 21 | Prep: | Cook: 15mins | Ready in:

Ingredients

- 1 8 oz. loaf of Sour Dough or French bread (baguette)
- 1/3 cup Italian dressing
- 1 lb plum tomatoes, seeded and chopped
- 1/4 cup chopped red onion
- 1/2 tbsp minced garlic
- 1 4 oz pkg crumbled feta cheese
- 3/4 cup fresh shredded parmesan cheese

Direction

- Preheat oven to 375.
- Cut bread into 1/2 inch thick slices. Brush one side of each slice with Italian dressing. Place in preheated oven until lightly toasted (about 5 minutes).
- Meanwhile in a medium bowl combine tomatoes, onion, garlic and feta and remaining Italian dressing.
- Spoon mixture onto each toast slice and sprinkle with shredded parmesan.
- Return to oven for 7-10 minutes or until toppings are heated through. Serve immediately.
- **You can increase or decrease the amount of Italian dressing added to the tomato mixture according to your tastes. I have also found that the "basil and sun dried tomato" flavored feta works extremely well in this recipe. **

350. Warmed Tomato And Garlic Bruschetta With Balsamic Syrup Recipe

Serving: 6 | Prep: | Cook: 5mins | Ready in:

Ingredients

- 6 slices Italian sourdough, ciabatta or focaccia (vegan)
- 2 large ripe tomatoes, chopped (increase amount according to how much you like tomato)
- 3 tablespoons olive oil
- 3 cloves garlic, finely chopped (not minced)
- fresh torn basil (about 1/4 cup)
- fresh flat-leaf parsley
- 1 cup balsamic vinegar
- freshly ground sea salt (about 1/2 - 1 teaspoon)
- freshly ground black pepper

Direction

- Prepare the bread: If the bread is a large loaf, you can even cut the 6 slices into halves.
- Put the chopped tomatoes in a bowl and stir in the salt. It might seem like a lot of salt, but like putting sugar on strawberries, salt on tomatoes has a kind of self-'macerating' action and they don't taste that salty in the end product.
- Put the balsamic vinegar in a small saucepan, bring to the boil, reduce heat and cook until reduced to approx. 1/4 cup.

- Put the olive oil and garlic into a small heat-proof jug or bowl and heat in the microwave for 30 seconds (1000w on high) or in a small saucepan, until quite warm but not so hot you can't touch it.
- Toss the tomatoes, basil, oregano, and oil mixture together.
- Toast the bread, and top with the tomato mixture. Crack pepper over the bruschetta, then drizzle the balsamic reduction over - about 1 teaspoon per slice should be plenty. Top with a good sprig of the parsley.

351. Wegmans Pumpernickel Bread And Beef Dip Recipe

Serving: 12 | Prep: | Cook: | Ready in:

Ingredients

- 16 oz. sour cream
- 1 1/3 cups mayo
- 2 TBSP. dill weed
- 2 TBSP. minced dried onion
- 2 TBSP. parsley
- 2 1/2 oz. jar of dried beef - cut into small pieced
- large round loaf pumpernickel bread

Direction

- Mix in a bowl all ingredients except the pumpernickel bread.
- Let stand overnight in the refrigerator.
- Next day
- Cut the centre out of the loaf of bread, forming a bowl...
- Leave 1 to 1 1/2 inches of bread around the sides and the bottom
- Cut a good size round hole in the top of the bread
- Take the bread that you scooped out and cut into 1 inch cubes
- Put the loaf of bread on a large plate
- Fill with the dip
- Either put the bread cubes around the outside of the plate or in a basket.
- To eat: scoop some dip onto a bread cube and pop into your mouth!

352. Whiskey Grapefruit Glazed Smoked Salmon Crostini Recipe

Serving: 8 | Prep: | Cook: 10mins | Ready in:

Ingredients

- 12 ounces smoked salmon
- ½ cup grapefruit, peeled, sectioned and roughly chopped
- 2 Tbls capers
- 4 oz cream cheese, softened
- 4 oz mascarpone, softened
- Leaves from ½ bunch of fresh thyme, finely chopped
- 1 Tsp finely ground Chipotle powder
- 2 Tbls Good EV olive oil
- 2 baguettes, cut on the bias into 1/4" slices.
- *********************
- glaze
- ½ cup Scotch whiskey (Preferably an "Islay" for its smoky flavor but any good Scotch will do.)
- ¼ cup grapefruit juice
- ¼ cup honey

Direction

- In a small pot, reduce the Whiskey, Grapefruit Juice and Honey until it becomes like thin syrup. Let cool slightly. It will thicken a little.
- Fit a cooling rack on top of a sheet pan and place the Salmon Strips on the rack. Brush the Salmon generously on all sides with the Grapefruit-Scotch glaze. Cover loosely with foil and refrigerate for 30 minutes.
- When Ready: Slice Salmon into 3/4-1" pieces and set aside.

- In a small bowl, whip the Cream Cheese and Mascarpone together; stir in chopped thyme. Set aside.
- In a separate bowl, gently toss the chopped Grapefruit with Chipotle Powder Set aside.
- Brush bread slices with olive oil and toast or broil both sides until lightly golden and crisp. Let cool to room temperature.
- Spread toasts with Cheese mixture. Divide Salmon evenly among Toasts, piling loosely. Top with Chipotle Spiced Grapefruit and a few Capers. Serve immediately.

353. White Bean Bruschetta Recipe

Serving: 16 | Prep: | Cook: 10mins | Ready in:

Ingredients

- 1 french baguette, cut in 16 (1/2-inch thick) slices
- 2 tablespoons olive oil
- 1 can (15 ounces) cannellini beans, drained and rinsed
- 2 tablespoons sun-dried tomato juliennes* in oil, drained
- 2 tablespoons chopped, fresh basil leaves or
- 2 teaspoons dried basil
- salt to taste
- 2 cloves garlic, halved
- *Juliennes are matchstick strips.

Direction

- Preparation Time: Approximately 10 minutes
- Cook Time: Approximately 10 minutes
- Preparation:
- Heat oven to 400°F. Brush one side of each bread slice with the olive oil. Place on a baking sheet, oil-side up. Bake for 8 to 10 minutes or until toasted. Meanwhile, mix beans, sun-dried tomatoes and basil in a medium bowl. Mash with a fork and mix well. Season with salt. Rub the cut sides of garlic over the tops of the toasts. Cover each toast slice with 1 tablespoon bean spread. Serve immediately.
- Servings: 16
- Nutritional Information per Serving:
- Calories 60; Total Fat 2.5g; Saturated Fat 0g; Cholesterol 0mg; Sodium 100mg; Carbohydrate 9g; Fibre 1g; Protein 2g; vitamin A 0%DV**, vitamin C 2%DV, Iron 4% DV
  **DV is Daily Value, used in labelling

354. White Bean Crostini Recipe

Serving: 4 | Prep: | Cook: 5mins | Ready in:

Ingredients

- 1 15 oz. can white beans, rinsed and drained
- 1 clove garlic, minced
- 1/2 tsp. Spanish smoked paprika
- a few sundried tomatoes, chopped fine (these are optional - I don't actually think they added that much to the final product)
- Approximately 1 tbsp. sherry vinegar
- olive oil to taste and for brushing bread slices
- 4 medium-sized slices Italian or French bread. (This is almost certainly one of the cases where it pays to get good bread.)
- 1 medium-sized tomato, chopped
- freshly-ground black pepper

Direction

- In a small bowl, combine the white beans, garlic, paprika, sundried tomatoes (if using), sherry vinegar and olive oil. Taste and add more garlic, paprika, vinegar, or oil as needed.
- Coarsely mash the bean mixture with a fork.
- Heat a skilled over medium-high heat. Brush each slice of bread with olive oil on both sides, and toast in the skillet until it is lightly charred on both sides. (1 minute per side or so.)
- Top each slice with some of the bean mixture, some freshly grated pepper, and some chopped tomato. Serve immediately.

355. White Bean Sun Dried Tomato Bruschetta Recipe

Serving: 8 | Prep: | Cook: 7mins | Ready in:

Ingredients

- 1 can cannelloni beans, juice reserved
- 2 garlic cloves, 1 thinly sliced & 1 halved
- 2 tbsp evoo
- ½ tsp chili flakes
- 8-10 basil leaves, thinly chopped
- 1/3 cup sun-dried tomatoes, chopped
- 2 tbsp parsley, chopped
- lemon juice
- salt and pepper

Direction

- Heat oil in a skillet over medium heat, add garlic sauté for 1 minute, and add chili flakes and sauté for 10 more seconds.
- Add basil leaves (do this carefully, so the oil doesn't splatter)
- Transfer the beans to the pan, adding 1-2 tbsp. of the bean liquid to the mixture. Mix.
- Take heat when the basil leaves are wilted.
- Add in the sun-dried tomatoes and parsley. Mix.
- Add the lemon juice and salt and pepper to taste.
- Serve warm on warmed slices Italian bread

356. Wild Mushroom Bruschetta Recipe

Serving: 410 | Prep: | Cook: 10mins | Ready in:

Ingredients

- 1 lb. wild mushrooms (whatever species are available, but chanterelle, black trumpet, porcini & hedgehog are the best for this recipe)
- 1 loaf French bread
- ¾ cup olive oil
- Grated parmigiano Reggiano
- fresh cracked pepper

Direction

- Mince the shroom. Add the oil to a sauté pan on medium heat. Add the minced shrooms and cracked pepper to taste. Sauté for about 15 minutes or until the water given off by the shrooms has cooked off.
- Slice the French bread lengthwise. Spread the mushroom mixture to your desired generosity (the more the merrier). And grate some parmesan cheese on top. Broil for 7ish minutes.
- A note on the wildness of mushrooms. Most of the mushroom species that are marketed as wild might have been wild at one time…a long, long time ago. Shitake and oyster mushrooms are frequently marketed as wild, but they are cultivated. This is not to say that there is anything wrong with cultivated mushrooms. But, truly wild mushrooms have a depth of flavour and nutrition that cultivated mushrooms cannot match. The mad scientists have not found a way yet to cultivate the following: chanterelle, porcini, black trumpet, hedgehog, lobster, morel, matsutake, and yellow foot, so you can be sure that those are wild varieties.
- Finally, mushrooms grow wild all over the US, but most of the ones that are commercially available come from the Pacific Northwest forests.

357. Wonderul Bruschetta Recipe

Serving: 24 | Prep: | Cook: 15mins | Ready in:

Ingredients

- 1/2 c. mayo or salad dressing
- 1 c grated mozzarella cheese
- 2 med. tomatoes, seeded and finely diced
- 1/4 c chopped pitted olives
- 1/4 c. grated fresh parmesan cheese (or 2 T dry)
- 1 tsp. dried whole oregano
- 1/4 tsp. dried sweet basil
- 1/2 tsp. pepper
- 1 loaf baguette bread
- 1/3 c butter or hard marg melted

Direction

- Combine first 8 ingredients in bowl. (Can be made ahead and refrigerated until needed)
- Cut baguette in 1 inch slices. Divide and spread margarine or butter on 1 side of each slice. Place, butter side up on ungreased baking sheet. Divide and spread tomato mixture on slices. Bake 350 oven for about 15 minutes until hot and cheese is melted. Serve warm.

358. Yummy Tomato Basil Bruschetta Recipe

Serving: 2 | Prep: | Cook: 15mins | Ready in:

Ingredients

- 1 large tomato seeded and diced small
- 1 large clove of garlic finely minced (see variation for less garlic flavor)
- 10-20 basil leaves (depending on their size) chopped chiffonade style
- 1-2 tbsp parmesan depending on your liking
- olive oil
- 6 slices of French bread or baguette
- OPTIONAL: balsamic vinegar

Direction

- Mix first four ingredients.
- Drizzle in the oil until everything is juicy- about 1/8 c.
- Let sit on counter while oven preheats to 400°.
- Toast bread in oven 5-10 minutes until just crispy and lightly browned.
- Top bread with bruschetta mixture.
- IF DESIRED you can drizzle a little vinegar over the bruschetta for a little sweet/tangy flavour.
- ALSO if you don't like a lot of garlic you can rub the bread with the garlic clove after it is toasted instead of adding to the tomato mixture.

359. Zesty Chicken Sombrero's Recipe

Serving: 6 | Prep: | Cook: 30mins | Ready in:

Ingredients

- 6 slices of whole wheat bread, crusts cut off
- cooking spray
- 1 tbsp canola oil
- juice of one lime
- 1 chicken breast, diced
- 1/2 red bell pepper, finely chopped
- 1/2 small onion, finely chopped
- 1 tsp minced garlic
- 1/2 zucchini, finely chopped
- 3 asparagus spears, finely chopped
- 1 tbsp low sodium taco seasoning
- a pinch of pepper
- 1/2 cup grated low fat cheddar cheese
- 1/4 cup salsa
- 1/4 cup plain yogourt

Direction

- Preheat oven to 375°
- Flatten bread with a rolling pin
- Spray a 6 cup muffin tin with cooking spray
- Press each slice of bread in the cups

- Bake in the oven for 5-7 minutes until crisp
- In a frying pan cook chicken on med/hi heat with the canola oil until cooked through (about 5-7 minutes)
- Add the red pepper, onion, garlic, zucchini, and the asparagus spears to the pan and reduce heat to med/low.
- Add the taco seasoning lime juice and pepper
- Cook until veggies are soft, about 7-10 minutes
- Spoon the chicken and veggie mixture into the bread cups.
- Sprinkle the cheddar cheese on each
- Bake for an additional 5 minutes, until cheese melts
- In a small bowl, mix the salsa and the yogurt together
- Take cups out of muffin tin and top with the salsa/yogurt mixture
- ENJOY!!

360. Zuchinni Bread Recipe

Serving: 3 | Prep: | Cook: 1mins | Ready in:

Ingredients

- Mix the following in a large bowl
- 3 C. Grated zucchini
- 3 C. sugar
- 1½ C. oil (canola works best)
- 2 t. vanilla
- 4 eggs
- Add
- 1 T. cinnamon
- ½ t cloves
- Add
- 4 ½ cups flour
- 1 ½ t baking soda
- 1 ½ t. salt
- ½ t. baking powder
- Bake 1 hour.

Direction

- Mix all ingredients in a large bowl until flour is incorporated.
- Prepare 3 med size loaf pans.
- I spray with cooking spray, then line with wax paper.
- Cook for 1 hour plus if needed, middle rack, at 325.
- The top of the bread turns out crispy.
- I love to serve this with softened cream cheese.
- To freeze...wrap in foil, then in a freezer zip lock bag.
- Take out a week later and POW!!! Flavour is great!

361. Cheesy Garlic Bread Recipe

Serving: 8 | Prep: | Cook: 10mins | Ready in:

Ingredients

- 1 1/2 c. mayo
- 1 c. shredded sharp cheddar cheese
- 1 c. thinly sliced green onion
- 3 cloves garlic, minced
- 1 loaf French bread, halved lengthwise
- 1/3 c minced fresh parsley (opt.)
- paprika (opt.)

Direction

- Preheat oven to 400.
- Mix mayo, cheese, onions, and garlic
- Spread on bread halves
- If desired, sprinkle with parsley or paprika.
- Wrap each half in foil
- Refrigerate 1 to 2 hours, or freeze.
- Unwrap and place on baking sheet
- Bake at 400 degrees for 8 to 10 minutes

362. In Your Face Garlic Bread Recipe

Serving: 12 | Prep: | Cook: 12mins | Ready in:

Ingredients

- 5 garlic cloves
- 2 sticks unsalted butter
- about a handful of cilantro
- pinch of pepper
- loaf of French bread

Direction

- Note-make sure the butter is allowed to reach room temp this allows for better mixing and spreading.
- Get the grill or even a grill plate heated you don't need a bonfire for this :)
- Grab a mixing bowl and a wooden spoon or spatula
- Begin to mince the garlic
- Place the butter in the bowl.
- Add in minced garlic and mix carefully
- Set aside and take the handful of cilantro and tear it up no need to be fancy.
- Now add it to the butter garlic mix and stir all ingredients together.
- Refrigerate the butter while dong the next step
- Take the loaf of French bread and cut it at an angle for presentation
- After the bread is cut spread the butter on both sides of the bread
- Very carefully place the bread on the grill or grill plate. Flipping over occasionally
- Now some of the bread will become very crispy on the outside but do not overcook and make the centre hard this is what makes the bread so wonderful because you get the crunch of the crust and the softness of the centre
- a word of caution watch the flames and try not to let the butter melt all the way it tastes so much better this way!

363. Mushrooms Over Bread Appetizer Recipe

Serving: 4 | Prep: | Cook: 10mins | Ready in:

Ingredients

- 1 10-ounce pkg of baby Portobello mushrooms
- Extra virgin olive to taste
- Dijon mustard to taste
- Fresh minced garlic to taste
- salt and pepper to taste
- 2 large slices from a round rustic white bread toasted
- extra virgin olive oil
- fresh chopped parsley for garnish

Direction

- In a large skillet with a few tbsp. of extra virgin olive oil, sauté sliced Portobello mushrooms until tender.
- Add the garlic and a few tbsp. of Dijon mustard to taste.
- Season with a bit of salt (mustard is salty too) and fresh grated black pepper.
- Cover and set aside.
- Take two long slices of fresh homemade white bread and toast slices in toaster oven or oven.
- Liberally cover with the mushrooms and any liquid.
- Drizzle over the olive oil and add some chopped parsley.
- Cut each piece of bread into two so you will have 4 appetizer pieces.
- Garnish with fresh chopped parsley.
- Serve immediately. Serves 2 to 4.
- If desired one may sprinkle on some fresh grated Romano cheese.

364. Spin Off Of Tastefully Simple Beer Bread Recipe

Serving: 8 | Prep: | Cook: 60mins | Ready in:

Ingredients

- 12 0z beer(not light or corona)
- 3 cups self rising flour
- 1/3 cup sugar
- 3 Tbl. melterd butter

Direction

- Preheat oven to 350
- Spray 9X5 loaf pan with baking cooking spray
- Combine flour and sugar
- Stir in beer (you might have to use your hands) Dough will be sticky
- Pour into pan
- Brush with melted butter
- Bake 50-60 minutes until brown
- Cool slightly remove from pan and continue cooling
- ENJOY!

365. Turkey With Dill Spread Canapes Recipe

Serving: 32 | Prep: | Cook: 10mins | Ready in:

Ingredients

- 1/2 cup mayo
- 1 tsp. fresh dill (minced) or 1 1/4 tsp. dry dill
- 1/2 tsp. season salt
- 8 slices dark bread or pumpernickel (crusts cut off)
- 3/4 LB. turkey breast sliced thin

Direction

- Combine Mayo, dill and season salt Blend well. Spread 1 tablespoon of mixture on each piece of bread. Top with turkey. Cut into 4 to 6 canapés and decorate with dill.
- Makes about 32 canapés

Index

A

Almond 3,4,11,12,23,57

Anchovies 4,41

Apple 3,6,15,22,26,96,101,113

Apricot 3,15,16,18

Artichoke 3,4,7,14,16,17,48,137

Asparagus 3,5,17,18,65,89

Avocado 5,7,18,86,149

B

Bacon 3,4,7,12,20,27,49,63,140,142

Bagel 3,21

Baguette 5,11,90,122

Baking 45,98

Basil 3,4,8,9,32,40,41,101,109,122,158

Beef 4,7,42,155

Beer 8,161

Berry 7,151

Biscuits 6,119

Blackberry 3,23,97

Blini 3,24

Boar 3,26

Bread 1,3,4,5,6,7,8,9,10,11,13,14,16,17,20,21,22,23,25,26,27,28,29,31,33,40,41,45,47,48,49,50,53,54,55,58,59,63,66,67,68,69,70,74,76,77,78,79,80,84,85,86,91,94,95,96,97,98,100,102,103,104,105,108,110,111,112,113,115,116,120,121,122,123,128,129,130,132,133,134,135,136,137,138,139,140,142,143,145,146,148,155,159,160,161

Brie 3,4,5,6,15,16,22,30,31,39,59,76,93,101,102

Brioche 3,31

Broth 6,120

Brown bread 13

Butter 3,5,7,22,30,32,45,68,96,144,146,153

C

Capers 156

Caramel 4,43,44

Cauliflower 3,28

Cheddar 4,44,45,46,52,58,68,76,117,153

Cheese 3,4,5,6,7,9,10,12,15,20,21,23,25,38,40,47,48,62,73,80,81,82,83,84,89,90,92,99,108,109,117,119,122,128,135,140,149,156

Cherry 3,4,13,25,33,37

Chervil 18

Chicken 3,4,7,8,29,49,51,52,144,147,158

Chipotle 3,12,22,130,155,156

Chips 3,21,22

Chorizo 4,5,61,81,82

Ciabatta 117

Cognac 53

Crab 3,4,5,6,7,32,55,56,94,98,119,136,137

Crackers 3,4,7,15,46,142

Cranberry 4,57,59

Cream 4,5,6,7,18,39,59,61,89,95,96,128,135,136,156

Crisps 4,35,43,44,57

Crostini 1,3,4,5,6,7,8,9,12,15,25,26,30,31,42,55,56,57,59,60,61,62,66,72,73,74,75,81,83,84,85,90,92,98,103,104,106,111,113,114,118,119,121,125,126,133,135,147,149,155,156

Crumble 26,40,54,106

Cucumber 4,5,59,64

Curry 5,7,64,65,144

D

Dijon mustard 46,52,55,56,90,101,120,135,152,160

Dill 3,4,8,24,59,161

Dried apricots 15

E

Edam 90

Egg 5,71,87

English muffin 52,119

F

Fat 13,24,156

Feta 3,5,7,22,28,33,73,123,139,154

Fig 5,6,66,73,84,94,113,122

Fish 6,111

Flatbread 5,88

Flour 15

Focaccia 6,124,127

Fontina cheese 74

French bread 9,12,13,14,15,16,17,22,23,25,26,28,35,36,40,45,46,49,55,57,58,64,66,67,68,69,70,72,73,74,77,80,87,91,94,97,100,103,104,108,109,115,116,118,124,125,134,135,137,138,139,140,141,143,145,146,147,149,151,153,154,156,157,158,159,160

Fruit 5,77

G

Garlic 3,4,5,6,7,8,9,11,32,39,50,55,60,63,67,77,78,79,80,95,101,106,116,117,136,148,154,159,160

Gorgonzola 4,5,6,39,74,79,85,100,113

Gouda 3,5,26,89,90

Grain 130

Grapefruit 5,7,88,155,156

Gratin 6,110

H

Halloumi 5,89

Ham 5,7,89,90,117,132,152

Heart 3,5,17,90

Herbs 131

Honey 3,5,11,12,15,33,85,88,92,155

J

Jam 3,4,6,30,40,113,122

Jus 23,28,51,93,128

K

Ketchup 27

L

Lard 45

Lime 3,22

Lobster 5,65,91

M

Manchego 135

Mango 4,59

Mascarpone 156

Meat 98

Mince 29,34,87,95,112,157

Mint 5,83

Mozzarella 5,6,9,23,47,61,75,88,102,103,104,105,138,139

Mushroom 3,4,5,6,7,8,28,29,30,45,60,65,83,84,95,105,106,107,120,145,157,160

N

Nut 12,13,36,64,73,103,108,116,118,151,156

O

Oil 3,4,5,11,18,23,32,56,82,91,94,95,107,148

Olive 3,5,6,7,11,18,32,33,89,94,95,103,104,108,109,123,135,148,150

Onion 4,5,6,7,38,43,48,64,80,95,96,110,117,138,148,152

Oregano 11,72,117

P

Pancetta 6,95,111

Parmesan 3,6,7,19,20,23,29,32,35,36,37,42,47,50,55,63,67,70,78,82,96,97,102,103,110,112,117,126,130,131,134,139,149,152

Parsley 3,28,89,92,96,117

Peach 4,5,6,62,76,113

Pear 5,6,92,113

Pecorino 6,113,114

Peel 19,21,41,71,81,87,92,128,149

Pepper 4,5,6,7,33,38,39,60,87,91,100,102,104,108,114,115,125,126,127

Pesto 5,6,33,90,97,109,116

Pickle 27

Pie 9

Pistachio 6,118,124

Pizza 4,5,6,7,36,41,52,93,99,100,116,117,140,150

Plum 11,148

Polenta 4,6,36,117

Pomegranate 6,118

Pork 6,119

Port 6,119,120,160

Potato 18

Prosciutto 3,22,26,122

Pulse 70,75,136,150

Pumpkin 15

R

Raisins 15

Raspberry 6,124

Rice 42

Ricotta 4,5,6,7,9,47,61,72,73,111,126,146

Rosemary 3,4,15,30,46,63,92,120

S

Sage 7,153

Salad 4,5,6,7,11,38,42,71,95,136,144,148

Salmon 3,5,6,7,18,24,70,107,128,129,155,156

Salsa 5,7,33,76,129

Salt 11,15,18,35,41,88,92,96,111,124,142,148

Sausage 3,7,14,129,130

Savory 7,130

Seafood 7,132

Seasoning 32,55,69,131,137

Seeds 15

Serrano ham 132

Sherry 6,110,136

Shortbread 7,131

Sourdough bread 96

Spinach 3,4,6,7,22,48,102,116,137,138,139

Steak 4,47

Sugar 13,24

Syrup 7,154

T

Tabasco 9,55,56,77,137

Tapenade 4,5,62,65,89

Tea 11,29,44,45,76,95,134

Thyme 92,117

Tilapia 3,11,12

Tomato 3,4,5,6,7,8,9,11,13,18,28,32,33,37,38,39,40,41,43,44,48,62,67,75,80,82,88,104,109,117,122,124,125,126,132,142,146,147,148,149,150,154,157,158

Truffle 4,56

Turkey 8,161

V

Vinegar 94,101

W

Walnut 6,7,113,152,153

White bread 120

Wine 6,96,101,119,124

Worcestershire sauce 64

Wraps 3,20

Z

Zest 8,41,158

Conclusion

Thank you again for downloading this book!

I hope you enjoyed reading about my book!

If you enjoyed this book, please take the time to share your thoughts and post a review on Amazon. It'd be greatly appreciated!

Write me an honest review about the book – I truly value your opinion and thoughts and I will incorporate them into my next book, which is already underway.

Thank you!

If you have any questions, **feel free to contact at:** author@oreganorecipes.com

Lucy Dickert

oreganorecipes.com

Manufactured by Amazon.ca
Bolton, ON